WAR ON OUR DOORSTEP

The Unknown Campaign on North America's West Coast

WAR ON OUR DOORSTEP

The Unknown Campaign on North America's West Coast

Brendan Coyle

Heritage House

National Library of Canada Cataloguing in Publication Data

Coyle, Brendan, 1957-
   War on our doorstep: the unknown campaign on North America's
west coast / Brendan Coyle.

Includes bibliographical references and index.
ISBN 1-894384-46-6

   1. World War, 1939-1945—Northwest Coast of North America.
I. Title.

D767.2.C69 2002   940.54'28   C2002-903702-6

Third printing, 2004

Heritage House acknowledges the financial support for our
publishing program from the Government of Canada through the
Book Publishing Industry Development Program (BPIDP), Canada
Council for the Arts, and the British Columbia Arts Council.

Cover painting: *Victory over Kiska*© by Rich Thistle
(www.richthistle.com)
Cover design: Darlene Nickull
Book design: Katherine Hale
Editor: Audrey McClellan

Heritage House Publishing Company Ltd., Surrey, B.C. Canada
#108 - 17665 66 A Ave., Surrey, B.C. Canada V3S 2A7

Printed in Canada

BRITISH
COLUMBIA
ARTS COUNCIL
We acknowledge the support of the Province of British Columbia
through the British Columbia Arts Council

The Canada Council | Le Conseil des Arts
for the Arts | du Canada

Contents

Foreword

Many British Columbians remember the day the war came to our coast. It was June 20, 1942, and the Japanese submarine *I-26* was on patrol off the west coast of Vancouver Island, intent on doing harm. Surfacing and laying down a smokescreen to mask their position, the crew of *I-26* readied their 5.5-inch (140-millimetre) deck gun for action. Two miles distant, on the shore, was the Estevan Point light. The lighthouse, established in 1907, had a wireless station. The Japanese commander of the submarine, Minoru Yakota, intended to knock that wireless station out, believing it was part of a radio-direction network working to pinpoint his location.

Chief Gunner Saburo Hayashi fired the first of 21 shots at 10:15 p.m. Half an hour later it was over. The isolated coastal lighthouse and its inhabitants, as well as residents of the nearby First Nations village, had come through the attack unscathed, but shaken. The first enemy shells to hit Canada's shores since the War of 1812 had made an impact, of sorts, on the sand—and a more indelible impact on the national psyche. Conscription, hotly debated in Parliament, was nudged into acceptance by the attack. And to this day, people still remember the day the war came here.

Some sceptics, looking at the conscription debate, suggest a conspiracy by Ottawa and the United States government—or just Washington, D.C., alone—to send in a U.S. Navy warship to "harmlessly" shell an ally to boost support for conscription. They are wrong, as the Japanese, including the crew and captain of *I-26* who survived the war, readily admit to the shelling. And there is proof for those who do not believe them: at least one shell did not explode. Discovered on the beach at Estevan on June 8, 1973, the shell was carefully examined and then destroyed by the Explosives Ordinance Division crew at CFB Comox less than a month later on July 3. People may lie, but as anyone who watches a good detective show knows, forensics don't. The shell was a 5.5-inch (140-millimetre) shell—a perfect fit for the deck gun of *I-26*. Even so, there is and ever shall be a determined group of true believers who will adamantly insist the Americans did it.

That's why we need to constantly examine our history, even that of more recent events. In terms of the war out here, a seemingly isolated and perhaps unimportant theatre in the global conflict of 1939–1945, Brendan Coyle has done a magnificent job in this comprehensive review of the war on the West Coast. No other single volume has so neatly tied together all the stories—from the submarine attacks and balloon bombings to the Japanese invasion of the Aleutians, from the joint U.S.–Canadian effort to drive out the Japanese, CANOL, and the naval battle of the Komandorskis to the myriad stories of how the war affected people in British Columbia, California, Oregon, Washington, and Alaska. Among the people affected, unfairly so, were loyal Japanese Canadians and Japanese Americans, stripped of their homes and property, and sent into exile by their governments in a racially charged atmosphere exacerbated by Japan's successful forays off our shores. That story alone is worthy of much reflection and emphasizes the need to remember the past so as to not repeat it, a lesson relevant in our own time as we grapple with the war on terrorism and the need in this conflict to protect the rights of our citizens and residents who happen to be either adherents of Islam or of Arabic origin or descent.

History is alive, history is relevant, and history is about us, the people. In the pages that follow, a number of connections to the present and lessons learned—and not learned—will spring to mind.

James P. Delgado
Executive Director
Vancouver Maritime Museum

Preface

While growing up on Canada's British Columbia coast, I'd heard stories about the Second World War that seemed to be based more on imagination than fact: rumours that a Japanese submarine had been sunk off Victoria after firing on the city; that a Zero had flown over downtown Portland, Oregon; and that the Japanese had actually bombed Anchorage in Alaska. I shrugged off these stories as so much fiction, and I forgot about them for the next twenty or so years.

In that time I picked up scraps of stories of veterans who had served in something called the Aleutian Campaign. I drew the mistaken conclusion that these soldiers had pulled an easy number, being posted to Alaska for a good part of the war. Alaska was, after all, right next door to British Columbia, and we were as far from the action as one could be, or so most everyone, including me, believed.

It was after reading Brian Garfield's excellent book *The Thousand Mile War* that I began to research further and seek out the veterans who had served in this unknown war. And far from being an easy number, it turned out that many of the soldiers, sailors, and airmen who went on to fight in Europe and the Pacific recall the extreme deprivation of fighting a war in the relentless weather of Alaska and the Aleutians. Here the North Pacific played no favourites, meting out equally harsh punishment to ally and enemy alike, claiming more casualties to weather than any other theatre of operations.

There was even some truth to the childhood rumours. While Japanese subs didn't shell Victoria, they did bombard the West Coast, not just once but on three occasions. An enemy aircraft did fly over Oregon and even bombed it in an almost totally unnoticed attack. And while Japanese Zeros didn't make it as far as Anchorage, they did bomb Dutch Harbor—an Alaskan fishing village 1,300 kilometres west—and occupied a tiny fraction of North American territory. All of these incidents were tied to this forgotten war in Alaska.

I have concentrated on Canada's involvement in the war in Alaska for the simple reason that this country was never given its due for its contribution. By no means do I seek to diminish the accomplishments of the United States in the Aleutians war. That nation was by far the major force in this theatre, as in many others, and there are several fine accounts of the monumental task it achieved in driving the enemy out of Alaska. Nor have I mentioned all units that were on duty in British Columbia, Washington, and Alaska during the war, but only those relevant to this story. Again, this omission is by no means meant to downplay their role in the defence of the West Coast.

It was difficult to piece together the actions of this obscure war. Some records give differing accounts of the same incident, while veterans struggle to recall events of 60 years ago. There is also some conjecture on my part when relating events, although what is described would have been a standard procedure. For instance, when submarine *RO-61* is pinned down to the sea bottom, there is a fairly rigid course of action any submarine crew would have followed, and that is how it is described.

That there ever was a war in the north was quickly forgotten because the campaign concluded as the bigger wars overseas carried on. What is left are the dog-eared squadron journals, the mud-brown photos of soldiers hunkered into the muskeg of treeless, subarctic islands, and the ineffaceable recollections of the few surviving grey-haired soldiers.

This book really is the effort of a lot of people, for without their help I would never have completed it. My brother, Fergus Coyle, took a manuscript I had all but given up on in exasperation. For taking time away from his wife, Cassie, and his two daughters to spend the better part of a year painstakingly editing this manuscript into a readable form, I wholeheartedly thank him. My wife, Melanie Arnis, and daughters Meghan and Rhianna put up with my endless hours working on this project while I was allowed to neglect the routine of family. I also want to thank those veterans of that unknown war who gave me their time, photographs, and memories, and the people at the National Archives and CSIS in Ottawa, Comox Air Force Museum and Major W.A. March of Air Command Headquarters, Department of National Defence, who searched through records on my behalf. Also, thank you to Harry Martin at Vimy House, Canadian War Museum; the 17th Division Association; Attu Veterans Association; Peter Vassilopoulos; and Len McCann and James Delgado of the Vancouver Maritime Museum, for their valuable time and assistance.

Brendan Coyle

Introduction

The Forgotten Front

Barren and windswept, the Aleutian Islands chain arcs for over 1,600 kilometres towards Asia from the Alaska Peninsula. Appearing as mere specks in the tempestuous North Pacific Ocean, the smallest of the far-flung islands is less than a kilometre in length. Dotted with seething volcanoes and hissing fissures, and subjected to daily earth tremors, this treeless, subarctic archipelago is the world's longest chain of active volcanoes. The warm water of the Japanese current colliding with the polar air of the Bering Sea shrouds the islands in an incessant fog, and the magnetic anomaly of the Aleutians wildly spins the compasses of ships and planes, making it a navigator's hell. Tumultuous seas hurl monstrous towers of water against the islands, once easily sweeping away a whole lighthouse in a freak wave over 30 metres high. Constant buffeting by the notorious williwaw—unpredictable winds that howl across the islands at 160 kilometres an hour—warns civilization away from this lonely corner of the world. This unmerciful archipelago, which seafarers aptly called "the terrible islands," became the most unlikely of Second World War battlefields.

In June 1942, at the height of its power, the Japanese Imperial navy struck north, capturing Attu and Kiska, two tiny islands at the western extremity of the Aleutian archipelago. Fourteen months later,

Aleutian Islands, Alaska

The Alaska / Aleutians Theatre
1942 - 1944

Japanese forces seize Attu and Kiska on June 7, 1942. This becomes the first U.S. soil occupied by an enemy since 1812.

Nome

Attu
St. Lawrence Isl.
Kiska
Pribiloff Isl.
Amchitka
Adak
Umnak
Unimak
Dutch Harbor
Kodiak
Anchorage

Alaska
USA

Yukon Territory
Canada
Whitehorse
Juneau

British Columbia
Canada

Prince Rupert

Pacific Ocean

Japanese planes launched from the aircraft carriers *Ryujo* and *Junyo* bomb Dutch Harbor in two attacks, June 3 and 4, 1942.

Vancouver
Victoria
Seattle

Washington
USA

a swarm of steel landing craft picked its way through the jagged rock pinnacles of one of Kiska's northern beaches, taking its bearings on Kiska's brooding volcano, the only prominent landmark that reveals there is indeed an island hiding within the cursed Aleutian fog.

In these vessels and those that followed was a combined Canadian-American invasion force of nearly 35,000 soldiers. What lay ahead on this remote Alaskan island was believed to be an estimated 9,000 desperate and suicidal Japanese troops.

While the Pacific war seemed well removed from the solitude of the West Coast, Japan brought it to our shores and grabbed a toehold in North America. Enemy submarines haunted the waters from Alaska and British Columbia in the north to Mexico in the south. And in final desperation, Japan launched thousands of bomb-carrying balloons against the continent. Thousands of Canadians went north with their American allies to fight far from the major spotlights of the Second World War in a campaign that even today remains virtually unknown to their countrymen—a war fought on the land and waters and in the air of North America.

This was the war on our doorstep.

A Japanese dual-purpose gun on Kiska today.

Enemy Offshore

On the great expanse of ocean between Hawaii and North America, a lone wooden steamer out of Seattle plodded south towards those volcanic islands. Loaded on its open decks was dressed lumber, cut and milled in the Pacific Northwest and bound for new military construction in Honolulu. The *Cynthia Olsen*'s 31 crewmen were oblivious to the juggernaut that was Japan's Imperial navy barrelling towards Hawaii, some 1,000 kilometres to the southwest, this morning of December 7, 1941.

Beneath the sea, Japan's newest submarine, *I-26*, ran her electric motors at flank speed on a course that would intercept the little steamship. Taking his eyes from the periscope sight, Commander Minoru Yakota[1] made a note of the hour—0319 Tokyo time. In nineteen more minutes Admiral Isoroku Yamamoto's carrier force would strike the United States Pacific fleet at Pearl Harbor and the two nations would be at war. Then and only then could *I-26* commence submarine warfare against American ships. A premature attack by one of Yamamoto's submarines might alert American forces of Japanese intentions before the American fleet at Pearl Harbor was put out of commission. Until that time Yakota could only shadow his quarry.

He chose to approach the steamer submerged in order to put his green crew through some practice attacks. As *I-26* had completed its sea trials only two months earlier, the new crew had not had time to polish its skills in submarine warfare. Compounding this lack of experience was dubious weaponry. Yakota's boat was the last to receive its stock of munitions and had been allotted only ten outdated torpedoes of questionable reliability.

The Cynthia Olsen *became the first casualty of the war on the West Coast.*

Again Yakota glanced at his wristwatch—0330 hrs (0800 Honolulu time).[2] The first wave of Yamamoto's attack planes should now be closing on Pearl Harbor's battleship row.

Yakota ticked off another five minutes and then gave the order to surface. The first officer relayed the order, initiating a sequence that blasted compressed air into the ballast tanks, purging the water that held the submarine down and bringing *I-26* to the surface in a froth of air and water.

On deck, Chief Gunner Saburo Hayashi's gun crew hoisted the firing block into the gun breech and loaded one shell into the 5.5-inch (140-millimetre) deck cannon. Yakota ordered one warning shot fired. It whistled across the *Olsen*'s bow. Unheeding or unseeing, the crew did not respond and the steamer casually followed its original course. Taken aback, Yakota ordered a second shot across the bow. This time the *Cynthia Olsen*'s crew noticed and heaved to. With the two vessels bobbing in the chop, Yakota allowed the crew to abandon the ship in two lifeboats. Not fearing any immediate enemy response, he then had his crew open fire with the deck gun and, circling the ship, put the crew members through various attack angles. This manoeuvre went on for several hours, but the stubborn *Cynthia Olsen*, held afloat by its cargo of lumber, refused to sink. Yakota ordered a torpedo fired, but it went wildly off course. He finally submerged his boat to observe the situation, believing American planes might now appear at any moment.

In the time allowed to abandon ship, *Cynthia Olsen*'s wireless operator sent off two SOS messages, alerting the Matson liner *Lurline*, 592 kilometres to the south, that they were under attack by submarine. *Lurline* in turn relayed the SOS to San Francisco, but the message was met with some confusion as no word had yet come over the airwaves about an enemy attack on Hawaii. For some as yet unexplained reason,[3] the initial reports of the Pearl Harbor attack came in 55 minutes after the *Cynthia Olsen*'s SOS. North America's first notice of war in the Pacific was the distress calls from the *Cynthia Olsen*.

After 35 minutes Yakota ordered the sub to surface again to fire more rounds into the ship. He remained there seven hours, surprised that he still had not spotted one American aircraft. With his quarry aflame and settling to port, Yakota was satisfied the ship was now a total loss. With a low grind of diesel engines, *I-26* proceeded to the northeast on a course that would bring it to the waters off Washington State and British Columbia.

After drifting for several days, *Cynthia Olsen*'s survivors were spotted by another Japanese submarine, *I-19*, which stopped to render medical assistance and offer navigational direction. This act of compassion by Commander Takaichi Kinashi was in contravention of the edict issued by the commander of the First Submarine Flotilla to kill all enemy survivors, similar to Adolf Hitler's decree that German submarines should surface to shoot the survivors of sinkings. This was an unpopular order, largely ignored by the German U-boat skippers. Likewise, a few Japanese I-boat skippers obviously chose to ignore their commander's orders, as some survivors did make it safely away in lifeboats without further harassment. In spite of *I-19*'s efforts, *Cynthia Olsen*'s crew was lost in the great Pacific Ocean—never seen again.

Japan's largest submarines, dubbed "I-boats" by the Allies, were formidable undersea craft. At 108.5 metres in length, the B1 class was more than a match for many coastal-type surface patrol ships, sporting a 5.5-inch (140-millimetre) deck cannon, two 25-millimetre machine guns, and six 21-inch (53-centimetre) bow torpedo tubes. Carrying extra fuel, the submarines had a cruising range of 35,000 kilometres, more than ample for conducting a patrol to North America's West Coast and back.

Forty-two of the I-boats had a watertight hangar forward of the conning tower or sail and were equipped to carry a collapsible, twin-

A Yokosuka E14Y1 Glen, much like that launched from I-25, in preparation for takeoff from an I-boat. Below is a drawing of a Glen.

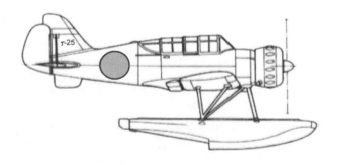

pontooned float plane, the Yokosuka E14Y1, which was dubbed "Glen" by the Allies. The Glen could be assembled in 55 minutes by the ship's mechanics and was launched by a compressed-air catapult. When the aircraft returned from its mission and landed next to the sub, it was retrieved by a crane.

Some of the I-boats were fitted to carry a two-man midget submarine—the Ho Kyoteki—or up to six Kaiten—a manned torpedo. This one-man suicide craft was used when Japan's Pacific fortunes had dwindled to the point where the navy was carrying out a desperate defence of the homeland itself.

Late in the war Japan built the massive I-400 class of submarines, which were 122 metres in length and could carry three of the new Aichi M6A1 float fighter planes. Slow to dive, the largest class of I-boat was never used to its full potential. As the war accelerated against Japan, much of its submarine fleet was consigned to ferry troops and supplies between beleaguered outposts.

One downfall of the Japanese submarine service was the lack of a consistent building program. Unlike the highly successful assembly-line production of the American and German fleet boats, the Japanese admiralty continually modified designs or changed models completely, leaving a large, inconsistent, and varied array of submarines. Furthermore, it was not until the closing stages of the war that Japan acquired any sort of surface radar. Before 1945, submarines lacking radar were easy pickings for American ships and planes with highly developed radar sets. The Allies had possessed the technology since the outbreak of war.

In December 1941, however, Japan's navy and army were enjoying phenomenal success, sweeping through Asia and the mid-Pacific. After the devastating attack on Pearl Harbor, Admiral Isoroku Yamamoto, commander-in-chief of the combined Japanese naval forces, and the Imperial navy were riding high on a wave of fanatical popularity.

But even with the Imperial navy's meticulous planning, all had not gone according to plan on December 7. Reconnaissance patrols over Pearl Harbor by submarine-launched aircraft had shown that the five aircraft carriers of the U.S. Pacific fleet were not tied up at the base, and subsequent patrols had failed to locate them. If they were not destroyed, the Americans would still have a powerful presence in the Pacific, so Japanese submarines were ordered to fan out from Hawaii in search of the carriers.

Early in his climb to the top of the naval hierarchy, Admiral Yamamoto realized that the aircraft carrier would replace the battleship

Commander Minoru Yakota surrounded by officers.

as the dominant surface vessel. In 1922, Japan launched the *Hosho*, the world's first aircraft carrier. With the exception of the United States, Axis and Allied naval powers were slow to accept the capabilities of the aircraft carrier, relying still on cruisers and battleships designed for old-style surface raiding. Yet it was the lowly Swordfish aircraft launched from the British carrier *Ark Royal* that had brought about the destruction of the great German battleship *Bismarck*. Aircraft-launched torpedoes disabled the ship, allowing the British surface fleet to sink her. Further evidence of the aircraft carrier's coming of age was the destruction of half the Italian fleet on the afternoon of November 13, 1941, after British naval planes found it at anchor at Taranto, Italy. These successes, carried out with relative ease by carrier-launched aircraft, further reinforced Yamamoto's faith in the aircraft carrier. He designed the modern Japanese navy around it, and the result was a force that emphasized the aircraft carrier replete with crews of highly trained airmen whose skills were honed in the art of naval air warfare.

Still, many voices in the naval powers, including Japan, clung to the old idea of battleships as surface raiders and the old tactics of ship against ship slugging it out. This lack of acceptance of new technology mirrored the reaction to the advent of the submarine in the First World War. It was not until Britain had suffered heavy ship losses from German U-boats that it acknowledged the submarine as a viable adversary. However, it continued to downplay the submarine well into the Second World War, when German U-boats employing wolf-pack tactics very nearly brought Britain to its knees.

In the United States, famed aviator Brigadier General Billy Mitchell had long been a proponent of aircraft carriers and also believed that they would one day replace the battleship as the dominant surface vessel. While there were those in the navy and Congress who did not share Mitchell's enthusiasm for the carrier, there was at least agreement that a force of aircraft carriers was needed for a well-rounded and ready capable fleet. As well, the impetus to build carriers came from an unlikely source. Following the First World War, the world's naval powers—France, Italy, the United States, Japan, and Britain—attempted to limit the size of battle fleets through the Washington Naval Treaty of 1922. Under the treaty, any number of warships under 33,000 imperial tons could be converted to aircraft carriers in the mistaken belief that this would limit each signatory's sea power, naval air strategy as yet being an unproven development. The United States had several cruisers already under construction, and to comply with the terms of the treaty it was obligated to either convert them to carriers or scrap them. This forced serious consideration of the carrier and its place within the fleet. By 1940 the Americans had assembled a sizeable fleet of aircraft carriers in the Pacific, and Japan had to eliminate them if it was to continue on its program of expansion and domination.

Not one to be blindsided by the propaganda that blurred the lines between ideology and reality—a condition many of his contemporaries had fallen prey to—Yamamoto publicly declared, in a 1940 interview with Shigeharu Matsumoto, a member of the Japanese cabinet, "In the first six to twelve months of a war with the United States and Great Britain I will run wild and win victory upon victory." And in the next breath he almost heretically claimed, "But if the war continues after that, I have no expectations of success."

Yamamoto clearly recognized that a strong naval opponent in the Pacific would be detrimental, if not fatal, to Japan, though a majority of his peers in the navy and, in particular, the army failed to see this in the heady aftermath of conquest. The admiral was also aware of the strategic disadvantage to being an island nation and the vulnerability produced by Japan's reliance on outside resources.

In the first months of the war, Yamamoto's faith in carrier warfare was borne out in victory after victory. On December 7, 1941, Japanese carrier-launched planes all but annihilated the American Pacific battle fleet at Pearl Harbor in their most stunning triumph. Only three days later, Japanese torpedo bombers sank the Royal Navy battleship *Prince of Wales* and the battle cruiser HMS *Repulse* near Singapore. In April 1942, 80 Japanese dive bombers quickly sank two more Royal Navy heavy cruisers. HMS *Dorsetshire* went down in eight minutes and HMS *Cornwall* in twelve minutes in the Indian Ocean without the loss of a single Japanese aircraft. It had taken the "inferior yellow man"[4] a few hours to send four major ships of Britannia's once-invincible navy to the bottom with childish ease. The enemy had lost only a few airplanes in the process. It was evident that the days of the big ship fleet were numbered.

In spite of these successes, Yamamoto was concerned about the American aircraft carriers that had eluded his planes at Pearl Harbor. He knew they were unlikely to return to Hawaii, which meant their probable destination was Australia or one of the mainland American bases: San Diego or San Francisco in California, the shipyards on the Columbia River in Oregon, or the base at Bremerton in Washington State. To intercept the carriers, Yamamoto sent a force of nine submarines to North America's West Coast, stationing them off every major port from Vancouver Island in British Columbia to San Diego, California.

Of great interest to the Japanese was the U.S. Navy port and shipyard at Bremerton, south of Seattle in Puget Sound. They believed the American carriers might be en route to Bremerton or already there. The Imperial navy was well aware that all marine traffic heading into or out of Puget Sound had one direct route to the Pacific Ocean—the Strait of Juan de Fuca, a 50-kilometre-wide body of water separating Vancouver Island in British Columbia and the Olympic Peninsula in Washington State. So when the *I-26* arrived with compatriot boats off the West Coast in mid-December 1941, Minoru Yakota took up station, patrolling from a point midway down Vancouver Island south to Cape Flattery at the northwest tip of the Olympic Peninsula. Shortly after his arrival, Yakota fired one torpedo at a merchant vessel off Vancouver Island. The torpedo missed and the unnamed freighter continued on, oblivious to its brush with war.

Commander Meji Tagami in *I-25* took up station off Juan de Fuca, patrolling as far south as the Columbia River. Separating Oregon and Washington states, the Columbia was of concern to the Japanese because it supported ship repair facilities and had deep-sea ports at Astoria in Oregon and at Longview on the Washington side. There was also a large army installation at Fort Stevens, as well as a radar and radio-direction-finding station at the mouth of the river.

Farther south, obvious targets were the waters off San Francisco and Los Angeles. Both were major ports, had large shipyards, and saw a good deal of navy traffic. San Diego was the main U.S. Navy base on the Pacific coast, while Santa Barbara was an important oil-producing region and a busy port for tanker ships. While the I-boats had been ordered to attack ships of commerce when they were encountered, their destruction was of secondary importance. The primary goal of the West Coast offensive was the destruction of the American aircraft carrier fleet. Before Christmas, *I-23*, *I-21*, *I-19*, *I-17*, *I-15*, *I-10*, and *I-9*, along with *I-25* and *I-26*, were prowling the coast from Vancouver Island south to the border of Mexico.

The Japanese employed the I-boats much more readily as surface vessels than the Germans did their U-boats in the Atlantic, preferring to shell rather than expend a torpedo—possibly due to the initial unreliability of the Japanese-made "fish." The I-boats were also ordered to shell important shore facilities such as navigational aids and military installations along the West Coast, which required them to move in relatively close to the enemy coast.

The Japanese had prior knowledge of many of these sites, such as radar and radio-direction-finding posts, due to some creative intelligence-gathering by the Imperial navy. During the build-up of Japanese marine forces, many officers were drawn from the ranks of the merchant service and were quite familiar with the West Coast ports because they had plied these waters during their merchant careers. The Imperial navy had also sent fishing vessels manned by navy sailors to reconnoitre the coast from Alaska to California. It is likely that merchant ships deposited spies in West Coast ports prior to the war, and these men were easily able to gather information on

The Japanese submarine I-26 *made two patrols of the West Coast, sinking two ships and shelling the radio-direction-finding station at Estevan Point on Vancouver Island, B.C.*

shore defences and military installations, or the lack of them. Large populations of first-generation Japanese had settled along the coast, and they would readily welcome visitors from the homeland. It is not unreasonable to think that information was passed, unwittingly or not, in casual conversation with visiting sailors and relatives. Prior to the war, this "subversive" gathering of information would not have been considered illegal.

As part of their West Coast agenda, Japanese submarines shelled land facilities in Hawaii, California, Oregon, and British Columbia, mainly military, transport, and communications targets, though there were also plans for the submarines to shell coastal communities at midnight on Christmas Eve. All nine submarines were to surface at a predetermined time and bombard villages along the coast from British Columbia to California in a synchronized attack. This was strictly a terror tactic, targeting civilians rather than military or industrial sites, and occurring on a holiday when businesses would be shut down, with families at home. Strategists believed the effect of such a bombardment on the continent so soon after the attack at Pearl Harbor would destabilize pubic morale and cause mass hysteria.

The submarines were busy in the weeks leading up to December 24. On December 12, around the same time *I-19* happened upon *Cynthia Olsen*'s survivors, *I-10* was on its way to the North American coast when it torpedoed the freighter *Donnyvale* east of where *Cynthia Olsen* had been sunk. Commander Yasuchika Kayahara then had *Donnyvale*'s survivors machine-gunned, killing 27 men in their lifeboats. In stark contrast to *I-19*'s humanitarian gesture, brutality would be typical of many Japanese submarine crews, as it would be of the country's military in general throughout the Asian and Pacific campaigns.

The lumber carrier *Samoa* was the first ship to come under attack along the West Coast. Southbound with a cargo of timber from Washington State to San Diego, *Samoa's* watch caught sight of the black shape of a submarine shadowing the freighter off Santa Barbara in the first light of December 18. Immediately the ship began an evasive manoeuvre. Not wanting to lose his quarry, *I-17's* commander, Kuzo Nishino, hastily fired a torpedo at the retreating freighter. Halfway to the target the torpedo exploded inexplicably—a sign of things to come for the I-boats. Nishino ordered his gun crew to shell the runaway freighter. In the anxious attempt to stop it, the crew lobbed five shells at the steamer before breaking off the attack. One shell connected, inflicting minor damage on *Samoa's* radio room.

That evening, *I-17* spotted the 6,912-ton oil tanker *Emidio* southbound off northern California. Nishino moved to intercept the tanker on the surface, but again was spotted by an alert watchman. The enemy submarine running on the surface quickly closed the gap between hunter and quarry to less than a thousand metres. The first mortar shot hit the midship fuel cargo tank, and the crew took to lifeboats, abandoning their doomed vessel. Ignoring the survivors, *I-17* continued to shell the wallowing tanker, connecting with six more hits to ensure *Emidio's* demise. A navy bomber en route to Seattle from San Francisco picked up *Emidio's* Mayday and caught the sub on the surface. One 300-pound (135-kilogram) anti-submarine bomb detonated perilously close to *I-17*, while a second, fortunately for Nishino, landed close enough to do damage but failed to explode. Nishino fired a single torpedo, which exploded under *Emidio's* stern, then retreated from the area, believing the victim was on its way to the bottom. Five of *Emidio's* crew died in the attack, and the hulk eventually washed onto the rocks at Crescent City, California, near the Oregon border, where it was declared a total loss. It remained hung up there until 1951.

On the same day that Nishino attacked *Samoa* and *Emidio* in California waters, Meiji Tagami, commanding *I-25*, took up station off the mouth of the Columbia River. Sometime after midnight on December 18, Tagami spied the outline of a merchant ship off Destruction Point on the Washington coast. It was the Union Oil tanker *L.P. St. Clair* running from the Pacific Northwest to the oil facilities at Santa Barbara. The tanker was already crossing the mouth of the river when Tagami ordered the crew to open fire with the deck cannon. When the first rounds sent up geysers of water alongside his ship, skipper John Ellison ordered an abrupt course change that took him into the river, as he knew the sub was unlikely to try to follow him there. *I-25* fired ten rounds, all of which missed, before *L.P. St. Clair* made it into the safety of the Columbia River.

On the afternoon of December 20, *1-23* attacked the tanker *Agwiwold* when it was off Santa Cruz Island. In a bold daylight surface attack, well within sight of the California mainland, *1-23* commander Genichi Shibata shot two 5.5-inch (140-millimetre) shells into the side of *Agwiwold.* First Officer Frederick Goncalves immediately undertook evasive manoeuvring and outran the sub to port, dodging eight more shells in the action.

Two days later Takaichi Kinashi's *I-19* carried out another daylight surface attack. On a sunny December 22, *I-19* surfaced off Point Arguello, 176 kilometres north of Los Angeles, to intercept the Standard Oil tanker *H.M. Storey.* In full view of beach strollers, *I-19* landed several shells on the 10,763-ton tanker. While *H.M. Storey* attempted to dodge the submarine's shells, Kinashi fired four torpedoes, all of which missed or failed to detonate. Sure that patrols would have been alerted, Kinashi broke off his attack and dived for cover. Although smoking, the tanker was able to make the safety of the tiny coastal resort community of Surf, California. Bombers arrived on the scene and peppered the area with anti-submarine bombs. However, *I-19* was safely submerged and creeping south to patrol the waters off Los Angeles.

On December 23, one day before the planned bombardment of West Coast communities, the I-boats surfaced along the coast under cover of darkness to await further orders. The brazen strike directly at America would bring prestige to the Imperial navy's submarine service. But it was not to be. At the designated message-relaying time around 0200, the faint tapping of wireless sets on the enemy submarines from British Columbia to California brought their skippers a discouraging message. The commander of the Advance Expeditionary Force—as the flotilla of subs operating on the West Coast was known—ordered that the Christmas bombardment was not to proceed. The admiralty was forced to concede that Japanese North Americans who populated some coastal areas might be killed during the attack. They might also become the target of a severe backlash in retaliation for the attacks on civilians. The subs were ordered to maintain patrols and continue to seek out the enemy carriers.

That same day, three more merchant ships came under attack. *I-17* made an unsuccessful attempt to shell the 7,000-ton freighter *Larry*

Doheny 128 kilometres southwest of Los Angeles, inflicting only minor damage before the ship slipped into the harbour of Long Beach.

The tanker *Montebello*, its holds filled with crude oil, was outbound from Los Angeles and heading north for Vancouver, British Columbia, when Kenji Matsumura on *I-21* caught it in his sights off Monterey, California. At 0540 the *Montebello*'s watch spotted the silhouette of a submarine shadowing them about a kilometre off the starboard quarter. Immediately Captain Olaf Eckstrom put his vessel into an evasive pattern, but a torpedo struck directly under the starboard bridge, blowing off the deckhouse, radio room, and forward mast. At once the ship began to settle by the bow, and Eckstrom ordered his crew away in the lifeboats. *Montebello* slipped under the waves at 0645. *I-21* fired at the survivors, splintering the wooden lifeboats, but miraculously hitting none of the crewmen. All 36 crew survived the torpedoing. In 1997, *Montebello* was discovered in 250 metres of water, less than two kilometres off the marine ecological reserve at Monterey Bay, her cargo tanks an environmental time bomb still full of crude oil.

Withdrawing south from the *Montebello* sinking, *I-21* came across the tanker *Idaho* off California's Long Beach and took up pursuit, firing several rounds, all of which missed. *Idaho* managed to elude Matsumura long enough to escape into the safety of Long Beach's harbour.

The following morning Kinashi, in *I-19*, spotted the freighter *Barbara Olsen* off Long Beach and lined her up for a torpedo attack. Again his torpedoes failed him and exploded short of the freighter. The alerted ship's crew outran the sub into Long Beach, and a frustrated Kinashi recorded four more torpedoes fired and four more misses.

Kinashi and other sub skippers would complain in their logbooks that the new Japanese torpedo, the Model 95, was fraught with problems. It was unreliable, exploding short of the target or not at all, or going off course. (These were the same complaints U.S. submarine skippers had about their newest fish.) Eventually problems with the Japanese torpedo were worked out, making it highly reliable, but it was too late for the submarine patrols of North America. If not for the initial unreliability of the Japanese torpedoes, more Allied boats would certainly have gone to the bottom along the West Coast.

Kinashi moved *I-19* into Catalina Channel off Point Fermin, and later that same day he spotted the 5,695-ton lumber freighter *Absaroka* heading south. He fired two torpedoes. Again the first officer ticked off the minutes on his stopwatch, shaking his head when time ran out on the first fish. As time clicked down on the second torpedo, the sharp rattle of an explosion reverberated through the sub's hull. Raising the periscope, Kinashi could see the ship had taken the hit amidships and was already settling in the water. He was lining up *Absaroka* for another shot when the appearance of a patrol plane forced him to dive before he could get off a parting shot. The freighter, buoyed by her cargo of lumber, was towed to Bethlehem Shipyards in San Francisco and repaired.

In Monterey Bay the armed yacht *Dorothy Phillips* was outbound on Christmas Eve when *I-23* opened fire. No match for a 109-metre submarine, the little gunboat sped back towards the bay and ran aground on the approaches. The sub, however, had given up the chase.

The appearance of enemy subs off the coast in the frantic weeks following the attack on Pearl Harbor set everyone on edge. In 1941–42, 147 submarine sightings were reported along the coast from the Columbia River to southern Alaska, and anti-submarine patrols were often needlessly sent out to investigate, straining valuable resources with sometimes disastrous results. Anxious comrades watched the hours pass as patrol planes failed to return in the wretched weather of northern B.C. and Alaska. Occasionally, an over-anxious aircrew bombed a submarine, only to confirm the target was an unsuspecting whale. (Sonar was an imperfect science at the time.)

The Japanese submariners contributed to the confusion by releasing hundreds of dummy periscopes—a buoyed bamboo pole with a weight at one end to hold the "periscope" upright. The Canadian army's heavy guns successfully "sank" one of these ersatz submarines when it appeared off Gordon Head near Victoria on January 31, 1941. This ruse effectively kept Allied anti-submarine forces on useless search-and-destroy missions long after the I-boats had withdrawn from the West Coast. It also partially explains the disproportionate number of submarine sightings and anti-submarine attacks recorded along this coast compared to the number of enemy subs actually employed here.

By December 27, only one Japanese submarine remained on the West Coast. The others had been recalled to the Japanese base at Kwajalein or ordered to Hawaiian waters to blockade those islands. Still patrolling off Oregon, Tagami in *I-25* attacked the 8,684-ton tanker *Connecticut* well into the Columbia River with a single torpedo. The fish struck home, and in the ensuing chase the tanker ran hard aground on a sand bar, taking on a port list as the tide receded. Believing the ship was sinking, Tagami withdrew and left the rainy Pacific Northwest to join his compatriots in Kwajalein. Miraculously, the torpedo did not ignite the tanker's explosive cargo, and the ship was later salvaged from the Columbia River bar that had kept it from sinking.

In January 1942 the I-boats concentrated on Hawaii, sinking five ships around the islands. On New Year's Eve, Hilo on Hawaii, Nawiliwili on Kaui, and Kahului on Maui were all shelled by enemy submarines. Surprisingly, when *I-7* launched its Glen aircraft over Pearl Harbor on December 18 and again on January 6 to observe the damage inflicted in the December 7 attack and check for the elusive American carriers, the plane was unchallenged.

In February 1942, two I-boats were ordered back to the West Coast. *I-8* patrolled the Port Renfrew / Cape Flattery area of the B.C.-Washington State coasts and *I-17* returned to its hunting grounds in California. Under cover of the predawn sky on February 28, Nishino guided his boat through Santa Barbara Channel to scout the oil installations along the shore at Goleta. As he made note of the pumping facilities, Nishino could plainly see vehicle headlights moving along the Pacific Highway. He then submerged to wait for nightfall.

For ten hours the crew whiled away the time, drinking hot tea and playing cards or games of *go maku* in the submerged boat. At 1900 hours Nishino brought his submarine back to the surface and ordered a three-man gun crew to station on the 5.5-inch (140-millimetre) gun. *I-17* then fired seventeen shells into the oil pumping station in a brazen strike at America—the first enemy shells to fall on the continent since the War of 1812. Fearing entrapment by anti-submarine forces between the Channel Islands and the mainland, the sub dived and proceeded north. On shore there was minor damage, and one U.S. artilleryman was injured the following day while deactivating an unexploded shell. He was awarded the Purple Heart for his injuries—the only serviceman injured by enemy action on the continental United States during the war.

The following day the *Los Angeles Times* reported in bold headlines the bombing of the Los Angeles area by Japanese aircraft. Others reported that the town of Santa Barbara itself was bombarded by enemy planes and cruisers. That night jittery anti-aircraft batteries around Los Angeles fired off 1,700 rounds of ammunition at flocks of birds and imagined enemy bombers. The physical damage *I-17* had caused amounted to about $500, but the propaganda wrought by media in North America stoked the embers of distrust against Japanese North Americans. Incidents real or perceived were unabashedly exaggerated and expounded upon by the media, and reporters who injected stories with their own biases helped turn attitudes against first- and second-generation Japanese North Americans.

On March 1 Nishino, nearing the end of his patrol, was at the extreme north point of his area—the waters off San Francisco's Golden Gate. Troop carrier *William H. Berg* was returning to San Francisco when *I-17* sent a torpedo under the ship's aft end. The submarine surfaced to attack with gunfire, but the troopship started firing back from deck-mounted guns. Nishino quickly dived, surprised at the quick reaction of the American crew. Nishino's *I-17* left the West Coast that same week.

The *I-8* under Commander Tatsunosuke Ariizume was anxious to record a kill on the West Coast, but it had lurked off Juan de Fuca Strait for a month with nothing to show for it. Ariizume was a highly experienced submarine skipper, having conducted patrols recently around the Hawaiian Islands. He and his I-boat would later gain infamy for one of the war's worst high-seas atrocities committed by submariners. After his crew sank the Dutch freighter *Tjisalak* in the Indian Ocean, the survivors, including a Red Cross nurse, were viciously tortured with swords and sledgehammers before being thrown over the side, while others drowned after they were bundled together and left to the sharks. Ariizume was eventually elevated to the position of squadron commander of four submarines, and crews under his direction boasted of consuming the flesh of "rescued" Allied prisoners. Like many of his compatriots, the bloodthirsty commander eluded justice after the fall of Japan by committing suicide at the Yokosuka navy base as Allied troops moved in. But in the opening days of the Pacific war he prowled the waters off southern Vancouver Island and Cape Flattery. Canadian anti-submarine patrols recorded more sightings at this time, possibly of *I-8*. Watchmen on the minesweeper HMCS *Outarde* spotted a submarine periscope in their wake, but when they turned on the target they came up empty-handed.

That same month, as a twin-engined Bolingbroke from the 8th Bomber Reconnaissance Squadron was returning to base at Sea Island near Vancouver, aircrew observed a submarine break the surface a kilometre astern of their aircraft. When the plane banked for an attack, the submarine immediately dived to safety as bombs were dropped on the area.

The *Moolack*, a tug consigned to the Fishermen's Volunteer Reserve (FVR), was towing a barge of explosives into the Strait of Juan de Fuca when it reported that a periscope had surfaced between the tug and its tow. The periscope immediately retracted as the barge closed over the site. An inexperienced watch officer on duty at Naden ordered the tug, unarmed and without any means of searching for a submerged submarine, to drop its tow and attack the submarine, much to the alarm of the tug's seasoned crew. After animated radio discussion, more experienced minds prevailed. In the fog and currents of the strait, a loose barge could easily end up on the rocks or collide with another vessel, which would have given Ariizume a kill in a very roundabout manner. Following a disappointing patrol, *I-8* left the Cape Flattery area without a single attack on an Allied vessel.

The ocean off the West Coast was rougher than what the crews of the I-boats were used to in the South Pacific, with generally foul weather and consistently strong currents that made it hard for them to manoeuvre. One submarine skipper recorded that the periscopes of Japanese submarines were too short, causing the boats to expose themselves in the West Coast swells.[5] Coupled with the unreliability of early Japanese torpedoes, hunting off the coast had been a disappointment to the enemy submariners. No aircraft carriers or major warships had been spotted along the coast, let alone attacked and sunk, and Allied anti-submarine patrols reacted much more quickly and were better prepared than the I-boat skippers had expected. Still, the enemy submariners gained a particular status amongst their comrades. They had brought the Pacific war to the very shores of North America.

And they would return.

Undefended Territory

During the brief history of European exploitation of the north, Alaska's Aleutian Island chain remained virtually unexplored and uninhabited. The Aleut people, distant relatives of the Siberian Eskimo, managed to eke out a living here, and traces of the Aleuts dating back thousands of years have been discovered on several of the islands. Ancient Aleut hunters established seasonal camps as well as burial sites throughout the chain.

When the Russian empire occupied Alaska in the eighteenth and early nineteenth centuries, the Aleutians became little more than a gulag. The Aleuts, sequestered in camps throughout the archipelago, were forced into slave labour as fur hunters and skinners. When the onset of winter ended the season's hunting, the Russians left many of the Aleuts on the remote islands to die.

In 1942, Aleut settlements were located on at least three islands: Atka, Adak at the centre of the chain, and at Chichagof Harbor on Attu, some 720 kilometres west of Adak at the western end of the chain. Attu was the site of a massacre of fifteen Aleuts in 1749 by Russian sealers at what is aptly named Massacre Bay. Now 42 Aleuts and two white missionaries lived at Chichigof. There had been an Aleut village at Constantine Harbor on Amchitka, but it was abandoned during Russian tenure of the islands. The only other inhabitants of the western islands were ten U.S. Coast Guard personnel at the Kiska weather station some 257 kilometres southeast of Attu.

Japanese submarines and fishing vessels doubling as spy ships had reconnoitred the western Aleutian islands of Attu, Agattu, Kiska, Shemya, Amchitka, and Adak in 1941. Although they found the islands to be desolate and mainly uninhabited, Admiral Isoroku Yamamoto saw their military potential. The most western of the islands lay only 965 kilometres from Japan's northern perimeter, Paramushiro in the Kuriles, and Yamamoto feared the Americans would eventually use them as bases from which to bomb Japan. He told Prime Minister General Hideki Tojo and the Imperial staff that it would be in Japan's interest to control the Aleutian Islands. They could serve as Japan's northern perimeter, and their occupation would prevent their use by the Allies.

Yamamoto's idea fit in with an earlier plan called the Greater East Asia Co-Prosperity Sphere (GEACPS)—a thinly veiled plan for Japanese expansion in Asia that was first conceived by Prime Minister Giichi Tanaka in the 1920s. The GEACPS was to arc halfway across the Pacific, encompassing the Aleutian Islands in the north, Midway and Hawaii in the mid-Pacific, and Australia and New Zealand in the south.

The Imperial generals scoffed at Yamamoto's Aleutian plan, saying the islands were too remote and too hostile for use by the Americans. Japanese troops would be put to better use in the South Pacific, where imperialist expansion was amassing new territory. They could not afford to waste troops on these "useless islands."

This view of the Aleutians changed on April 18, 1942, when Lieutenant Colonel James Doolittle's B-25s bombed Tokyo and the Yokosuka navy base in a daring daylight raid—something Tojo had promised the Japanese people would never happen. The only land controlled by the Allies within bombing range of Tokyo was the Aleutians, and Yamamoto believed this was where the bombers had originated.

Doolittle's medium-range bombers had in fact been launched from the carrier *Hornet*, 950 kilometres east of the Japanese coast, and struck directly at Japan's capital city. Without enough fuel for a return trip to *Hornet*, the bomber crews' unorthodox plans were to carry on and ditch their planes over Manchuria. From there they were to make contact with Chinese nationalists who would arrange for their escape from the occupied territory.

Under interrogation, a captured airman of Doolittle's raiding party revealed that the bombers came from an aircraft carrier and not from a base in the Aleutians. Still, the raid showed Japan's vulnerability to such an attack, and it must have convinced the chiefs of staff that it was only a matter of time before the United States built air bases in the Aleutians and commenced bombing runs on the motherland. Shortly after Doolittle's raid, approval was given to Yamamoto's plan to occupy the Alaskan islands.

Yamamoto still had to contend with the American carrier force that had escaped destruction at Pearl Harbor. Subsequent submarine patrols off Hawaii, North America, and Australia had failed to locate and destroy the carrier fleet, which was in waters south of Hawaii, and this meant the United States remained a powerful opponent in the Pacific. Doolittle's Tokyo raid showed just how decisive an opponent the aircraft carrier was becoming in naval strategy.

Yamamoto and his admirals devised a two-fold plan to carry out both offensive and defensive aims. Japan would initiate a carrier-launched attack on Alaska at Dutch Harbor—a fishing village in the eastern Aleutian Islands, 1,280 kilometres west of Anchorage. An assault force would then occupy Attu and Kiska in the west of the chain, Adak at its centre, and eventually Dutch Harbor itself. When the aircraft carriers of the U.S. fleet steamed north to defend Alaska, they would be met and destroyed at Midway by a superior Japanese force. Midway, 2,200 kilometres north of Hawaii, was a minor U.S. possession supporting a garrison of marines and an assortment of fighter planes. Japan had long desired this Pacific atoll, which would be the geographic centre for the GEACPS and pivotal as a base from which to launch further attacks on Hawaii.

Thus the attack on Alaska would finish off the U.S. Pacific fleet; put Japan in control of Midway, from which it could stage an invasion of Hawaii; ensure Japan was not threatened by enemy bases in the Aleutians; and cut the northern supply route from North America to Russia. Japanese bases in the Aleutians could be used as staging points for direct action against North America. Japanese warships would be free to cruise North America's West Coast with impunity. Long-range bombers and warships could hit the Boeing aircraft plants and shipyards located at Seattle and Vancouver. Once cities along the West Coast had been bombed, American desire to hold on to its South Pacific territories would be greatly undermined. Certainly the American public would desire to negotiate peace with Japan, and the United States would be forced to cede control of the western Pacific. Early in 1942, Yamamoto was given priority to proceed with his Midway / Aleutian plan.

Even at this early stage of the Pacific war, however, ingenuity and some good fortune on the part of the Allies helped in the fight against Japan. U.S. cryptographers achieved a most significant milestone in this theatre of the war when they developed Magic, an ultra-secret code-breaking unit, to decipher the secret messages transmitted by the Japanese navy. From radio interceptions, American intelligence learned that Yamamoto was planning simultaneous attacks in Alaska and at Midway north of Hawaii. Some in American intelligence believed (correctly) that a Japanese feint at Alaska might only be a diversion to draw out the American carrier force into a decisive battle at Midway. Others believed an attack on the north would be a prelude to a larger invasion of the North American continent. Both scenarios held equal weight in military circles. But no one knew just where in the north the Japanese would strike, and any of the coastal villages from Ucluelet on Vancouver Island's west coast to Nome in Alaska's north were considered possible targets of attack. The very real possibility of enemy troops landing in the north brought home the fact that until the approach of war, Alaska, northern British Columbia, and Canada's north had been ignored. Now it appeared the enemy would soon be pounding at the gates.

As early as the 1930s, Alaskans had urged Congress to approve some form of military presence for Alaska, but these requests were ignored. In 1935, Brigadier General Billy Mitchell professed to Congress that "Alaska is the most strategic place in the whole world, the jumping off point to Asia and Japan." Fairbanks, at the centre of Alaska, was within 6,400 kilometres of every important northern capital. Mitchell already viewed Tokyo, which was then staking claims in Manchuria, as the new threat in the Pacific. From Fairbanks, the Japanese capital was within fifteen hours' flying time, as was New York. The Aleutian Islands could provide the stepping stones for an invading army from Asia right to North America, and whoever controlled Alaska could control the world.[1]

By and large, Mitchell's prophecies were ignored. Only in the year before the attack on Pearl Harbor did the U.S. Congress begin to take any notice of Alaska's defence. Prior to 1940 there was virtually no American military presence in the territory.[2] U.S. defences there consisted of one army outpost on the Canadian border at Haines, the Chilkoot Barracks. This fort had been built to maintain order over the Klondike gold rush and housed a small garrison armed with First World War helmets and rifles. There was no armament larger than a .303 rifle. Throughout Alaska, there were only a few hundred soldiers posted to guard the whole vast territory.

In 1940, however, Congress decided some form of military expenditure was needed for the northern territory, and it formed the Alaska Defense Command, which would direct all aspects of land, sea, and air defence. The task of putting together the newly created force fell to Lieutenant General Simon Bolivar Buckner Jr.—a high-achieving West Point graduate from Kentucky, whose father had been a Confederate Army general in the American Civil War. Buckner was well suited to Alaska, with an ability to skirt protocol and conventions of formal command to get what he needed—a requisite for survival in the north. He got the go-ahead to construct air bases at Anchorage, Yakutat, Kodiak Island, and Annette Island, 65 kilometres north of Prince Rupert, B.C., in the Alaska Panhandle. Naval seaplane bases were also slated for Dutch Harbor, Kodiak, and Sitka.

In 1922 the U.S. had agreed not to fortify the Aleutian Islands. This was another part of the Washington Naval Treaty, which also limited Japan's naval strength to half that of Great Britain and the United States. The Aleutian agreement was an attempt to allay Japanese concerns over a possible American naval presence so close to the homeland, but the hawks in Japan's navy were not appeased. In 1934 Japan renounced the treaty. It was not until 1940, however, that Congress approved construction of the Fort Meares army base at Dutch Harbor and a navy base at Makushin Bay. Two secret air bases also got the green light. Disguised as a salmon cannery called Saxton & Co., a base was erected 280 kilometres east of Dutch Harbor at Cold Bay on the Alaska Peninsula, while 65 kilometres west of Dutch Harbor, at Umnak Island, another crude airfield went up as the Blair Packing Co. By June 1942 the small army outpost of Fort Meares was nearing completion.

In 1940 Alaska's communication system consisted of a series of wireless operators and a few radio transmission sites. In many regions of the north, messages were delivered to a radio transmission station by boat or dogsled or on foot over long distances. This was obviously an unreliable method, and there were often long delays in receiving messages. To run an army in the vast north, Buckner needed to greatly improve upon what little was available and extend electronic communications to areas where none previously existed. To this end, the U.S. Army leased a cable-laying ship, the *Brico*, from the British Columbia Telephone and Telegraph Company and pressed it into service until the end of the war. By V-J Day the *Brico* had laid 50,000 kilometres of undersea cable, venturing as far north as Nome at the edge of the Arctic Ocean and west into the Aleutians.

The largest cable-laying ship in the world, *Restorer*, belonging to the Commercial Pacific Cable Co., was brought north from Victoria at

The Brico, *chartered by the U.S. Army from the B.C. Telephone and Telegraph Company to lay communications cable in Alaska. The ship now spends its days as a restaurant on the Old Island Highway near Courtenay, B.C.*

the end of May 1942 and crewed by Canadian merchant navy sailors and the U.S. Army Signal Corps. It also spent the entire Pacific campaign laying communications cable in the far reaches of Alaska. Eventually it operated as far out into the chain as Amchitka Island—an area patrolled by Japanese submarines and planes and only 112 kilometres from the main enemy base at Kiska.

Buckner was initially given the 4th Infantry Regiment, totalling nearly 800 men, which had arrived at Anchorage in June 1940. The first personnel of the 11th Army Air Force, which came to be known unofficially as the Alaskan Air Force, also began to arrive. They were under the command of Colonel Everett S. Davis.

In 1940, the U.S. Navy's Pacific fleet, under Admiral Chester Nimitz, created the Alaskan Sector of the Seattle Naval District and placed this small command under Captain Ralph C. Parker. His "Alaskan Navy" consisted of eight First World War-era destroyers armed with 3-inch (76-millimetre) guns and a fleet of wooden "YP" (Yard Patrol) boats. These were essentially fishing boats. Some had a machine gun mounted forward, but their usefulness was limited to little more than coastal patrol. The navy posted six S-boats—vintage First World War-era submarines—to stand watch far out into the Aleutian Islands. The S-boats were obsolete, cramped affairs, 69 metres in length, that

The cable ship Restorer.

the submariners aptly dubbed "pigboats."[3] They had no food freezers, only one toilet and shower for 55 men, and no air conditioning. Condensation was thick inside the subs, and after a time at sea it produced fungus over the bulkheads, blankets, and electrical equipment. Cockroaches made themselves abundantly at home on the pigboats. On the list for decommissioning, several of the tired old submarines were recalled from training status and sent to Alaska once the United States entered the war. At this point only one ship, the *Gillis*, a seaplane tender, had radar, and there was only one wireless set, at Dutch Harbor. Six navy PBYs—the military version of the Catalina flying boat—were also based at Dutch Harbor. All Coast Guard vessels fell under the command of the Alaskan naval sector.

By the time Japanese bombs fell on Pearl Harbor, Alaska had a little over 2,000 air force personnel, 22,000 soldiers, and fewer than 600 navy personnel. After the strike, the vulnerability of Alaska and the north finally hit home to those in Washington. Since the navy had few ships to spare after the loss of the battleship fleet at Pearl Harbor, one option given serious consideration was to abandon Alaska to the Japanese and mount the entire defensive to hold Midway—the key target. Nimitz correctly concluded that Yamamoto would again use his carriers as his main thrust at Midway, rather than engage in a duel of big guns. Thus it was to Midway that Nimitz directed his remaining carriers, *Hornet* and *Enterprise*.[4] However, he was not of the mind to simply abandon the north to the Japanese, so he bolstered Alaska's meagre naval force with the addition of five cruisers and four more old four-stack destroyers. With the addition of the cruisers, the Seattle Naval District's Alaskan Sector was reformed into the larger North Pacific Force. On May 21, 1942, this force of nine ships under the command of Admiral Robert A. Theobald steamed out of Pearl Harbor. Nine days later the squadron dropped anchor at Kodiak, Alaska, with orders to "defend at all costs."[5]

In 1940, in response to Japan's increasing militarism and the uncertain aspirations of the Soviet Union, Canada and the United States signed the Pacific Joint Agreement on Defense. Simply put, the agreement stipulated that each nation would supply troops, ships, and planes for reciprocal defence of its neighbour. This particularly applied to Alaska, which the United States would find difficult to defend without Canadian co-operation. Under the terms of the agreement, Canada would make contingents of its army, navy, and air force available for the defence of Alaska if the territory was threatened.

When Magic revealed the very real threat of a Japanese attack on Alaska, the United States invoked the terms of the joint agreement. However, the Americans had kept Magic a tightly guarded secret—its allies would not know of the code-breaking unit's existence until the war had ended—and by spring 1942 the U.S. had still not informed the Canadian government of the planned Japanese attack on Alaska, information gleaned by Magic. As a result, the Canadians could not understand the urgency the Americans were placing on the defence of the remote northern territory. Somewhat reluctantly, the Canadian government complied with American requests for military support, asking few questions, though many of the Canadian military brass rightly cried foul.

Almost immediately, the Canadian navy assumed a very large share of the responsibility for running escorts for convoys bound north to Alaska or returning south. This entailed taking over the escort of ships from the Americans off Cape Flattery or Seattle and shepherding them as far north as Dutch Harbor and eventually out to Adak and Amchitka when the war moved into the Aleutians. This was a crucial role from early on, as much of the northern-bound material was destined for Russia as part of the Lend-Lease program—one of the first vital steps by the western alliance to keep the Soviet war effort alive.

The West Coast fleet of the Royal Canadian Navy (RCN) was largely composed of escort and harbour defence vessels. The largest warships on the coast were three converted Canadian National steamships, the armed merchant cruisers *Prince Henry, Prince David*, and *Prince Robert*. The *Prince Robert* had successfully intercepted and captured the German freighter *Weser* and her crew off Mexico in the Pacific in September of 1940. It also had served to transfer Canadian troops from Esquimalt to Hong Kong in the ill-fated defence of the British colony. *Prince Henry* followed up by intercepting two German freighters that attempted to make a break out of Peru, where they'd been holed up since the outbreak of war. The crews of *Munchen* and *Hermonthis* scuttled their ships at the point of capture, and Germany was denied the much-needed raw materials they were transporting. Despite these actions, the armed merchant cruisers, like most of the current inventory of warships in the Pacific Northwest, were no match for the highly efficient carriers and cruisers of the Japanese Imperial navy should a confrontation arise.

Other significant RCN vessels based on the West Coast station for at least part of their wartime career were the corvettes *Quesnel, Dawson, Vancouver, Edmunston*, and *New Westminster*. Minesweepers *Outarde, Quatsino, Ingonish, Canso, Bayfield, Courtenay, Kelowna, Guyesborough, Caraquet, Comox, Chignetco*, and *Miramachi* alternated duties between the Prince Rupert Force, which operated as far north as Dutch Harbor in the Aleutians, and Esquimalt Force, which operated between Washington and Prince Rupert.

Completing the regular navy roster was an assortment of auxiliary vessels such as submarine chasers and Fairmiles—boats designed by the British Fairmile Engineering Company for anti-submarine response and vessel interdiction. The Fairmiles replaced the ageing fleet of armed trawlers and resembled a cross between a luxury yacht and a motor torpedo boat.

Near Victoria the RCN operated from its main base, HMCS Naden at Esquimalt, and the base for northern operations at Prince Rupert. Secondary bases were also located at Comox for training and at HMCS Discovery in Vancouver for liasion with the air force. The base at Esquimalt was protected by gun emplacements at Fort Rodd Hill at

The Canadian National steamships Prince David *(top),* Prince Henry *(middle), and* Prince Robert *(bottom) were converted to armed merchant cruisers and served in the Alaska / Aleutians theatre under U.S. Navy control.*

the entrance to the harbour. This updated British fort was originally built in 1858 and sported two 6-inch (150-millimetre) disappearing guns, which were updated by modern twin 6-inch guns, anti-aircraft batteries, and searchlight posts. The sheds housing the searchlights were painted to appear as fishing shanties complete with two-dimensional dories to fool enemy observers. Inside each fish shack was a searchlight, 80 centimetres in diameter, that had a range of over 25 kilometres. With powerful searchlights also at Fort Worden and Port Angeles on the American side, the entire 50-kilometre width of the strait could be covered by high-powered lights and gun batteries.

Fort Rodd had originally been constructed in response to the threat of another group of invaders coming down from Alaska—Russians, who in the 1850s controlled the Alaskan territory and were at war with Britain on the Crimean Peninsula. During the lucrative West Coast fur trade, Britain feared a Russian fleet might try to seize Vancouver Island because of its wealth of fur-bearing marine mammals.

Overlooking the Juan de Fuca Strait, Albert Head had three 9-inch (230-millimetre) guns, a rail system to feed them ammo, and a self-contained ventilation and electrical system bored into the rock cliffs of the fortification. Two 8-inch (200-millimetre) guns were mounted at Christopher Point at the southern tip of Vancouver Island, while 6-inch (150-millimetre) guns were deployed at Macaulay Point, Mary Hill, Ogden Point, and smaller batteries around the city. The Americans reciprocated on their side of the strait with 10-inch (260-millimetre) heavy guns and an array of 6-inch (150-millimetre) guns at Fort Worden near Port Townsend, Washington.

An important but much overlooked facet of the Canadian navy was the Fishermen's Volunteer Reserve (FVR). Fishermen already possessed a good knowledge of the bays and coves where they worked, and they had excellent seamanship skills. It made sense for the navy to employ that knowledge. As fishermen were involved in a vital war industry—food production—they did not have to sign up for overseas service. The formation of the FVR solved several problems for the government. The fishermen continued to work in their field for the war service and their boats served as patrol vessels for the resource-strapped navy.

In 1939, Lieutenant Commander Colin Donald, a retired Royal Navy officer living in British Columbia, was commissioned by the RCN to organize the volunteer unit. He was given use of the tug *Skidegate*, in which he travelled up and down the coast, signing up new recruits. Going from the starched halls of the Royal Navy to dealing

One of the searchlight emplacements at Fort Rodd Hill, near Victoria, B.C., disguised as a fisherman's shanty. Note the two-dimensional plywood dory in front.

with gruff fishermen on the remote coast of British Columbia would no doubt have given the commander some culture shock. But Donald was easy-going and well liked by the recruits, although he endured some good-natured ribbing along the way.

The fishermen were an eager and somewhat rebellious addition to the navy. They had their own version of regulation dress—British pussar uniform with gumboots and trademark Cowichan Indian sweater over top. If they didn't like an answer from a superior officer, they questioned it. Seasoned fishermen gave professional advice and opinions, requested or not, to some of the navy's "prairie sailors." This attitude did little to endear them to the regular navy officers, some of whom considered the FVR the "bastard child" of the fleet. In spite of the members' shortcomings with protocol, however, there was no denying their professionalism as sailors. Ships of the FVR were the only vessels to carry out continual patrol from Cape Flattery to Alaska in all weather, 24 hours a day, seven days a week, while the main fleet ships of the navy were port-bound. By doing this, the FVR freed the navy from routine patrol for the more urgent matters of escort and anti-submarine patrol. Some of the FVR vessels were purchased outright by the navy, but a great many were fishboats

One of the 6-inch disappearing guns at Fort Rodd Hill.

Anti-submarine netting left from the Second World War at Fort Rodd Hill.

Ruins of a Second World War 6-inch gun pit near Victoria, B.C.

confiscated from the Japanese-Canadian fishermen who lived along the coast. These served as gate vessels (a guard vessel at the entrance to a harbour) or ran supply and performed police and surveillance duties at some of the more remote stations.

On one occasion in July 1942 off the Queen Charlotte Islands, an FVR vessel encountered what the crew assumed was an odd, round buoy that had got loose from its mooring. The crew machine-gunned it till it sank out of harm's way. When they reported its description, they learned it was one of the new Japanese horned-type anti-ship mines—a calling card perhaps left by one of the prowling enemy submarines. Mines began to turn up with more frequency off the north coast, carried on seasonal currents from Asia or the Aleutians. One of the deadly devices was recovered as late as 1972, washed up on the west coast of the Queen Charlottes. For this added danger, FVR reservists were paid an extra 25 cents a day when working in the area.

As the FVR had over 400 vessels, keeping tabs on them could have been difficult, as it was not feasible to supply them all with radios due to shortages and imposed radio silence. The FVR came up with the idea of using carrier pigeons on the majority of boats so headquarters could keep track of their whereabouts. Ingenious in its simplicity, the system was nearly impossible to intercept, could travel over long distances without relay stations, and required little maintenance except daily feeding. The birds, with coded messages attached, could be released from any point on the coast to relay a ship's status and maintain the link between ship and base.

Besides being a low priority for military expenditures, the defence of British Columbia's 6,400-plus kilometres of coastline was also a logistical nightmare. Air Vice-Marshall Leigh Stevenson of the Royal Canadian Air Force (RCAF), an air corps veteran of the First World War, was placed in charge of Western Air Command (WAC) in January 1942. One of Stevenson's first tasks was to figure out how to defend the skies over this expansive territory on a shoestring budget. Much of the north's hinterland had never been explored, and charts that did exist of the remote areas were at best incomplete. It would be a daunting task to try to cover all of the tens of thousands of square kilometres of the B.C. and Alaska coast with air patrols. Besides, the aircraft and crews were more badly needed in Europe, where the war took precedence over home matters.

To alleviate this concern, a system of remote radio-direction-finding posts was established in a rapid construction program in 1942 along the west coast of Vancouver Island, the Queen Charlotte Islands, Johnstone Strait, Prince Rupert, and as far north as Nome, Alaska, on the Seward Peninsula. Radar and radio-direction-finder stations with the most up-to-date equipment were installed at the remotest coastal points: Langara and Marble islands; Cape St. James on the Queen Charlottes; and Cape Scott, Ferrer Point, Hesquiat, and Jordan River on Vancouver Island's west coast.

A radar installation was built at Guise Bay on the northern tip of Vancouver Island and manned by the RCAF. Its only real moment of excitement was when radar watchers sounded the alarm after mistaking a flock of Canada geese, flying in their distinctive V pattern, for attacking enemy aircraft.

Complementing these outposts were approximately 1,500 civilian coast watchers, many of them aboriginal people, who inhabited the remote villages of the coast from southern B.C. to northern Alaska. Trained by the army in aircraft and warship identification and issued one pair of army field glasses each, fully conversant coast watchers could visually identify 55 types of enemy aircraft and all classes of Japanese warships and submarines. These remote villagers, trappers, fishermen, and lighthouse keepers were a workable system of eyes and ears for the armed forces, relieving the government of deploying much-needed men and support services to far-flung outposts.

Prince Rupert
and the
Inside Passage

The Inside Passage runs along the West Coast from Seattle to Alaska. This naturally protected water highway begins at Puget Sound in Washington State and continues up the east coast of Vancouver Island. Between Prince Rupert and Juneau, Alaska, it is sheltered by myriad large islands. The passage became crucial for shipping materials north during the Second World War, as its many bottlenecks and uncharted shoals made it nearly impenetrable for enemy submarines attempting to conduct any sort of patrol.

When Japan began her conquests of Asia in the mid-1930s, the Canadian government cast a wary eye to the undefended Pacific coast. To protect the strategic Inside Passage from intrusion by enemy ships, the Dominion government in 1937 commissioned a fort at Yorke Island, 6.5 kilometres east of Kelsey Bay on northern Vancouver Island. Yorke held a commanding position overlooking the 10-kilometre-wide gap of Johnstone Strait between Vancouver Island and mainland British Columbia. Initially two pre-First World War, 4.7-inch (120-millimetre) guns were installed in 1938. They could lob 45-pound (20-kilogram) shells a distance of eight kilometres. A garrison of 55 men of the 85th Battery—the 15th Coast Brigade, Royal Canadian Artillery—was deployed to the fort. There were few amenities on the island and only a small barracks for the construction party, so the crew had to build accommodations and supplement rations with wild game—not a bad situation considering the rationed foods that soldiers would later have to endure.

After the attack on Pearl Harbor, the fortification was upgraded to house 260 personnel, searchlight emplacements, a generator powerhouse, radio buildings, workshops, an armoury, and ammunition bunkers. By war's end, Yorke had become an impenetrable fortress with 62 buildings in place, making it larger than many of the villages of the central coast. The 4-inch (120-millimetre) guns were replaced with two 6-inch (150-millimetre) guns that could lob seven 100-pound (45-kilogram) shells a distance of thirteen kilometres each minute. Ten-centimetre lead plating was also installed on the bunkers housing the guns.

Gun emplacements were commissioned around Vancouver at Ferguson Point in Stanley Park and on the north shore across the First Narrows at the entrance to Burrard Inlet. The University of B.C. sported 6-inch (150-millimetre) coastal guns above Wreck Beach. All of these gun sites were complemented by searchlights housed in heavy concrete bunkers, which can still be seen today. It is unlikely this array of coastal batteries would have been any match for the big guns of the Japanese navy had it successfully breached the West Coast defences, however. The newest battleship of the Yamato class sported 18-inch (460-millimetre) guns that could throw a 1,000-pound (454-kilogram) projectile at a target 72 kilometres away—the distance from Nanaimo to Vancouver.

With the Inside Passage protected, General Buckner of the U.S. Army established a system of embarkation ports and staging bases to rush men and equipment to Alaska, and devised land, sea, and air routes to convey Lend-Lease supplies to the Soviet Union. Prince Rupert in northern British Columbia played a pivotal role. The town, linked to the south by its port and a single rail line, was the most northerly rail terminus on the West Coast and boasted a fine natural harbour. It could be used to alleviate the overburdened ports in the south from Vancouver to San Francisco. Troops and war material could be shipped to Prince Rupert by rail, cutting out much of the sea route with its exposure to enemy submarines. Citing these strategic advantages, the United States officially designated Prince Rupert a military sub-embarkation point to Alaska on April 5, 1942, which meant the city could be militarized and which put its port and rail facilities at the disposal of the American army.

Prince Rupert, a town of about 7,000 people before 1941, saw great improvements to its existing port facilities funded through the largesse of the United States when that country entered the war. The harbour was fortified with guns and a permanent army garrison. Additional gun emplacements were built on Digby and Kaien islands, and submarine nets were strung across the harbour. The town also housed a large U.S. Army camp atop Acropolis Hill and maintained a processing camp for troops fifteen kilometres north at Port Edward.

Prince Rupert's vital Canadian National Railway link followed the Skeena River, hugging sheer cliffs and running over several trestle bridges, which made it a vulnerable target for sabotage. The Canadian government gave serious consideration to the threat of a Japanese submarine landing a commando unit unseen near Prince Rupert with orders to take out trestles or tunnels, and in response it commissioned an armoured train to provide a mobile defence along the 130-kilometre run between Prince Rupert and Terrace. On July 29, 1942, No. 1 Armoured Train made its first operational patrol to Prince Rupert. Built in Winnipeg, it consisted of eight specially designed rail cars and an armoured locomotive. In the centre were two cars that housed the command post, infirmary, and one platoon. Two more infantry platoons were housed in two other rail cars. Four rail cars each carried one 75-millimetre gun, a diesel generator, searchlights, four 40-millimetre Bofor anti-aircraft guns, as well as four mobile mortar cannon and machine guns. Revetments of heavy armour were constructed on the platforms to protect the men from enemy sniper fire and weather. The train could quickly deploy about 120 infantry to engage an enemy landing party. The train remained in the Prince Rupert area until 1944, when the unit disbanded and the train was broken up in Winnipeg.

With the increase in ship traffic to and from Prince Rupert and the confirmation of enemy submarines on the West Coast, the town was in need of air defence from the already stretched Western Air Command (WAC). Air Vice-Marshall Stevenson was responsible for the air cover for the northern terminus, and he faced a couple of problems. There were no airfields in the north from which a fighter unit could be readily based to Prince Rupert, and Canada's air forces were already highly committed overseas and in the U-boat war on the East Coast. Compounding this, the United States had still not told anyone in the Canadian government, Stevenson included, that Japan was planning an attack in the north. As far as the Canadian government was concerned, an aerial attack on Prince Rupert was highly unlikely, so if Stevenson had tried to convince Ottawa to divert money from its war budget to furnish airfields in the hinterland of B.C.'s north, Ottawa might have begun to question Stevenson's competency.

As soldiers in the north soon learned, it was easier to go around the government than through it. Stevenson found a solution that would get him a fighter strip for Prince Rupert while raising few eyebrows

Canada's No. 1 Armoured Train, built to defend the 130 kilometres of rail line between Terrace and Prince Rupert from commandos landed by enemy submarines. The train was decommissioned in 1944.

back east. The U.S. Army Air Force (USAAF) needed to supply air cover to southeast Alaska, but was in the process of moving available squadrons farther north, where they were anticipating a Japanese attack. Stevenson could supply a fighter squadron to Prince Rupert, but there was no proper airstrip to be had. The U.S. Army had established an airfield on Annette Island, just 65 kilometres north in the Alaska Panhandle, but could not spare a squadron to man the field. In February 1942, Stevenson proposed to General John L. DeWitt, who oversaw all western defence for the United States, that a Canadian fighter squadron assume the field at Annette and take over air defence and anti-submarine patrol to Ketchikan and Yakutat, quickly extend them to cover Anchorage, the Gulf of Alaska, and Kodiak to Dutch Harbor, and later share duties with the Americans patrolling out of Nome to the Siberian coast. DeWitt gladly accepted this arrangement.

A fully operational fighter squadron, the 115th, was to be transferred to cover Prince Rupert. Up to that time the 115th had been flying air support for the Esquimalt navy base as well as anti-submarine patrol and vessel identification from Pat Bay near Sidney, B.C. The "fighter" designation was something of a misnomer, since the 115th's main aircraft was the twin-engine Bristol Bolingbroke, a Canadian version of the British Blenheim medium bomber. The "Boleys" had been fitted with racks of fixed, forward-firing, .303-calibre, armour-piercing machine guns as well as reconnaissance cameras for vessel identification. They could also be armed with an array of 250- and 500-pound (110- and 225-kilogram) anti-submarine bombs. The squadron began extensive cold-climate training for Alaskan operations in March 1942 to prepare for the severe conditions it would encounter in southeast Alaska.

By May 10 the first ground crew and a Canadian army unit, the 112th Light Anti-Aircraft battery of the 6th LAA Regiment, arrived on Annette Island to set up camp. Upon disembarking they found the term "base" could only be used in its loosest interpretation to describe their new home. The only residents of Annette were the inhabitants of Metlakatla, a Native village about two kilometres from the base, and some U.S. Army personnel. One year earlier the U.S. War Department had received consent from the Metlakatla to use the island reserve.

The first RCAF support personnel to arrive at Annette found the incessant rain of the region had turned the dirt runways to mud. Few permanent structures had been erected, so the Canadians lived in tents. Latrine, bathing, and laundry facilities were non-existent. The night they arrived was all the more memorable because the ammunition dump

Canadian aircrew of the 115th Squadron at Annette Island, Alaska.

caught fire—presumably set by an aircraft landing flare—and went off in a profusion of explosions and bullet shots. Fired by the rumours of invasion, all took cover—laying low for the night until confident that Japanese troops were not invading the island. The 115th Squadron's arrival in Alaska in May 1942 wrote two minor footnotes in American military history. Canada became the first and only Allied foreign power to set up a military base on United States soil and the only foreign nation to directly assume defence of American territory.

This growing Allied front in the North Pacific was governed largely by the United States. The American military directed the operational control of Canadian army and navy contingents in northern Alaska, and they were used as the Americans saw fit. One exception was Annette Island, where the units came under direct Canadian operations. As well, the air force retained much of its autonomy. The Americans had to request the deployment of Canadian squadrons through RCAF Headquarters in Vancouver. (This was not a new situation for Canada, as much of this country's involvement in the two world wars had been directed by Great Britain.)

Ironically, when the United States entered the war in Europe, it was also given operational control over Canadian convoy escorts in the North Atlantic, even though Canada's Atlantic escort force far outnumbered the Americans and the Canadians had already been at war for over two years. The arrangement caused much dismay in the Royal Canadian Navy and some tension between the brass of the two forces.

In the North Pacific, however, the relations between the Canadian and American forces were less formal and remained cordial throughout the campaign. While the United States wanted to assume overall command of West Coast defences, Stevenson adamantly opposed the idea on the grounds that Canada was better prepared and had the larger force from the Alaska–B.C. border to the Columbia River. Eventually the U.S. let the matter drop. Defence of the Pacific Northwest from Alaska to Oregon was to be mutual, and RCAF members were stationed with the navy, army, and air force in Seattle. Likewise, American officers were stationed with Pacific Command in Victoria and at RCAF Headquarters at Jericho Beach in Vancouver.

Ottawa was understandably reluctant to divert much-needed men, equipment, and especially experienced squadrons to Alaska, a point the American brass found exasperating. To the Canadian military, Alaska was of minor concern and the American preoccupation with it seemed far out of proportion to other fronts. It was not until May 21 that the U.S. War Department told the Canadian government that the Japanese were indeed going to launch an attack in the north and an invasion might follow. The Canadian chiefs were incredulous, as the Americans had agreed to keep them fully informed of all pertinent developments in matters of defence. To the consternation of Air Vice-Marshall Stevenson, the U.S. would breach this agreement on several occasions, in spite of possibly dire consequences. For example, the U.S. Navy was supposed to inform WAC in Vancouver of all large ship movements, convoy or otherwise, so RCAF patrols could identify them. When part of the damaged U.S. fleet was en route from Pearl Harbor to Seattle, orders were to keep silent and not even inform the Canadians of their transit. A patrolling RCAF Canso encountered the fleet at night some 640 kilometres west of Cape Flattery and challenged with the appropriate signal flares. At first the fleet refused to answer, then gave the incorrect reply to a second challenge. This caused some excitement at WAC. Everyone was expecting an invasion by the Japanese, and now an unidentified fleet of warships was heading towards the coast. The Canso, still tailing the convoy, again challenged the fleet and after some hesitation received the correct recognition signal by Aldis lamp with the following message: "Please do not break w/t [wireless telegraph] silence." When reproached by Stevenson, the U.S. Navy's Admiral Fletcher, overseeing the fleet movements, apologized but added that he had orders not to inform the Canadians. Apparently reciprocal goodwill could be a one-way street.

In May 1942, Magic's increased interception of Japanese messages indicated to American Intelligence services an attack on or invasion of the North Pacific coast was imminent. Brigadier General William Butler, who had assumed command of the U.S. 11th Army Air Force in Alaska on March 8, 1942, ordered all of his available squadrons forward to new fields closer to Dutch Harbor. Once dispatched, they left a gap in anti-submarine and reconnaissance patrols between Yakutat and Anchorage. Anticipating an enemy submarine offensive in the Gulf of Alaska, Buckner requested additional units of the RCAF be transferred to Alaska in preparation for an attack and possible invasion of the mainland.

However, when plans for a Japanese attack in the north were finally made known to the Canadians at the end of May, Vice-Marshall Stevenson's primary concern was Prince Rupert. Because of its strategic value as a sub-embarkation port, it could be targeted for attack by enemy submarines and possibly for aerial bombardment. Stevenson and other WAC officers argued that they barely had the resources to maintain anti-submarine patrol along Canada's own West Coast. If a raid was about to be made on the Pacific coast, they asked, why leave British Columbia exposed for the benefit of Alaska? They balked at Buckner's request for two Canadian squadrons and at first refused. Lieutenant-General Kenneth Stuart, the Canadian chief of the General Staff, concurred with his officers. Diverting Canadian squadrons to Alaska would create a gap in British Columbia's air defence, leaving the north coast vulnerable.

Instead, Stevenson decided to immediately bolster the air defence of Prince Rupert and ordered the 8th Bomber Reconnaissance Squadron (flying Bolingbrokes), from Sea Island south of Vancouver, and the 111th Fighter Squadron (flying P40 Kittyhawks), from Pat Bay, to Annette Island for coverage of Prince Rupert.

The dispatch of these two squadrons would leave a gap in anti-submarine defence around the approaches to the Strait of Juan de Fuca and Vancouver Island. To strengthen the southern areas, the 14th Kittyhawk Squadron would move from its base on Sea Island near Vancouver to Pat Bay. At the end of May, the 118th Fighter (Kittyhawk) Squadron was ordered from Dartmouth, Nova Scotia, to Pat Bay, some

P40 (Kittyhawk) fighters of RCAF 118th Fighter Squadron, based at Annette Island, Alaska, from 1942 to 1943.

6,400 kilometres across the country; and the 132nd Fighter (Hurricanes) training squadron was ordered to Sea Island from Rockcliffe in Ottawa. The 118th already had extensive anti-submarine experience in the Atlantic hunting German U-boats, so the threat to the West Coast was obviously taken quite seriously if the air force was willing to move a fully operational squadron from the menaced East Coast waters.

Some of the air force personnel were already battle-hardened veterans pulled from other theatres and rotated to the unit. Squadron Leader Arthur Yuile of the 118th had flown in the Battle of Britain and had several kills to his credit. He had been shot down once, shot up once, and wounded once. At the height of the air blitz over England, Yuile had flown three gruelling sorties in seven hours, fighting off German bombers, for which he received the Distinguished Flying Cross.

As the Canadians now seemed determined to provide coverage primarily to Canadian territory, an irritated General DeWitt prevailed upon Washington to reiterate the terms of the Pacific Joint Agreement on Defense to Ottawa. After some discussion, the Canadian chiefs reluctantly agreed to Buckner's request to send Canadian squadrons farther north for the defence of Alaska. At the end of May, WAC ordered the 8th Squadron to immediately proceed to Yakutat rather than Annette, while the 111th's move north was put on hold.

So far the war had proceeded pleasantly for the men of the 8th Bomber Reconnaissance Squadron, flying anti-submarine duty out of Sea Island near Vancouver. They enjoyed weekend dances with plenty of female company at the Palomar and Cave dance halls in Vancouver and were sometimes treated to dinner by local families. Plenty of American liquor and smokes could be picked up on refuelling stops at

McChord and Whidby air stations in neighbouring Washington State. As Harry Bray, a pilot of the 8th, reminisced, "War wasn't exactly hell."[1]

These amenities came to an abrupt end when the 8th's commanding officer informed the men that a Japanese invasion force was about to strike at Alaska and they were being sent north to help out the U.S. Army Air Force. The squadron would fall under direct control of the Alaskan Defence Command and was to proceed north as soon as possible. The Boleys were fitted with new American .50-calibre turrets on the fuselage, and after a stop at Paine Field in Washington to be refitted for American bombs, twelve bombers of the 8th headed north on June 2. On a stopover at Annette, the armaments crew found that none of the bombs stored in Alaska would fit the bomb adapters of the Canadian planes, so new adapters had to be designed and flown up to meet the squadron.

The flight north was a series of base-hops, taking the 8th through some of the most isolated airstrips on the continent. The aircraft left Vancouver as quickly as the planes could be outfitted with the new gear and armaments, making refuelling stops at Port Hardy, Bella Bella, Terrace, and Annette Island before continuing north to Juneau and then Yakutat.

At each town the 8th's bombers set down along the way, the Alaskans treated the Canadian aircrew like liberating heroes. Nothing was too good to lavish on the RCAF, with the Alaskans showing their appreciation in the form of free drinks, dinners, and souvenirs. When the squadron moved on to Anchorage, one Juneau business owner had

The P40 was the main Allied fighter in the Aleutians war. This fine vintage Kittyhawk of 118th Squadron is owned by George Maude of Sidney, B.C.

One of the hazards of Alaskan flying was landing. A Kittyhawk of the 118th cracked up after landing on the dirt runway. Rain left the airstrips a mire of rocks and mud, causing many accidents.

to sheepishly request from the Canadians the return of the deed to his store. Apparently, even Alaska's renowned generosity knew some limits.

Already partway across the country, the 118th received orders to divert to Annette Island in Alaska (the 132nd continued on to Sea Island). The 118th's new duties were to reinforce the 115th, already in residence at Annette, which was now redesignated a bomber squadron, and to provide fighter support for Prince Rupert. After an arduous five-day, transcontinental flight from their base in Dartmouth, Nova Scotia, fifteen Kittyhawks[2] and two Hudson aircraft landed at Annette Island. This was believed to be the longest overland flight by a fighter group ever undertaken, and two P40s were lost after they had to make forced landings en route.

When the squadron arrived at Annette that first week of June, a U.S. customs agent balked at the Canadians importing aircraft and weaponry without proper duties being paid—and refused to allow the Canadians to leave their aircraft. This left the RCAF pilots sitting idle in their planes for several hours while the red tape was unwound. After some telephone calls from an embarrassed General DeWitt to the State Department, U.S. Secretary of State Cordell Hull granted the Canadians "Distinguished Visitor" status and exempted them from U.S. customs laws.

Life quickly fell into monotonous routine on Annette. Initially there were no hangars for aircraft, so ground crews worked in unheated tents draped over the planes' engines and performed maintenance in highly disagreeable weather. Besides the pressures of maintaining combat-ready squadrons, artillery, and infantry units, the personnel had to cope with conditions reminiscent of those faced by early settlers. Facilities lacked such basics as running water, electricity, bunks, and barracks. Men had to thaw water when the temperature dipped below freezing and keep a steady supply of firewood chopped for the wood stoves. The unpaved runway was full of rocks, roots, and potholes, and the constant rain caused aircraft to sink into the field to the depth of their landing wheels. If men opted to cut across the "parade square," they had to contend with the mud—because of which few drills or musters were ever called. The mud also ruled out wearing uniforms much of the time, as it was impossible to keep them presentable. Eventually a wooden boardwalk connecting most of the buildings provided some relief from the quagmire.

When anti-submarine flights, maintenance, instruction, and target practice were done for the day, the Canadian crews put in extra hours building a basic camp with material they begged or borrowed from the Americans. The military constructed a road to Metlakatla so it could use the village's landing wharf. Six-inch (150-millimetre) gun emplacements and machine-gun bunkers for defence were placed around the island, while a 75-person infirmary and wooden barracks with generators were added by 1944.

Still, facilities were sparse, and endless boredom, bad weather, and a spartan lifestyle were the order of the day for those men serving on Annette Island. Many veterans could see no point sitting in the wilds of Alaska and requested, but were denied, a return to overseas posting. There were no women there until nurses arrived much later in the war, and no dances or the like enjoyed by troops currently training in Britain. Prince Rupert was over 65 kilometres south by boat, and Ketchikan, Alaska, a town about the size of Prince Rupert, was even farther north, so the men were generally confined to the island for most of their posting. Rain appeared endless to those not used to the weather of the northwest coast. "If it wasn't raining it had either just finished raining or was about to rain," complained Donald Stewart of the 115th.

If unchecked, the doldrums of northern postings could break out in tragedy. After the Canadians and Americans on Annette Island celebrated Christmas dinner together, a black private from a construction

Anti-submarine patrol off northern B.C. / southeast Alaska in 1942–43. The aircraft is from RCAF 115th Squadron, based out of Annette Island, Alaska.

battalion shot himself through the head at the end of the runway. The isolation of the north and the abrupt change in climate, which particularly affected those men from the south, were never addressed, with the result that the number of suicides in the desolate Alaskan bases averaged one per day—many of these within the black construction battalions from the southern United States.

Relations remained fairly cordial on the base between the Canadians and their American counterparts, although there were problems inherent in having two distinct chains of command using the same facility. The commanding officer of the Canadian units on Annette, Wing Commander Dean Nesbitt, a veteran of the air war over Britain, wrote WAC about the attitude of certain American officers. The RCAF squadrons on Annette Island, the only land-based units south of Yakutat, had assumed the main air defence duties of southeast Alaska, and while the Canadians operated the two squadrons in place of USAAF units and were by far the largest contingent on Annette Island, the Americans controlled supplies, construction, transportation, building use, and fuel.

The American construction officer considered the Canadian needs of secondary priority and he had no orders to let them use the American facilities. Few construction materials were made available to build the new camp, and the Canadians could use the construction equipment only if the Americans had finished with it for the day. As late as August 1942, 650 Canadians were crowded into facilities meant to support 150. A tent camp was to be built to support the influx of Canadians, and the aircrews were required to work in construction at the end of the day on top of their regular duties. When 200 Canadians were told by Colonel D. Christiansen, the American CO on Annette, that they would have to

RCAF's Western Air Command band parades through Ketchikan, Alaska, in 1943.

move to a partially completed tent city so newly arriving U.S. troops could use their barracks, Nesbitt refused. There was no latrine or wash hut available at the new camp, and suitable drinking water was already at a premium. The aerodrome and parade square were 3.5 kilometres away from the camp, across boards floated on the mud. There were few vehicles available, and at times the weather made the roads to the ludicrously distant aerodrome impassable, rendering a quick response to enemy action impossible. When a state of readiness was called for, aircrew and ground crew camped by their aircraft to maintain the standard. Nesbitt's steadfast refusal to move, and his request to WAC, led to General DeWitt stepping in to speed construction of a new Canadian camp less than two kilometres from the aerodrome and airfields. However, in letters to WAC dated as late as December 1942, Squadron Leader Gordy Diamond, who took over from Nesbitt in late August 1942, indicates many necessities were sadly lacking at the new camp.

The use of the aerodrome and facilities became another thorn for Nesbitt and Diamond. The American captain in charge had no orders allowing the RCAF use of the aerodrome, so he sharply curtailed the Canadians' access or barred them altogether when it suited him. It consequently sat empty while Canadian crews worked on their aircraft outside in rain, snow, and subzero temperatures. Nesbitt protested again to WAC in his weekly report, writing, "[The American captain] is none too co-operative and has found occasion to point out to us that there is a war on," adding dryly, "he thinks it started last December." Nesbitt then requested that the Canadians assume total control of the aerodrome and its facilities, and General DeWitt was again forced to overrule his own officer. It was not until November, though, that the RCAF was allowed full use of the aerodrome and other necessities such as fuel, transportation, and machine shops. The Canadians were, after all, conducting patrols over American territory on behalf of the United States.

Flying in southeast Alaska and northern B.C. called for piloting by the seat of one's pants, and the units posted there suffered a disproportionate number of losses due to the weather. In the good months, rain and fog forced pilots to fly at treetop level, and when they were over water to "whip the waves"—a dangerous manoeuvre practised to put planes under the cloud ceiling but just above the water. The point of the manoeuvre was to make it impossible for a surfaced sub or radar to spot the aircraft, giving the flyers the element of surprise, but more often it was used because the fog hung on the water, and whipping the waves was the only way for pilots to keep a bearing on the sea. The manoeuvre was aptly named because the aircraft would be so low to the water that the propellers would whip up spray off the ocean. When the sea got rough, as was usually the case, a plane's prop could, and did, dig in and flip the craft. This killed several airmen serving in the North Pacific.

The merciless North Pacific claimed more lives and aircraft due to weather and hazardous flying conditions than any other theatre of the

The Norseman aircraft that killed pilot Fred Currie and five members of a United States Overseas (USO) tour group at Annette Island. The air groups in northern B.C. and Alaska were subjected to the worst weather of any Second World War theatre.

Flying in the wretched weather of northern B.C. and Alaska was fraught with problems, as shown by the wreckage of this Canadian Stranraer flying boat.

war. Air war operations had never taken place in this kind of climate. A Kittyhawk flown by Petty Officer G.A. Baxter disappeared without a trace and was believed to have crashed into the sea near Ketchikan on October 12, 1942. At Baxter's funeral another Kittyhawk pilot, an American in the RCAF, crashed and died when his plane went into a barrel roll during a flypast. Apparently he had not taken into account the 250-pound (110-kilogram) anti-submarine bomb recently added to the P40's underbelly. An RCAF Stranraer flying boat crashed while attempting to land at Annette, killing all five crewmen. A Norseman single-engine bush plane also went down, killing pilot Flying Officer Fred Currie along with his passengers, three female performers and two male officers of an entertainment troupe on their way to the base. A Bristol Bolingbroke crashed in a fiery takeoff, igniting the .303 ammunition for the plane's machine guns. Two men were thrown clear while three remained trapped inside. American construction workers first at the scene pulled two of them clear at the insistence of Petty Officer John "Digger"Wallace, who barely escaped himself as the plane "blew to a million pieces."[3] It was Wallace's third air crash since joining the RCAF, and he was subsequently awarded the U.S. Air Medal for "extreme coolness and courage in the face of probable death."

RCAF Stranraer flying boat No. 951 of the 120th Squadron disappeared mysteriously while on anti-submarine patrol off northern Vancouver Island on August 23, 1942. Hours after taking off from the seaplane base at Coal Harbour near Port Hardy, the big, bi-winged plane was forced to put down at sea 144 kilometres southwest of Cape Scott and sent out an SOS. A long-range search plane spotted the stricken aircraft, but engine trouble and deteriorating weather forced the would-be rescuers to return to base. Mountainous waves, reported in excess of nine metres (not unusual off Cape Scott), forced back the RCAF's high-speed crash boat *Malacite*, while Fishermen's Reserve boats volunteered to go out but were overruled. During the night the radio signal from No. 951 ceased. Over the following weeks all available ships and aircraft searched, to no avail. Oddly enough, the official Air Force inquiry into the disappearance mentions an enemy submarine spotted heading in the direction of the downed plane but gives no more detail. This coincides with a patrol of *I-25* in which the sub had departed Japan on August 14 and a submarine sighted off Langara Island around the time of 951's loss. Petty Officer Everard T. Cox, Flight Sergeant Mervyn Cram, F/S Lawrence Horn, and Sergeants Adolf Anderson, Charles Beeching, Kenneth Hope, Leslie Oldford, and Robert Bruce Stuart in No. 951 vanished without a trace of wreckage ever found.[4]

The RCAF marine division service boat *B.C. Star* disappeared off northern B.C. with all hands between July 24 and August 3, 1943, en route from Bella Bella to Cape St. James on the southern tip of the Queen Charlotte Islands. Much time passed before anyone realized the vessel was missing, as schedules were deliberately not kept to deter enemy interception. An air-sea search found three bodies without life jackets or rafts, and it remains a mystery what caused the boat to founder so quickly.

The RCAF marine vessel B.C. Star, *which mysteriously disappeared with all hands off the southern Queen Charlotte Islands in late July 1943.*

A Boley in winter at Annette Island. At bases as far north as Nome, shortages of British-made parts reached serious levels, and all planes of the 8th Squadron were cannibalized to keep just two flying.

In November 1942 Vice-Marshall Stevenson flew to Annette Island to look into charges that the squadrons were using the excuse of bad weather to avoid regular anti-submarine patrols. The complaints had come from Air Group 4, headquartered at Prince Rupert, to which the Annette squadrons belonged. Stevenson found the reasons for the long periods of no-flying well-founded. After concluding his investigation he was grounded on Annette Island himself for four days because of bad weather.

Even in that remote bush country of southeast Alaska, the two squadrons managed to see some action, however limited. From their advance base at Paramushiro in Japan's northern Kuriles, enemy submarines were venturing into the waters of southern Alaska and northern British Columbia.

On July 7, 1942, Flying Officer W.E. Thomas and his crew of Bolingbroke No. 9118 were on anti-submarine patrol off Prince of Wales Island with clear weather and a calm sea, 216 kilometres northwest of their base. The second observer reported what appeared to be churning water and white smoke puffs a kilometre off the starboard wing. Turning 180 degrees, the bomber came in directly over the target and scored a direct hit with a 250-pound (110-kilogram) bomb. "The object they attacked was cigar-shaped and well over one hundred feet long breaking the surface in a dark outline with no indication of conning tower or guns but having what appeared to be an elevator rudder in the stern."[5] As there was no debris after the attack—only a large patch of discoloured water, which spread out for about 125 metres—the aircrew concluded they'd bombed a whale. A second aircraft sent to the area reported two steady streams of three-inch bubbles about a foot apart coming to the surface. The following morning, two American Coast Guard cutters arrived on the scene and reported a strong smell of diesel in the area. They then released depth charges in a co-ordinated attack on the site, which they believed resulted in a definite sinking.

On July 9 the U.S. Coast Guard cutter *McLane*, just east of the area of the purported sub sinking two days earlier, reported an attack by an enemy submarine. *McLane*'s skipper reported torpedoes had been fired across the cutter's stern and that they were undertaking evasive action. P40s of the 118th Squadron, dispatched from Annette Island, peppered the area with anti-submarine bombs but came up empty-handed.

While Japanese submarines did reconnoitre the waters from Alaska to the Pacific Northwest, Japanese records surrendered after the war

Was this the enemy submarine sunk by the RCAF's 115th Squadron on July 7, 1942, 130 kilometres northwest of Ketchikan, Alaska? The Japanese claim none of their submarines were sunk in northern B.C. / southeast Alaska. Still unidentified, the sub resembles a Soviet D-class boat. It is possible that subs of the Soviet Pacific fleet were conducting patrols of the West Coast and that one was mistakenly sunk. There appears to be an explosion forward of the conning tower. There is also an "86" spray-painted on the conning tower. Jim Johnston was the photographic technician on Annette for the entire war and supplied this photograph.

A Hawker Hurricane of RCAF's 135th Squadron, based at Annette Island from August to November 1943.

indicate no submarine losses in that area. Both Japan and the Soviets had old British Vickers-designed submarines of the same class in their fleets, built between 1921 and 1937. It is possible that a sub of the Soviet Pacific fleet, with no war to fight in the North Pacific, was prowling the waters of Alaska and B.C. when it was unwittingly sunk by the Canadian plane. The Russians still remain tight-lipped about their submarine activities, so there is much conjecture about the identity of the intruder. Whatever occurred in the "Battle of Annette Island," Flight Officers Leonard Hylary, John Shebeski, and William Evans of Bolingbroke No. 9118 were credited with an enemy sub kill and received citations from the USAAF and the RCAF.

More typical of the enemy engagements in southeast Alaska, a Boley reported enemy submarine contact 56 kilometres off Annette Island and dropped a 250-pound (110-kilogram) anti-submarine bomb on the target. Closer inspection revealed the enemy to be a large log with a tall branch sticking up. The following morning the plane's crew found a log had been painted under the Boley's cockpit where the "kill" credits are applied. In February 1943, a formation of planes passing over Prince Rupert was fired upon by confused ack-ack gunners, leading one crewman to remark afterwards, "If it weren't for those gunners around Rupert shooting at us occasionally, we would get no excitement at all!"[6]

In keeping with the practice of rotating squadrons on remote bases, the 118th Fighter Squadron was replaced by the 135th (Hawker Hurricanes), and the 115th Squadron by the 149th Bomber Squadron in Lockheed Ventura bombers in August 1943.

Despite other wartime commitments and the budget allotted the Pacific coast, Canada's forces did an admirable job of covering the West Coast and its approaches from Oregon as far north as the Aleutians. Considering the numbers and the length of patrols of Japanese submarines off the coast, it is surprising they did not claim a greater percentage of shipping. Canadian and American countermeasures can take much of the credit for this. But despite a fairly comprehensive system of patrols for the vast coastal hinterland of British Columbia and Alaska, one fact was clear to those involved in the security of that territory: "A wilderness could not be defended."[7]

The Nikkei Story

Even before Pearl Harbor and U.S. entry into the Second World War, some 20,000 Japanese Americans had joined the war in Asia under the Rising Sun. Several Japanese-Canadian fishermen from British Columbia also felt it their duty to go to Japan and enlist as navy reserves. They received basic training and a uniform before returning home to Canada. Local fishermen protested that some of the Japanese fishermen wore their navy uniforms and flew the Rising Sun from their little gillnetters.

After December 7, 1941, Japanese North Americans (Nikkei) who remained in Canada and the U.S. found themselves the target of negative sentiments—for obvious reasons. The U.S. Pacific battle fleet had been all but destroyed in the surprise attack, and over 3,500 Americans were killed. Thousands of Commonwealth troops, including 2,000 Canadians, had been killed or captured at Hong Kong as Japanese forces moved down the far east coast of Asia, and now Japanese submarines were off the West Coast, attacking shipping in our very own waters. One had only to be of Japanese descent to arouse suspicion.

A month before, in November 1941, U.S. president Franklin Roosevelt had commissioned State Department representative Curtis Munson to investigate the loyalty of Japanese Americans. Munson noted in his report that there were three distinct groups of Japanese Americans. The Issei, first-generation Japanese, had been born in Japan but had made a decent living in North America, raised their families here, and would have become citizens had they been allowed to do so. Life in America had considerably weakened their loyalty to Japan, and their devotion to their god and emperor was challenged by their allegiance to the United States.

Nisei were second-generation Japanese North Americans. They had received all their education in North America and were genuinely loyal to America despite the fact they were considered by the government to be Japanese. Munson noted they considered themselves Americans. To them, Japan was a foreign country and the Japanese looked down on them as foreigners. Munson added that encouragement and acceptance of this group would go a long way to swing them away from any lingering romantic longing for old Japan. In 1941, when Pearl Harbor came under attack, the Hawaiian National Guard was made up almost entirely of Nisei soldiers, but in January 1942 nearly all Japanese Americans were discharged unceremoniously from armed service or were assigned only menial labouring duties. In that same month, the California State Personnel Board voted to bar from all civil service positions any descendants of nations with whom the United States was at war. This act was only enforced against Japanese Americans and did little to instil in them patriotism for a country that was now denying them basic rights.

The Kibei were a portion of the Nisei population who had been born in North America and who had received some or all of their schooling in Japan. It was the Kibei who troubled Munson, as their loyalty could be questioned.

After December 7, 1941, 5,560 Americans of Japanese ancestry renounced their U.S. citizenship and left the country to volunteer for service in the Imperial forces. Other Nikkei who served Japan may have done so unwillingly. Many of them were in Japan when war was declared on America. If they returned to North America they faced internment or expulsion to Japan. If they remained in Japan they faced forced enlistment. Japan was, after all, a totalitarian state ruled by fear, where an act of disloyalty could mean death or years of hardship. Conscription into the emperor's army was the lesser of two fates.

The statistics do not reveal the numbers of Nikkei who threw off any lingering attachment to Japan in disgust following the attack on Pearl Harbor and the declaration of war against the United States. However, two cases that gained prominence following the war gave those in favour of interning the Japanese North Americans justification for their position.

The most notorious case involved Tomoya Kawakita, an American citizen who joined the Japanese army following the start of the war. Surviving prisoners of war indicted Kawakita as a camp guard and interpreter who actively participated in the torture and death of at least one American soldier—a survivor of the notorious Bataan Death March.[1]

Another example was Sergeant Inouye Kanao, a Canadian citizen of Japanese ancestry, known to Canadian prisoners at the Sham Shui Po camp in China as the "Kamloops Kid," a reference to his home town in the British Columbia interior. It was not an endearing term, and for Canadians, Kanao's treason was unfathomable. His father had served proudly with the Canadian army in the First World War and received the Military Medal for Bravery. Kanao himself had signed on with the Imperial army in 1938, and because his first language was English and he was fluent in Japanese, he earned himself a position as the camp commandant's personal interpreter. Kanao took particular delight in targeting Canadian prisoners, unmercifully beating hapless POWs held by two other Japanese goons in retaliation for some indignity, perceived or real, he had suffered while a boy in Canada.

Following the war, Kanao's camp superior Commandant Tokunaga and his comrades received twenty-year sentences for war crimes. In an attempt to avoid their fate, Kanao argued his Canadian citizenship exempted him from being tried as a war criminal. The British trial judge agreed and instead sentenced Kanao to death for high treason. He was executed three days later on April 25, 1947—perhaps the only Canadian executed for treason in the Second World War.

Events in local waters also cast suspicion on the Nikkei. In early 1942, Fishermen's Reserve sailors searching a fishing camp owned by a Japanese Canadian in Sidney Inlet on Vancouver Island's west coast found a large tank, filled with diesel fuel, submerged in the inlet. A filling pipe leading to the tank was hidden in the brush at the shore's edge. The camp had been shut down but was being investigated for possible enemy activity. A squad of soldiers from Victoria, led by a team of RCMP, set up machine-gun posts around the inlet and maintained a constant vigil as they believed the inlet, with its hidden tank, was a secret refuelling and rendezvous point for enemy submarines. Several weeks passed uneventfully except for the arrival of a black bear that stumbled into the camp and was killed by an overzealous soldier who dispatched it with a machine gun. No submarine made an appearance at the site, and in retrospect it seems unlikely that Japanese submarines, with their massive fuel-storage capacity that enabled them to make non-stop patrols to North America and return, would need such an unreliable and questionable source of fuel.

But even such innocuous "evidence" shed a bad light on the Japanese North Americans, and the resulting rumours did little to endear the local Japanese populations to their non-Japanese countrymen. Many unfounded and outright racist charges were levelled at the Nikkei. There were groundless accusations that the close-knit communities were forming a fifth column to promote anarchy and carry out terrorist acts. The largest concentrations of Japanese-Canadian and Japanese-American communities were along the West Coast, where the men worked as fisherman and owned outright a good percentage of the vessels making up the West Coast fishing fleet. This led to suggestions that Japanese-Canadian fishermen were rendezvousing with enemy subs off the B.C. coast to pass information and spies. Even more preposterous was the accusation that the Japanese community protested too much—an "obvious" sign of its guilt.

Further proof of Japanese duplicity was the discovery that in the Asian colonies captured by the Japanese during the 1930s, many of the cooks, waiters, bartenders, and barbers employed at British bases just prior to the war were actually high-ranking Imperial army officers. These spies worked on the bases at any job that would bring them into casual conversation with European officers, who innocently passed information to the spies. The West Coast could easily be infiltrated in this manner as well. Air Vice-Marshall Stevenson, concerned that remote stations along the coast were open to attack and sabotage, wrote Air Force Headquarters in January 1942, "[Security] cannot rest on precarious discernment between those who would actively support Japan and those who might at present be apathetic."

Despite Munson's sympathetic findings that "there is no Japanese problem on the coast" and "there will be no armed uprising of Japanese," President Roosevelt signed Executive Order 9066 on February 14, 1942, making Japanese Americans wards of the government.

In Canada, Parliament passed Order in Council 1486 on February 24, 1942. It allowed police to search, confine, enforce curfews on, and eventually confiscate the property of the Japanese Canadians. Major newspapers and community groups enthusiastically encouraged the imprisonment of the Nikkei. By mid-March 1942 their fate was sealed and evacuation orders enacted.

General John DeWitt was charged with overseeing the removal of the Nikkei populations from the coastal United States, and over 110,000 civilians were moved to ten camps in California, Arizona, Wyoming, Idaho, Utah, Colorado, and Arkansas. Some 23,000 Canadian Nikkei were relocated away from the West Coast to six camps in the inland Kootenay region of British Columbia. Initially, local populations of the Nikkei in the Lower Mainland were held at Hastings Park

Fairground before the move inland. Families were split up at the Canadian camps, with men sent to work on road crews in B.C. or at sugar beet farms in the prairies alongside German POWs. A few Nikkei who were considered security threats were sent to prisoner of war camps at Angler and Petawawa, Ontario.

The property of the Canadian Nikkei fell under the "protection" of the wartime Security Commission. Real estate, farms, livestock, homes, fishing boats, and all manner of property was seized and sold at a fraction of its worth. Many white fishermen grasped the opportunity to snatch up Japanese-Canadian assets. This ended the Nikkei domination of the fishing industry and supplied the new owners with fishing boats and equipment at fire-sale prices. To add insult to injury, internees were required to pay the cost of their internment and an "appropriate" sum deducted by the commissioner. It was not until 1949, four years after the war's end, that the Japanese Canadians were allowed to return to the coast.

In the United States, Nikkei who had been leading a peaceful life on the coast now found themselves being shipped to inland internment camps and treated as common criminals. At the Lordsburg Camp in New Mexico, Private Clarence Burleson shot two critically ill internees— Hirota Isomura, a fisherman, and Toshio Kobata, a farmer—for no apparent reason. The report said they were "shot while trying to escape," although there was no serious inquiry and no autopsy made available. Other inmates noted that the two men were so ill they were lagging behind in the march to the camp. Burleson took this as an attempt to escape and killed both men with shots at very short range. Two Nikkei made to dig graves for Isomura and Kobata were told by their guard, "Work quickly or I will make you dig two more graves."

The Manzanar Camp, west of Death Valley in California, was the most infamous of the camps, and several deaths and shootings occurred there. Evacuees were housed in a searing desert with no arable soil and little protection from the heat in summer and cold in winter. In May 1942, Hikoji Takeuchi was shot and killed while trying to escape. A non-fatal shooting in which the guard claimed the prisoner was trying to escape followed this. A simple inspection of the wounded evacuee's shirt revealed a bullet hole through the front and not through the back as would be the case if he were fleeing. No charges were laid against the guard.

The most notorious incident occurred at Manzanar. Protest began among the evacuees after one Nikkei leader was jumped and beaten by

NOTICE TO ALL
JAPANESE PERSONS
AND PERSONS OF
JAPANESE RACIAL ORIGIN

TAKE NOTICE that under Orders Nos. 21, 22, 23 and 24 of the British Columbia Security Commission, the following areas were made prohibited areas to all persons of the Japanese race:—

LULU ISLAND (including Steveston)	SAPPERTON
	BURQUITLAM
SEA ISLAND	PORT MOODY
EBURNE	IOCO
MARPOLE	
DISTRICT OF QUEENSBOROUGH	PORT COQUITLAM
	MAILLARDVILLE
CITY OF NEW WESTMINSTER	FRASER MILLS

AND FURTHER TAKE NOTICE that any person of the Japanese race found within any of the said prohibited areas without a written permit from the British Columbia Security Commission or the Royal Canadian Mounted Police shall be liable to the penalties provided under Order in Council P.C. 1665.

AUSTIN C. TAYLOR,
Chairman,
British Columbia Security Commission

A copy of the notice ordering the removal of Japanese Canadians from areas of the Lower Mainland.

Japanes-Americans at the Owens Lake Internment Camp.

a group of assailants. The beating was believed to stem from group rivalries among internees themselves, and Nikkei leaders levelled charges that a racketeering scheme was being run by prisoners and some camp administrators. A series of work stoppages ensued, followed by more accusations and the arrest of one organizer, Dick Miwa. By evening, two agitated blocs had formed up in the camp town centre under the gaze of soldiers. As the tense crowd of evacuees pushed towards the line of police and armed soldiers, they were ordered to disperse. Tear gas was fired into the rebellious crowd, which quickly re-formed to challenge the police and send an unmanned car crashing through the walls of the police station. In the chaos, soldiers opened fire on the crowd, resulting in the deaths of two young Nisei and the wounding of ten more.

Several more killings occurred in the American camps. S. James Okamoto, a Tule Lake, California, camp trustee, was shot to death by a guard after getting out of the truck he was driving. The guard was fined one dollar for misuse of government property—the bullet.

James Wakasa, who had immigrated to the United States in 1903, was in his 60s when he was shot while purportedly trying to escape from the Topaz Camp in Utah. The bloodstained earth where he died showed Wakasa was clearly within the camp boundary and the bullet had entered his body from the front and exited through his back. A court-martial found the guard who shot Wakasa "not guilty."

In an effort to prove their loyalty to the United States and Canada, many Nikkei joined the respective services of their countries when the ban on their enlistment was lifted in February 1943. Their fluency in the Japanese language meant many Nikkei were used to monitor Japanese radio transmissions. They also fed false information back to Japanese commands in the South Pacific and were used as interpreters during interrogations of Japanese POWs. "All-Japanese" regiments formed up in the U.S.; Japanese-Canadians were allowed to enlist, and many served with distinction in the European theatre.

In the 1980s, almost 50 years after orders for removal of Japanese Canadians and Americans were enacted, internees received an acknowledgement of their ill-treatment from their respective governments and were awarded $20,000 each. No Japanese North American was ever convicted of spying for Japan.

Highway
to Tokyo

Both the Canadians and Americans had long considered building a road connecting the wild northern territories with southern civilization. In 1905, the Northwest Mounted Police, forerunner of the Royal Canadian Mounted Police, blazed a trail nearly 640 kilometres from Fort St. John, B.C., towards the Klondike before the end of the gold rush cut short the project at the Stikine River. In the 1930s, B.C.'s pro-western premier Duff Pattullo hounded the federal government to fund a highway to Alaska with the idea it would open up northern B.C. for development. The Canadian government was not anxious to pour money into a road that it felt would mostly benefit the United States, and when Pattullo's attempts to initiate a northern highway project met with the immoveable force of Prime Minister Mackenzie King, he turned to the Americans, finding a sympathetic listener in U.S. president Franklin Roosevelt. While many Americans supported a road through Canada as the only way to connect Alaska with the continental United States, many in Congress opposed the idea. They did not want to pay for a road that they believed would mostly benefit Canadians.

The Canadian government admonished Pattullo for his overtures south of the border on the grounds that such an American-funded highway would threaten the Dominion's security and sovereignty. Out of respect for its northern neighbour, the United States did not push the issue. Pattullo wanted his highway, however, and stoked the fires of western discontent by pointing out the priority given projects in the east over those in the west, particularly British Columbia. Pattullo again pressed the Americans, proposing private entrepreneurs cover the cost of road construction. Again the federal government scolded the upstart premier and refused to consider a road through Canada's north funded by U.S. dollars. Plainly Ottawa did not want a large U.S. presence or investment in its northern territory.

Pearl Harbor, and the intercepted Japanese transmissions indicating that Alaska would be the likely target of an invasion force, changed everything. It was no longer a matter of *when* to build a road to Alaska, but *how long* it would take to build it. Highway access to the north would allow troops to defend North America's northern perimeter against invasion by Japan via Alaska, or possibly by Germany through Siberia should the Russian front fall. (At its narrowest, the Bering Strait separating Siberia and Alaska is less than 64 kilometres wide, and in deep winter it sometimes freezes, narrowing the gap even further for an invading army—literally putting it at North America's back door.) An Alaskan highway could also be used to ferry much-needed equipment to beleaguered Soviet troops. Not least, a road through Canada's north was seen as a major step to bring about the downfall of the Japanese empire. It would make it easier to send large numbers of troops to Alaska, where they could use the Aleutian Islands as stepping-stones to the Kuriles for an invasion of Japan.

In January 1942 the American and Canadian members of the Pacific Joint Board on Defense recommended that a highway be constructed linking Alaska to the continental United States. By February the American Cabinet War Committee concurred and approved initial funds and the survey of a route for the new highway, even though the U.S. had not been given, nor even requested, Canadian approval for a road that would pass over 1,900 kilometres of Canadian territory.

If the Canadian government was reluctant to build a northern highway before 1941, the threat of an invasion by Japan via the North Pacific finally prompted Ottawa to change its mind, but with this sobering warning: "The highway goes both ways, to be used by us...or an invading army."[1]

When the bill was tabled in Parliament, Ottawa was quick to give agreement and was perhaps even glad to have the Alaska Highway annoyance finally resolved. The Americans were shouldering the greatest portion of the cost and problems associated with a construction project of such magnitude in the unforgiving north. Canada agreed to waive all import duties and taxes on equipment and personnel; provide the right of way through Canadian territory; and allow the use of timber, gravel, and waterways as required for construction. The United States would assume the cost of construction and maintenance up to a period of six months after war's end, at which point the Canadian section of the highway would be turned over to Ottawa. The U.S. Army Corps of Engineers would be responsible for the initial survey and cutting out a rough road, while the U.S. Public Roads Administration would take responsibility for straightening and grooming the pioneer road.

Three routes had been proposed, but the Dawson Creek through Whitehorse to Fairbanks route was chosen over a shorter coastal route because it would parallel an existing series of rough airfields extending from Edmonton, Alberta, to Whitehorse in the Yukon—the Northwest Staging Route. The weather inland was much more stable than that of the coast and, significantly, a coastal highway would be vulnerable to enemy attack from the sea and by carrier- or submarine-launched aircraft.

By mid-March 1942, a corps of U.S. Army engineers had descended on Fort St. John in British Columbia to begin survey work for what was dubbed "Highway to Tokyo." The new road would have its southern terminus at Dawson Creek and end 2,470 kilometres away at Fairbanks, Alaska. Much of the groundwork on the first leg of the Alaska Highway was already done for the American army engineers. Knox McCusker of the Dominion Land Survey of Canada had completed surveying and mapping a route in the north Peace River district and had roughed out a 75-kilometre road between Dawson Creek and Fort St. John. As well, the Dominion Land Survey had come up with a method of road surveying using an aircraft as a sighting platform. The Canadian engineers who devised this method were brought on board and were responsible for much of the initial routing work on the Alaska Highway.

Seven United States Army construction battalions did the initial road clearing through the wilderness. Three of them were totally composed of black enlisted men from the American Deep South (commanded by white officers), as it was assumed in the U.S. Army at the time that black men were only fit for support duty. The sudden movement of these men to the north was devastating, as they had been given no opportunity to acclimatize to the harsh northern weather and the relentless building schedule, and there were significantly more suicides among the black soldiers than among their white compatriots.

Road construction had to be kept up for 22 hours a day to meet the rigorous deadline, much of this in the cold months when temperatures remained well below zero. When the temperature fell to -50° Celsius, the stocks of antifreeze for the heavy machinery froze solid. In the summer, men worked in the sucking, waist-deep muskeg under relentless swarms of black flies and hoards of mosquitoes "as big

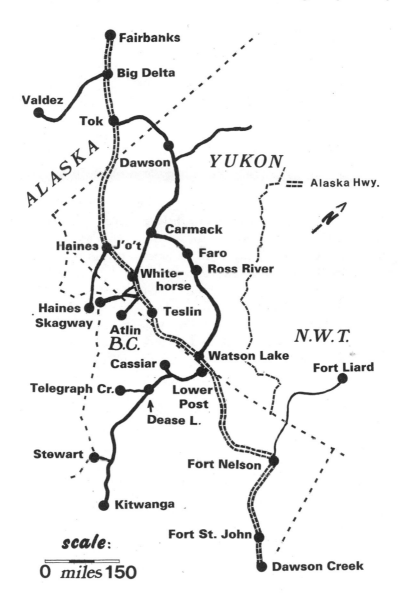

The Alaska Highway, a two-lane road carved through the wilderness was informally dubbed the "Highway to Tokyo." Its primary purpose was to ferry troops and equipment for an invasion of Japan via British Columbia, the Yukon, Alaska, and the Aleutians. Its main use was as a lifeline for the Lend-Lease program to the Soviet Union.

as Zeros" (a reference to the Japanese fighter plane). There were also predatory bears and cougars. The rugged country provided its own dangers. Seven men were killed when their log raft overturned as they shot the rapids of a river, while others died as vehicles and earthmoving equipment slid down embankments or overturned on the soft muskeg.

The road roughly followed the path of the Northwest Staging Route (NWSR), a series of rough airfields that had been hewn out of the wilderness from northern Alberta through B.C. to the Yukon Territory in the late 1920s. The Canadian government established the NWSR to service the remote areas of Canada's western lower north. It was intended to join up with a string of American airfields planned for Alaska through the Aleutians and on to the Orient to form the much-touted Great Circle Route. By the time war came, the Americans had instituted a crash program to develop airfields in Alaska for its military defence.

The NWSR originally passed through Grande Prairie, Alberta; Fort St. John, Fort Nelson, Prince George, and Smithers in northern B.C.; and Watson Lake and Whitehorse in the Yukon Territory. After 1941 it was expanded from Montana to Fairbanks and eventually Nome. Edmonton became the major southern terminus. Smaller emergency landing strips were roughed in along the route as well, parallel to the new Alaska Highway.

While it was used to rush men, supplies, equipment, and aircraft to vulnerable sectors for use against Japan in the expected Alaskan war, the route served a much larger role in the Second World War. Over 8,000 aircraft were moved north along the route to Nome, Alaska, as part of the Alaska to Siberia Lend-Lease program to the Soviet Union. In Nome and Fairbanks, Soviet pilots would take possession of the aircraft and fly them across the Bering Strait to Siberia and on to the Russian front in the desperate struggle for survival against Germany. Once the air route was fully established it was no more unusual to see Bell Aircobras and Dakota DC3s with the red star of the Soviet Air Force passing north through Montana, Edmonton, and B.C. than it was to see planes with the American star or the RCAF roundel. At Nome there were as many Soviet officers as American in town, desperately stocking up in the small stores and shops before heading home to war-starved Russia.

As more men and equipment moved north, lack of a reliable supply of petroleum threatened to grind the war effort to a halt. Alaska needed petroleum imported in significant quantity by tanker ships from the south, but neither the United States nor Canada could provide enough tankers and the warships or planes to escort them along the Pacific coast. If the Allies were to eventually launch an invasion of Japan via Alaska and the Aleutians, they would need a steady, protected, and preferably local supply of oil in the north.

The Americans turned their attention to Norman Wells in the Northwest Territories, where huge reserves had been discovered in 1920. A small refinery existed there, but it only produced enough to supply local needs. Pumping stations, pipelines, and a larger refining capacity were needed to maintain the defences of Alaska and the Canadian north. The United States requested and received permission from the Canadian government to develop the fields as well as to construct a refinery at Whitehorse some 800 kilometres south. In May 1942, a complete, operational refinery in Texas was dismantled and shipped north via Prince Rupert and Skagway, then reassembled at Whitehorse. At the same time the pipeline and the Canol Road (an access road from Norman Wells on the Mackenzie River to Whitehorse) were built by the U.S. Army Corps of Engineers and a consortium of companies, later to become BPC (Bechtels, Price, Callaghan), which was head-quartered in San Francisco. Construction took twenty months, and oil production at the refinery began in April 1944.

Detractors in the U.S. Senate later launched an investigation into Canol, claiming the project had been conducted secretly and ended as a $100 million waste of American war dollars. Furthermore, they said, the money had been spent developing a Canadian oil project with no foresight to negotiate post-war rights for the United States. Canol, however, produced over a million barrels of oil for the war effort and would have been invaluable had the Allies chosen to invade Japan by way of Alaska.

The war barely affected the Native people of the Yukon until the intrusion of northern megaprojects like the Alaska Highway, NWSR, and Canol. The locals got seasonal work on the highway construction project in traditional roles as suppliers of game and firewood or as casual labourers. But it was the invading armies of construction crews, who brought north with them the ills of "civilized" society, that most profoundly impacted Native society. While hospitals in Fort St. John and Whitehorse were expanded to the benefit of the Natives, diseases brought north by outsiders boosted their need for such facilities. Epidemics of mumps, measles, influenza, meningitis, whooping cough, dysentery, diphtheria, and tuberculosis ran rampant through Native populations living close to the new highway. Infant mortality among Native infants peaked at 47 percent in 1943–44, triple its pre-war rate. Among a test group of local Natives, 49 percent were infected with TB, while others living in outlying areas were unaffected by these new maladies.

In the frontier setting of highway towns, alcohol passed freely from road crew to Native as a means of bridging the cultural gap. Outsiders entered into short-term relationships with Native women, resulting in an explosion of illegitimate children, who were then abandoned when their fathers returned south or moved on. In a span of less than one year, as the Alaska Highway was bulldozed through their traditional territory, the lifestyle of the Yukon Natives was dramatically and forever changed by a war thousands of kilometres away.[2]

In Whitehorse the population swelled from about 400 to over 7,000 inhabitants within a year, while almost overnight Dawson Creek boomed from 400 to 4,000 people. A tent city was erected at Dawson Creek, and necessities like water and firewood were trucked in to support this instant town. The number of American personnel, both army and civilian, in Canada's north eventually numbered nearly 50,000, and they were cordially referred to by northerners as the "army of occupation."

The huge American troop presence in Canada's north did not go unnoticed, nor was it taken lightly. The British High Commissioner to Canada, Malcolm Macdonald, pointed out to the Canadian government the seriousness of having such a large foreign presence in its north. Macdonald was suspicious of American motives for constructing such megaprojects as the Alaska Highway, Canol, and development and upgrades to the NWSR. Perhaps with such heavy investment in the Canadian north, compared to the lack of it by the Canadians themselves, the U.S. could claim sovereignty in those parts. If the Americans decided to stay put once the war was over, Canada would be able to do little about it.

Prime Minister William Lyon Mackenzie King decided that a Canadian authority should be in place to protect the interests of Canada, and he appointed Major General W.W. Foster to oversee American activities in the north. The matter of U.S. involvement came to a head when Imperial Oil denied Foster access to information, saying that it first had to clear access through United States authority. Foster applied for the information again and was refused, this time on grounds of national security. The matter went to the highest levels of the two governments before Foster's authority was established.

While Macdonald was right to question the integrity of American intentions in the north, he also made suggestions that put the matter to rest. Canadians needed more participation in their own northern territory on these megaprojects, their government deemed, and for this it paid the Americans nearly $124 million—a phenomenal sum to be diverting from the war acquisition budget. It gave Canadians control of their section of the Alaska Highway and won permanent improvements to the Northwest Staging Route from the Americans, who in effect became contractors to the Canadian government. Ultimately, this expensive but prudent manoeuvre removed any question of Canadian dominion in the north.

Even by today's standards the Alaska Highway is a feat of modern engineering. It was officially opened on November 20, 1942, above Kluane Lake, Yukon, at a spot respectfully named Soldier's Summit. Winding 2,228 kilometres from Dawson Creek, B.C., to Fairbanks, Alaska, the road was officially opened for public use in 1946.

Return of the I-Boats

6

By March 1942, all Japanese submarines operating along the continental West Coast had been recalled and dispatched to the waters around Midway and Alaska to carry out reconnaissance in anticipation of the upcoming assaults on those areas. Around the Aleutians and Kodiak Island, submarines *I-9*, *I-15*, *I-17*, *I-19*, *I-25*, and *I-26* concentrated their attention on Dutch Harbor, Adak, and Kodiak, which had an air base and a naval anchorage. The Japanese were unaware of the secret American bases at Cold Bay and Umnak Island.

In March, *I-19* attempted to launch its Glen off Kodiak Island, but lost its half-assembled float plane when the sudden appearance of a destroyer forced it to dive. Two months later, Meiji Tagami's *I-25* successfully launched its Glen aircraft over Kodiak, manned by pilot Nobuo Fujita and his observer Petty Officer Shoji Okuda. At the navy anchorage in Woman's Bay they reported only minor American war vessels. Tagami, as well as Yakota's *I-26*, then headed south to the B.C. and Washington coast, taking up position once again off Cape Flattery.

While they were en route south, several witnesses spotted *I-25* off Langara Island in the Queen Charlottes, including the lighthouse keeper on Langara. While some locals were evacuated, others remained to keep a watch on the I-boat, which appeared to be observing the activity on shore. After some time the boat submerged without incident.

Eventually a U.S. Coast Guard cutter and the Fishermen's Reserve vessel *Moolack* arrived to carry out a cursory search for the intruder. Witnesses told a shore party from the two vessels that the sub had remained for some time before diving and that it was unmistakably a submarine, not anything else. This was consistent with Tagami noting years later that his boat had been spotted off Langara Island and that he dived, assuming aircraft would have been alerted.

On June 7, Minoru Yakota's *I-26*, which had claimed the first American merchant ship in the Pacific war, lay in wait at the mouth of the Strait of Juan de Fuca off Vancouver Island's southern extremity, hoping to intercept the elusive American aircraft carriers, should they be docked at Seattle, when they moved north to defend Alaska once it was attacked.

It was shortly past noon on June 7 when Coastwise Steamship Lines' *Coast Trader*, outbound from Port Angeles to San Francisco, came into the lens of Yakota's periscope 40 kilometres off Port Renfrew on Vancouver Island's west coast. Shadowing the freighter at periscope depth, Yakota closed to within 750 metres of the freighter, sounding off co ordinates to senior torpedoman Takeji Komaba as he manoeuvred his submarine into attack position. *Coast Trader* glided into the parallels worked out by the torpedo officer and he was ready to fire. On Yakota's command, two torpedoes whined their way to the target, followed minutes later by two terrific explosions on the ship's port side. Aboard the *Coast Trader*, ruptured steam lines filled the engine room with burning, choking vapours. The sea immediately flowed in through buckled hull plates and busted valves, dousing the engines and generators.

Verne Wikert, a twenty year old who had just signed on as an oiler, was knocked out as he was blown headfirst against a steel bulkhead by the terrific blast. When he came to he was immersed in diesel fuel and water and in total darkness. His head still reeling from the impact, he found a ladder and hung on, but figured he was done for—until he saw daylight penetrating from above. The impact had knocked the blackout screen off the ventilation tube. Pulling himself through the shaft and onto the listing deck, Wikert struggled into a life jacket and slipped over the side into the cold water. The ship was aflame and settling at the stern, with oil and debris littering the water. Wikert slipped in and out of consciousness as fellow sailors grappled him into a lifeboat. When he awoke, *Coast Trader* had already disappeared beneath the surface on her way to the ocean floor. All 36 crewmen managed to get away safely to lifeboats, but one died during the night from burns and exposure. Wikert's boat was rescued by the fishing vessel *Virginia 1* and towed into the Indian reservation at Neah Bay near Cape Flattery. The following morning the Canadian corvette HMCS *Edmunston* picked up two more life rafts with survivors and discharged them at Port Angeles. *Edmunston* and aircraft from Sidney, B.C., and Washington carried out a systematic search for the enemy submarine, but the deep, cold waters of the Pacific Northwest concealed the sub as Yakota made his way north to wait out the hunt off Vancouver Island's Barkley Sound.

Meanwhile, *I-25* skipper Meiji Tagami was also in Pacific Northwest waters, also off Cape Flattery. Tagami had been running on the surface under cover of darkness to recharge the sub's batteries and compressed air cylinders. Just after midnight on June 20, *I-25*'s watch caught sight of the freighter *Fort Camosun* steaming 112 kilometres south of Cape Flattery. The ship had just been built at the Victoria Machinery Depot for the British Ministry of Transport, and it was headed south on its maiden voyage with a load of lumber and raw materials for the manufacture of munitions. The *Fort Camosun* was to take up duties in the European theatre, via the Panama Canal. By 0230 Tagami had lined up the 7,126-ton freighter and fired a single torpedo that ripped *Camosun*'s hull under the port bridge. Immediately Number 2 and 3 holds filled with water, dousing the ship's engines, auxiliary generators, and steam-powered steering motors as the vessel began to settle evenly in the water. Half-naked crewmen, wakened by the shock of the explosion, spilled into darkened passageways yelling, "Torpedo! Torpedo!"

As crewmen pulled away in lifeboats, a shell whistled over the freighter's bow. A second landed against her side, opening up the hull to more sea. Fearing aircraft had been alerted by now, Tagami dived and broke off the attack.

The *Fort Camosun* did manage to get off a distress call, but the nearest help—the Canadian corvettes *Edmunston* and *Quesnel*—was six hours' steaming time away. As dawn broke the two corvettes found the stricken freighter wallowing on an even keel, her main deck nearly awash but held afloat by her cargo of lumber. Tagami had returned to the scene and shot his scope up for a quick look at the rescue attempt. HMCS *Quesnel*, under Lieutenant John A. Gow, detected the sounds of the submarine still in the area and began laying depth charges to force the I-boat away while *Edmunston* picked up two lifeboats of survivors and began salvage operations. HMCS *Vancouver* and the American armed yacht *Y-994* arrived later to join in the search for the submarine, but by noon all contact had been lost.

When the Canadian salvage tug *Dauntless* and U.S. Navy tug *Tatnuck* arrived in the late afternoon they found the *Edmunston*, under command of Lieutenant Raiffe Barrett, struggling bravely to tow the unwieldy *Camosun* to safety in a rising sea, with the freighter's main deck only centimetres above water. Late the following day, as the flotilla

Fort Camosun *under tow off Neah Bay, Washington, photographed from the tug* Nemanook. *Note the torpedo hole where water is pouring out of the deck.*

rounded Cape Flattery, it was decided to beach *Camosun* at Neah Bay on the American side. All four vessels were struggling to keep a handle on the tow as waves began breaking over the wounded ship and it settled lower in the water. After reaching the safety of the bay, temporary repairs were made and the tug *Canadian National No. 2* arrived and towed *Fort Camosun* to the graving dock at Victoria, where a large piece of a Japanese torpedo was discovered in the twisted metal.

On the day *I-25* attacked the *Fort Camosun*, Yakota was proceeding aboard *I-26* on a northerly course eight kilometres off Barkley Sound on Vancouver Island's west coast. At dawn the sub had been forced to dive after the fishing vessel *Talapus*—a member of the Fisherman's Volunteer Reserve—spotted it from about six kilometres astern. In fact, *Talapus*'s crew did not realize they were following a submarine until it dived, as its silhouette resembled another FVR vessel—the *Marauder*. After several hours, Yakota resurfaced and continued north. It was almost the longest day of the year, so at 10 p.m. the setting sun still illuminated the western horizon.

I-boats patrolling the West Coast had orders to shell important shore-based installations as well as ships. To Yakota's starboard lay Estevan Point, where, just beyond the lighthouse, he understood a radar / radio-direction-finding installation existed. The subs had orders to destroy these direction-finding locators, as they could home in on the submarine's wireless transmissions.

By 2217 hours, the sky to the west still cast its fading light over Hesquiat, the Nootka village nestled behind Estevan Point's lighthouse. Yakota, standing atop the conning tower, ordered Chief Gunner Saburo Hayashi to commence firing with the 5.5-inch (140-millimetre) gun. The first shell landed 550 metres short of the lighthouse and sent up six-metre geysers of water. Yakota scolded the crew to aim higher. Several more shells landed around the lighthouse as the gun crew adjusted the range. Following shots went high over the Indian village, landing in a hilly area beyond the community. As the shells exploded, lights were doused in the tiny village and the gun crew could hear the frantic squealing of pigs coming from the village.

On shore, wireless operator Edward T. Redford radioed "WE ARE BEING SHELLED!" Shells were missing the lighthouse but landing all around the village five kilometres away. Lighthouse keeper Robert

Fort Camosun *under tow after being torpedoed by* I-25, *112 kilometres southwest of Cape Flattery, Washington.*

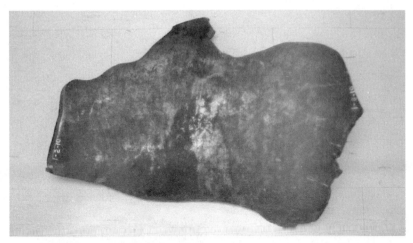

A Japanese torpedo fragment pulled from the hull of Fort Camosun *at the Esquimalt graving dock, June 1942. Photographed at the Canadian War Museum, Vimy House.*

Lally hurled himself up the spiral staircase of the tower to douse the thousand-watt light that had been kept burning in spite of submarine threats because of the treachery of waters off Vancouver Island's west coast. From his vantage point Lally logged the second and third salvoes, noting that they exploded with such force the lighthouse tower shook and three of the lantern windows were taken out by flying debris. *I-26* got off about 21 shots before Yakota ordered the sub away, having done little other than alert the enemy to his presence.

An air force bomber peeled down the airstrip at Pat Bay, but spun out, cracking up and blocking the runway so no other craft could take off. It was 30 minutes before an aircraft from Coal Harbour near Port Hardy flew over the area, but it turned up nothing. In the days following, as panicked headlines reported the attack on British Columbia by Japanese submarines, a contentious conscription bill easily passed through Parliament.

I-26 remained off B.C.'s coast until mid-July and returned to Yokosuka via the Aleutians without finding any more targets. By shelling Estevan Point, however, Minoru Yakota unwittingly earned himself a tiny footnote in Canadian history: His was the first enemy attack on Canadian soil since the War of 1812.[1] And because of the Japanese submariner's actions, lighthouses along the West Coast were finally blacked out, causing the Russian freighter *Uzbekistan* to crash onto the rocks at Pachena Point with a load of Lend-Lease materials in April 1943.

Meanwhile, Meiji Tagami in *I-25* had moved south to his old hunting ground off the Columbia River in Oregon. Guarding the river mouth is Fort Stevens, just west of Astoria. This concrete fortress built into the bluffs overlooking the river mouth and the sea had four batteries housing 6-inch (150-millimetre) disappearing guns and 12-inch (300-millimetre) mortars.

Meiji Tagami, commander of the I-25.

Fort Stevens had been established during the American Civil War to counter the sizeable Royal Navy base in Victoria, B.C. While the Union Army was occupied fighting the Confederate forces, the Americans feared the British might attempt to seize territory at the mouth of the Columbia. This gave Fort Stevens the distinction of being the only Civil War fort west of the Missouri River, but it was about to gain further notoriety.

On June 21, the day following *I-26*'s attack on Estevan Point, Tagami slipped his submarine through homebound fish boats to within eight kilometres of Cape Disappointment, which marks the river entrance. Sometime before midnight he brought *I-25* to the surface and lined the submarine up, deck cannon facing directly aft and bow pointing to open sea. On shore he knew there was some sort of military base, and he had the approximate location of the radio-direction-finding station.

Tagami gave the order to fire and Sadao Iijima let loose with the 5.5-inch (140-millimetre) cannon, landing the first shots in front of Battery Russell, which was off active duty that evening. The explosions broke the sleep of the soldiers encamped in tents behind the battery, and confusion reigned as men in undershorts ran about in darkness lit up by exploding mortars. Several observation posts, as well as the armed yacht *Manana II*, radioed alarms to the fort's control centre, which by now was well aware of the submarine.

Author's rendition of the attack on Estevan Point by Minoru Yakota's I-26, June 20, 1942.

Along the beach in front of the fort was a string of observation posts manned with searchlights and machine guns. The furthest post, at the south jetty, was eight kilometres from the main fort. An exploding shell cut the telephone line connecting the fort to the three northern beach emplacements. When the control centre at Fort Stevens was unable to raise the beach posts, it assumed the Japanese had landed, cut the communication lines, and captured the placements.

I-25's position would have been less than five kilometres from shore, directly in line with the wreck of the *Peter Iredale*, an iron-and-steel sailing ship that grounded on the shore in 1906 and whose remains can still be seen today. The fire control centre at Fort Stevens calculated the sub to be out of range for the battery's big guns, so it never gave the order to fire or even turn on the searchlights. This was an odd assumption since the submarine's comparatively small gun was landing shells on the shore and had a range of only eight kilometres—far less than the range of the fort's large guns. For Tagami it proved a fortunate error in judgement. Had he any idea of the number and size of guns aimed in his direction, he later wrote, he would never have risked his ship or the lives of the 108 sailors aboard. As it was, gunner Iijima estimated that he fired seventeen shots in the direction of the fort.[2]

On Delaura Beach Road a shell landed metres short of a home owned by the Hitchmen family, leaving a three-metre crater where Mrs. Hitchmen's garden had been moments before and splintering a tree. Another shot sailed over the house and exploded just outside the new cemetery about a kilometre inland. Tagami retreated north, slipping past the blacked-out shapes of the *Manana II* and the Columbia River

A round that failed to explode. This shell was discovered amongst wood debris at Estevan Point. It was found to be a Japanese make, putting an end to speculation that the point was fired on by a "friendly" gunboat.

lightship, to leave the confusion onshore behind. *I-25* arrived again in the waters off Dutch Harbor on June 26, but finding no worthwhile targets he set home for Japan, though *I-25* would later return to the West Coast on a very special mission.

In May, three Japanese submarines—*I-7*, *I-9*, and *I-15*—were still on reconnaissance patrol in the stormy waters of the eastern Aleutians around Kodiak and Unalaska, and in the Gulf of Alaska, preparing for the Dutch Harbor attack. *I-9*, patrolling in the gulf, had surfaced to shell the *General W.C. Gorgas*[3]—a 119-metre cannery ship converted to an army troop carrier. The submarine landed two shells on the *Gorgas* but was outmanocuvred by the old cannery boat, which managed to slip away.

To the west, the Dutch Harbor assault force under Rear Admiral Kakuji Kakuta slipped out of Ominato in northern Honshu on May 25 and proceeded east under cover of a swirling mass of fog rolling towards North America, followed two days later by Admiral Hosogaya's Aleutian invasion force. On May 30 the three Japanese submarines remaining in Alaska were ordered to station around Dutch Harbor.

This monument marks the site where one of seventeen shells fired by I-25 landed only metres short of the Hitchmen family home near Fort Stevens, Oregon, June 21, 1942.

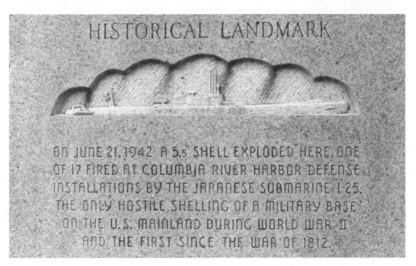

Fort Stevens today, near Astoria, Oregon. The fort was shelled by I-25 on June 21, 1942.

An 8-inch gun at Fort Stevens. Had the fort returned fire, I-25's 5.5-inch gun would have been no match for the fort's equipment.

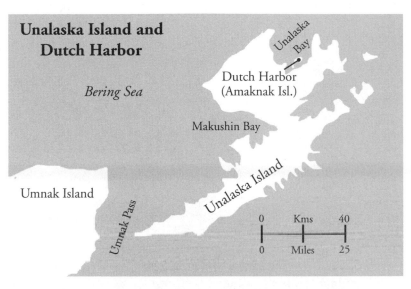

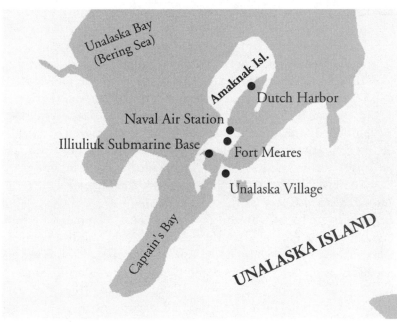

The Enemy Strikes North

7

In the far north of the Pacific Ocean, a type of storm known only to that hostile and lonely corner of the world gathered east of the Komandorski Islands off Siberia's coast. Ice fog—minute crystals of frozen moisture—formed as the warm water of the Japanese current collided with the arctic atmosphere and coated the ships' steel with ice. Storms like this are frequent and routinely move in a freezing, swirling mass from west to east with the rotation of the earth. On June 3, 1942, the cyclonic mass intensified as it swept over the barren, volcanic islands of the Aleutian archipelago, barrelling towards the Alaska Peninsula.

Shrouded by that tempestuous blanket was a squadron of warships of Imperial Japan's formidable navy. The aircraft carrier *Ryujo* and the Imperial navy's newest carrier, *Junyo*, sailed with the heavy cruisers *Takao* and *Maya* and a screen of three destroyers, the *Akebono*, *Ushio*, and *Sazanami*, as well as the fleet oiler *Teiyo Maru*. Below decks, *Ryujo* carried 16 Mitsubishi Zeros and 21 Nakajima Kate light bombers, while *Junyo* had 24 Zeros and 21 Aichi Val dive bombers. Commanded by Rear-Admiral Kakuji Kakuta, the squadron was the Second Carrier Striking Force and part of Vice-Admiral Moshiro Hosogaya's Northern Striking Force. Kakuta was to deliver the attack on Dutch Harbor, then soften up and occupy Adak with a small force of ground troops. At the same time, Hosogaya would be standing by in the heavy cruiser *Nachi* between Japan's northern Kurile Islands and the Aleutian islands of Attu and Kiska with an invasion force of 2,500 troops. Once Adak was under Japanese control, Hosogaya's troops would provide reinforcements on the island, from which they could leapfrog to Dutch Harbor if necessary.

Imperial Japanese navy aircraft carriers Ryujo *(above) and* Junyo *(below) formed the Second Carrier Striking Force of Admiral Hosogaya's Northern fleet, which attacked Dutch Harbor, Alaska, on June 3 and 4, 1942.*

At the same time, 1,100 kilometres directly south, the First Carrier Striking Force of Vice-Admiral Chuichi Nagumo steamed towards a decisive confrontation with the American navy at Midway. Admiral Isoroku Yamamoto, commander-in-chief of naval forces and architect of the Pearl Harbor attack, directed both operations from his flagship *Yamato* at a point northeast of Midway.

In the north, Yamamoto believed the closest air bases to Dutch Harbor were at Anchorage and Kodiak Island. Reconnaissance missions by submarine-launched planes had not scouted the islands west of Dutch Harbor, and the American air bases built as fish canneries at Umnak Island and Cold Bay on the Alaska Peninsula remained undetected.

On the bridge of *Ryujo*, Rear-Admiral Kakuta grew impatient with the weather. A ceiling of cloud hung ominously over the fleet, and radio silence made him unsure of the whereabouts of his other ships, none of which had radar (it was still in its experimental stages with the Japanese). The sun was to rise at 0258 in the northern latitudes, but at nearly 0230 the sky showed no sign of lightening. Outside, the mercury stood at 7° Celsius, and the sea spray froze in slick sheets on the flight decks. Aviation Officer Lieutenant-Commander Masatake Okumiya argued against launching an attack under such conditions and advised giving it more time.

Below decks the aircrews in the ready rooms nervously joked and smoked cigarettes. Some tried to sleep. They had received their latest briefing, their aircraft engines were already warmed up with fuel tanks topped, and they could now do nothing but wait as apprehension gave way to boredom. Kakuta's warships ploughed on through the ghostly fog to Dutch Harbor at 22 knots. If he was unable to launch his planes and the fog lifted, Kakuta feared enemy aircraft or submarines would surely spot his attack fleet and thereby jeopardize Yamamoto's entire operation at Midway. Bad weather or not, the strike would go ahead, he resolved; the success of Midway depended on his actions.

In the grey inkling of first light, the watch reported carrier *Junyo* 900 metres off the port side. With the lifting of fog, Aviation Officer Okumiya informed the admiral that it would be safe to launch his planes. Kakuta nodded to Lieutenant Commander Okada, who then gave the order to launch the attack. On the decks of the two carriers, pilots climbed into their planes and stood ready, their engines breaking the morning silence with an ever-growing war cry. At 0243 the signal came, and one by one the fleet of 35 bombers, dive bombers, and legendary Zeros took off into a ceiling of cloud at only 223 metres. In the rolling sea, *Ryujo* went bow first into the trough of a wave just as a bomber was lifting off, throwing it into the sea. The single propeller dug into the water and the plane started sinking nose first into the frigid water. The two crewmen escaped as the plane disappeared under *Ryujo*'s bow and were spared an icy death by the swift action of an escort destroyer.

The airborne planes circled the two carriers, waiting to group, the glory of the epic aerial attack on Pearl Harbor beckoning the pilots on. Today they would have the honour of delivering the second carrier-launched strike directly against American territory. After the last planes had joined them, the two formations headed north for Unalaska Island.

Patrolling the waters 256 kilometres south of Unalaska, a lone PBY stumbled into a break in the fog and was immediately pounced upon by Lieutenant Yoshio Shiga leading a pack of Zeros. Shiga's planes shot it down, killing three of the crew instantly. The remaining five airmen got a life raft away into the freezing waves and crawled aboard it. Two more crewmen, including the pilot, died shortly after from bullet wounds. The cruiser *Takao* later plucked the three survivors from the icy North Pacific, giving them the dubious distinction of being the first prisoners taken in the Alaskan war.

Shiga had lost valuable time chasing the American plane, and with his air group once again in the fog, he became hopelessly lost and radioed *Junyo* for permission to return to the ship. Alaska's unpredictable weather was not to give the Japanese pilots the same easy victory they enjoyed at Pearl Harbor six months before.

The fog also made it impossible for *Ryujo*'s planes to maintain formation, compelling flight leader Lieutenant Masayuki Yamagami to order them to break formation and find their own way to Dutch Harbor, where they would regroup before the attack. Kakuta's aircrews had only outdated maps of Unalaska and Dutch Harbor, copied from old Russian whaling charts. There were many gaps in the drawings where shorelines were unexplored, so that the pilots did not even know the outline of Dutch Harbor from the air. Still, they managed to find it.

American Intelligence had correctly figured that Dutch Harbor was the likeliest target for a diversionary attack by the Japanese in the north, and anti-aircraft guns, manned 24 hours a day, were placed around the harbour. At 0405 the seaplane tender USS *Gillis* signalled the radio tower overlooking Dutch Harbor of a group of unidentified aircraft heading towards the base. The air-raid siren sounded, sending troops with First World War rifles and helmets running from the barracks of the navy base and Fort Meares army base to the trenches and gun batteries around the harbour.

They had run through the drill many times before during practice and false alarms, which this also appeared to be. As Allied aircraft movements were not broadcast, it was common to have an air-raid alert on the side of caution. As the planes passed over Unalaska's Pyramid Peak and reformed over Captain's Bay, the soldiers assumed them to be another patrol from nearby Fort Glenn, the secret base on Umnak Island, and relaxed their guard. There had been an air-raid drill already that morning, and some troops didn't even bother to respond to this one. Suddenly a Zero peeled off to strafe the barracks at Fort Meares. Behind, a Kate let loose its bombs on the wooden barracks, killing 25 men.

Machine gunners on the ground opened fire as two more Zeros swooped down on a lumbering Catalina flying boat that was attempting to take off. Bullets tore into the mail plane, killing the two civilian passengers as the seaplane erupted in flame. Tracers strafed two more PBYs moored in the harbour, while one flying boat crew managed to get airborne. Climbing over Captain's Bay, the PBY came up under a Zero emerging from a run on the base. The waist gunner opened fire at the same time as machine gunners on the ground, hitting their mark. The Zero burst into flame and plummeted into the harbour as the trundling, ungainly PBY disappeared into the fog between two mountains, pursued by angry Zeros.

In the radio shack overlooking the harbour, the navy signalman could not get a response from Fort Glenn. The wireless telegraph set at the secret base had failed, and the fighter pilots, only 66 kilometres west of the action, were unaware of the attack. The radioman on duty at Cold Bay, 288 kilometres east, picked up the distress signal and sent fighter pilots running for their P40 Curtiss Warhawks and roaring off west to Dutch Harbor.

Back at Dutch Harbour, a Kate light bomber dropped a 500-pound (225-kilogram) bomb on the radio tower, blowing gaping holes around the radio shack and shattering its windows. Rattled but unhurt, the signalman resumed his tapping of the wireless set moments later.

Soldiers in First World War helmets take to the trenches during the attack on Dutch Harbor, June 3, 1942.

In Anchorage, Juneau, and Ketchikan, civilians had been advised to take shelter in the vast wilderness of surrounding forests in the event of an air raid, while Prince Rupert had drilled to whisk schoolchildren away to the safety of the rain forest. It now appeared the rumours, jawed over coffee and around the dinner table, of an attack by the Japanese were coming true. The north was under attack.

After tearing up the village of Dutch Harbor for twenty minutes, the Japanese planes disappeared into the mist over the vast sea. When the fighters from Cold Bay finally roared in some twenty minutes later, the barracks at Fort Meares were in flames and an inky cloud of smoke billowed from a burning army truck below. The enemy was long gone.

As the Japanese pilots withdrew over Makushin Bay, they noted the four old destroyers in the bay and radioed ahead to *Ryujo* for reinforcements. Kakuta ordered *Junyo*'s planes back into the air to find and destroy the American ships. Four Pete float planes were catapulted from *Maya* and *Takao* to act as scouts for *Junyo*'s bombers, but as the weather worsened, *Junyo*'s planes again found themselves lost and had to return to their carrier.

In a squall over the North Pacific, *Ryujo*'s planes headed south to meet the carrier force. The driving rain streamed across the cockpit canopies, and the warm breath of the pilots fogged the inside of the clear shell to make visibility even worse—it was now only 50 metres as the heavy black cloud ceiling forced them perilously close to the breaking waves. Salt spray whipped up by the planes' propellers threatened to choke the engines, and the pilots had to break formation to find their own way back to the carriers. Incredibly, all but the plane lost at Dutch Harbor returned safely.

The squall had by now passed over Fort Glenn on Umnak Island, and men there could see smoke billowing up from Dutch Harbor. Umnak scrambled 21 P40s to investigate. Into the clear skies over Umnak stumbled the four lumbering Petes launched by the Japanese cruisers. Two Warhawks immediately machine-gunned one Pete, sending it to the water in pieces, while the others headed to the receding storm for cover. The P40s raked them with machine-gun fire and a second Pete crashed into the madly churning sea south of Umnak. The two remaining scout planes somehow managed to elude the pursuing fighters and sent frantic calls to the Japanese ships. Badly damaged, they crash-landed next to *Takao* and sank as their riddled pontoons and fuselages filled with water.

Both pilots clambered to safety on a boarding net let over *Takao*'s side. In a debriefing, they described how they'd been jumped by American fighters over Umnak Island. Kakuta concluded that prior air reconnaissance had not been thorough enough. Somewhere in the islands was a secret American air base. The Japanese immediately roused the three Americans taken prisoner when the PBY went down. Slapping them about, they demanded to know where the P40s had suddenly appeared from. Then they brought the captives on deck and threatened that unless they divulged information about a secret fighter base, they would be thrown over the side. The prisoners denied knowledge of any such air base. Their captors apparently believed their pleas of ignorance, for the Americans were returned to *Takao*'s brig, where they spent three more weeks, ending up in a Japanese prison camp for the duration of the war.

On June 3, twelve bombers of the RCAF's 8th Bomber Reconnaissance Squadron had just arrived in Yakutat from Vancouver when the aircrews were informed of the Japanese attack at Dutch Harbor and ordered to depart immediately for Anchorage, where the enemy might strike next. Reports of submarine sightings were coming in, and a force of Japanese warships lurking somewhere in the fog was poised to strike at a target or targets unknown. The Boleys' exhausted crews immediately refuelled and headed out. With radio silence now in effect across Alaska, and with sketchy charts and minimal visibility, they made their way by dead reckoning across the tip of the Kenai Penninsula— staying just above the waves before circling over the Kenai Glacier at the head of the inlet and dropping into Anchorage.

In the blinding fog the radio operator of the lead Boley received an SOS from one of the 8th's planes that was lost and low on fuel. He lost contact when his own plane's trailing antenna was knocked off as they flew so low the antenna hit a trestle bridge. But the stray Boley kept trying. It had pulled into a steep climb to avoid crashing into the wall of a rock face or glacier, but when it came up into sunshine, the crew had no idea where they were. Radio contact was vital if they were to get down through the jagged peaks of the Kenai, so Flying Officer Pappy Deeks took a chance and broke radio silence. After several desperate calls to the radio range at Cordova south of Anchorage received no reply, he radioed, "I know you're down there. We need that range. If you don't turn it on and we survive, you damn well won't!" The radio range came abruptly back on the air, allowing Deeks and his crew a safe passage to Anchorage.[1]

Dutch Harbor, Alaska, under attack from Japanese carrier-launched planes, June 3, 1942.

Two of the 8th's planes arrived in Anchorage well ahead of the others, and it seemed ten Canadian bombers had disappeared somewhere along the treacherous route from Yakutat. An enemy task force was also somewhere near the Gulf of Alaska, and jittery sky watchers were seeing every plane as the enemy. It did not help that the Canadians were flying unidentified types of aircraft from out of the west with big orange roundels on the fuselage that could easily be mistaken for the large red sun emblazoned on Japanese planes. For once the bad weather was a help rather than a hindrance; as the Canadians were forced to fly low to the water, they were unnoticed as they passed the American ack-ack gunners posted around Cook Inlet on the approaches to Anchorage. All but one of the missing Boleys made it safely to Anchorage. The exception crashed into a rock embankment during an emergency landing from which the crew miraculously walked away.

On June 3, 900 kilometres southwest of Kodiak, American Lieutenant J.D. Campbell's PBY stumbled on the Japanese carriers. Five Zeros flying cover for the force closed in and shot his plane up so badly he had to ditch it in the roiling sea. The crew escaped and was later picked up by the U.S. Coast Guard cutter *Nemaha*. Concerned that the downed PBY might have radioed his fleet's location, Kakuta ordered a withdrawal to the northwest. Almost as one, the ships turned to port and slipped back into the swirling mass of cloud that had delivered them to North America's shores.

8

The Second Strike

Awet, grey blanket still lay draped over the North Pacific as morning broke on June 4. Rain squalls occasionally washed across *Ryujo*'s flight deck, cutting visibility to less than 100 metres as fog steamed off the ocean. Admiral Kakuta had successfully carried out the first half of Yamamoto's Alaskan offensive with the attack on Dutch Harbor, and his Second Carrier Striking Force now moved west to attack a second American target—Adak Island, 880 kilometres west. Rear-Admiral Senatori Omori's occupation force of 1,200 troops was sailing east from the Kuriles to occupy Adak after a pre-invasion bombardment by Kakuta's planes and cruisers, and was to quell any resistance that might exist on the island. To the south, the First Carrier Striking Force was due to launch its attack on Midway in a matter of hours.

In the war room of the *Ryujo*, Aviation Officer Masatake Okumiya apprised officers and pilots of the Adak operation. Among them was Admiral Kakuta and his senior staff officer, Commander Masanori Odagiri. As usual, the weather was bad, Okumiya lectured, and it appeared to be deteriorating as the fleet moved west. The fleet's speed was now reduced to ten knots, he added. He told the men that somewhere in the eastern islands the Americans had successfully installed a secret fighter base. That alone could thwart Omori's invasion of Adak and would most certainly make the island difficult to hold once it was taken. The weather over Dutch Harbor was likely better, as the easterly storms tended to slow towards the Alaskan coast, and Okumiya suggested they make a second strike against Dutch Harbor rather than attacking Adak. The pilots now had a good idea of Dutch Harbor's layout but knew little of Adak's. Kakuta was convinced and gave the order; the invasion of Adak would be postponed for now. They would attack Dutch Harbor a second time instead. A message was relayed to Admiral Hosogaya, and a course change ordered to the northeast, towards Dutch Harbor again.

At noon a U.S. Navy PBY discovered the fleet and attacked, only to be shot up by flak bursts from the Japanese guns. It managed to limp away. Another PBY soon came across the Japanese fleet, but a cover of Zeros brought it down with all hands. One by one, American planes found and lost the enemy fleet as it slipped in and out of the Aleutian fog. A lone B-26 Marauder launched a torpedo at *Ryujo* but missed. The bomber returned hastily to Cold Bay to re-arm and refuel, then went back out looking for the fleet. The crew found it but was never heard from again. The wrecked plane was discovered some time later on the Alaska Peninsula; it had apparently crashed after being shot up and trying to return to Cold Bay.

By now, every available aircraft in the area, American and Canadian, was airborne, searching for the

Zenji Abe was the youngest of the Japanese pilots involved in the attack on Pearl Harbor, December 7, 1941. He flew an Aichi Val dive bomber in the strikes against Dutch Harbor. Abe retired as a colonel from post-war Japan's Self-Defense Force.

elusive Japanese fleet hiding somewhere in the fog off the Alaskan coast. When two B-17 Mitchells ran across the fleet and attacked, one was blown out of the sky and the other, wounded, flew back to Cold Bay. Three Marauders also found the Japanese and dropped their torpedoes, but the angry swells took them off course. For all the dogged attacks by American planes, the Japanese fleet remained unscathed.

Below decks of *Junyo*, Petty Officer Zenji Abe listened to the commander of flight operations go over his pre-attack briefings.

The Northwestern *burns after being hit by Japanese bombs in the second attack on Dutch Harbor, June 4, 1942.*

Hailed as the youngest of the Japanese pilots in the attack on Pearl Harbor, Zenji Abe and his brother pilots now received a dressing-down from their superior because only *Ryujo*'s planes had made it to Dutch Harbor in the first strike. The charge must have stung Abe as unfair. After all, a Kate light bomber could bomb in level flight, while the Val dive bomber he flew had to pick its target and dive from 3,200 metres—and the cloud ceiling over Dutch Harbor had been only a few hundred metres.

Rain washed across the *Ryujo*'s flight deck, pelting the canopies and wings of planes as they readied for take-off. The Mitsubishi's propellers drove the water back across their windscreens, rendering it nearly impossible for Flight Petty Officer Tadayoshi Koga to make out the signalman at the end of the flight deck. Koga, a brash young airman with a great dislike for Americans, felt honoured to be chosen as one of the 28 pilots assigned to make the second attack on Dutch Harbor.

Koga had been indoctrinated into the military school of thought that held up Japan's pilots as modern-day Samurai. By tradition, he had left clippings of his hair, fingernails, and toenails with relatives in Japan so they would have something of him to bury if he should not return from battle. At a sign from the signalman, Koga's Zero roared to the end of *Ryujo*'s deck and lifted off into the black sky to join a force of 27 other Zeros, Kate bombers, and Val dive bombers headed to finish off Dutch Harbor.

Smoke pours from the tank farm as 3.4 million litres of fuel oil burn after being struck by Japanese bombs, June 4, 1942.

At Fort Meares, civilian construction crews that had been on the job since 6 a.m. were about to take the last coffee break of their twelve-hour workday on board the SS *Northwestern*, an old Alaska Steamships vessel appropriated for use as a floating barracks, mess, and generating plant. Two waves of Zeros suddenly swooped down over Unalaska Island, firing as they roared across Dutch Harbor. Bullets tore up the loading dock next to the old steamer as work crews raced for safety. From 3,300 metres above, one pilot put his Val into a screaming dive with the *Northwestern* in its crosshairs. Releasing his 500-pound (225-kilogram) bomb, he pulled his plane away from the attack as the old liner exploded into flame amidships. Bombs from the Kates demolished the wooden wharf of the naval air station as Zeros strafed the meagre pickings around the harbour. Bombs killed the four-man crew defending an anti-aircraft battery and all but destroyed the wood-frame hospital in a burst of flying timber and glass. An explosion lit up the village as a rack of bombs ignited 3.4 million litres of fuel stored in wooden tanks. The roar shattered windows all over the island and sent a black mushroom cloud billowing skyward.

The blast could be heard at Umnak, 65 kilometres west, and a squadron of P40s, the Aleutian Tigers of the 11th Air Force, scrambled to investigate. In the ensuing dogfight the Tigers knocked out two Japanese bombers and two Zeros over the cluster of islands, while two of their own planes were shot down. With the sudden appearance of the American fighters, and with their second mission complete, the Japanese attack planes swarmed south for *Ryujo* and *Junyo*.

When the smoke over Dutch Harbor had cleared, the toll for the Americans was 78 dead and fourteen aircraft lost in the two attacks. The Japanese lost fifteen airmen and eleven planes.

Escorting a Nakajima Kate over tiny Unalga Island, northeast of Unalaska, Tadayoshi Koga and five wingmen spotted a lone PBY turning back towards Cold Bay. Flown by Pilot Albert E. Mitchell, PBY 42-P-4 had been warned away from the area moments earlier as the second attack on Dutch Harbor was under way. Immediately the six Zeros swooped down on the lumbering flying boat and opened fire, sending it plummeting towards Unalga Pass below. Even as it went down, the stricken craft's waist gunners continued to fire back, hitting Koga's Zero. Army observers at nearby Brundage Point on Unalaska watched in horror as survivors from the PBY who made it into life rafts were all machine-gunned to death by the circling Zeros.

Koga's Zero took a bullet through an oil pressure indicator line, and the overheating engine began to sputter and stall. Confident, Koga broadcast an SOS that was picked up by one of the Japanese submarines standing lifeboat duty around Unalaska Island that day. He then glided his plane to Akutan Island, just north of Dutch Harbor, and put his wheels down for what should have been a perfect landing. The landing gear dug deep into the soft Aleutian muskeg, flipping the plane and breaking Koga's neck.

A mushroom cloud rises from the burning fuel storage tanks at Dutch Harbor.

A Japanese Zero fighter, piloted by Tadayoshi Koga, crash-landed on nearby Akutan Island following the attacks on Dutch Harbor. The Zero was salvaged from the muskeg and made to fly again.

For five weeks the dead pilot and his Zero lay undisturbed until spotted by an observant PBY crew. The Alaskan muskeg, so troublesome to the military, had won it a valuable prize. Salvaged and sent to the army's aeronautical testing facility in California, the Zero was found to have suffered only minor damage and made to fly again. American pilots and engineers were consequently able to thoroughly study the principles of what was then the fastest, longest-range, and deadliest of all fighter planes. This was the beginning of the end of Japan's fighter superiority in the Pacific. Allied fighter tactics and future aircraft could

The Zero with American markings. The plane was studied for tactics, and the F4F Hellcat design was based on it.

now be designed to capitalize on the Zero's advanced technology as well as its shortcomings and would eventually chase Japan's wonder plane from the Pacific.

As the second attack on Dutch Harbor drew to a close, Admiral Yamamoto was suffering a crushing defeat at the hands of Admiral Raymond Spruance's carrier fleet at Midway, from which Japan's navy would never recover. Yamamoto had lost the element of surprise the day before when an American PBY spotted a Japanese troop convoy making for Midway, shadowed it for two hours, and reported its movements. The easy victory the Japanese expected over the American navy quickly turned into catastrophic defeat for Japan. In the debacle, infernos raging aboard the carriers *Kaga, Soryu*, and *Akagi* put three of the four carriers in the south out of action. Yamamoto radioed terse new orders to Admiral Kakuta on *Ryujo* about 190 kilometres southwest of Dutch Harbor: "Second Carrier Striking Force will join Admiral Nagumo's First Carrier Striking Force at Midway as soon as possible. Landing operations in the Aleutians postponed."

As the last of the aircraft touched home on the carrier's flight decks, Kakuta radioed back that the Second Carrier Striking Force would immediately proceed south and refuel the morning of June 6 before joining the First Task Force. That would not put the Second Carrier Force at Midway until the afternoon of the 8th, Yamamoto calculated, and shortly after he received another radio message that sounded the death knell to Japan's Midway folly. "Carrier Hiryu hit by bombs and set afire, 1930 hrs."

Japanese troops file ashore on Attu, June 7, 1942.

In the early morning of June 5, Yamamoto ordered the withdrawal of what remained of his Midway force. In that horrific battle he had lost four carriers, two heavy cruisers, and 332 aircraft. Had carriers *Ryujo* and *Junyo* been added to the force, rather than used for the feint in Alaska, the outcome of Midway might have been very different. As it was, the war was lost for Japan with this battle, and from now on it would wage a desperate fight to keep the enemy from its shores.

In Alaska, however, a quiet war would drudge on. To salvage some measure of victory, however small, from the Midway debacle, Yamamoto ordered Admiral Hosogaya's Northern Striking Force to resume the Aleutians operations and to proceed with the capture of the islands of Attu and Kiska.

At the time, 42 Aleuts and 2 white civilians made up the population of Attu's tiny village overlooking Chichagof Harbor. Foster C. Jones maintained a weather station for the U.S. Weather Bureau, and his wife Etta taught school to the Aleut children comprising about half the settlement's population. The Joneses were also missionaries. When he heard of the attacks on Dutch Harbor, Jones expected the Japanese to land on the island at any moment. He had stashed supplies in the hills, where he and his wife would try to hold out as long as possible against the Japanese.

Early in the morning of June 7, Aleut villagers saw planes with Japanese markings fly over their island, not knowing a contingent of Japanese troops had already landed at Massacre Bay, eight kilometres south, with many warships standing by. Shortly, enemy soldiers surrounded Chichagof, firing their weapons. They hit one woman in the foot and wounded one of their own soldiers. Foster C. Jones destroyed his radio before he and Etta were rounded up, and the Aleut men were placed under house arrest. The Japanese took Foster away the next day. It was the last his wife ever saw of him. The Aleut prisoners later whispered to her that her husband had been shot and some of the local men had buried him in the yard of the little Russian Orthodox Church in the village.

The Japanese landed 1,200 troops in the first days of Attu's occupation. At first they rummaged through the Aleuts' homes, took their stocks of dried fish and food supplies, and roughed up the menfolk. But order was restored when Major Matsutoshi Hozumi, who spoke excellent English, came ashore the following day and ordered them to return the Aleuts' food and stay out of the village. After several days Etta Jones was sent south and interned near Yokohama, where she survived the war, while the Aleuts were put to work supplying fish for the occupation force. Army engineer Kishichiro Miyazaki recalled of the Aleuts, "They looked so much like us, the only difference being the language."[1]

The Aleuts were eventually sent to the city of Otaru on Hokkaido, where they were paid, albeit a meagre sum, for their labour. Conditions were bad. Their diet consisted mainly of rice, with never enough food or medicines, according to Steven Mike Hodiakoff, an Aleut teen at the time. Of the 42 Aleuts interned in Japan, 16 succumbed to foreign disease and the gradual decay wrought by immersion in a strange culture so far from home. Throughout the rest of the Aleutians, inhabitants who were relocated to mainland Alaska at the war's outset fared no better. Among those newly settled by the United States government in southeast Alaska, tuberculosis, culture shock, and the same neglect suffered by their compatriots in Japan killed off half the populace in some of the camps.

At 0115 hours on June 7, 290 kilometres southeast of Attu, 500 Japanese marines of the Maizuru Third Special Landing Force silently went ashore at Kiska. This island was of strategic importance to the Japanese. It had the finest deep-water harbour in the Aleutians, from which the terrain abruptly rises more than 1,000 metres up the side of a simmering volcano. As a bridgehead to mainland Alaska, it could easily be defended against land and air attack and would serve as the vanguard of Japan's northern defences.

Under Captain Tekeji Ono, the advance force silently made its way towards the island's only habitation, a ten-man U.S. Coast Guard

On June 7, 1942, Japanese troops captured Attu and Kiska, Alaska. This Japanese war footage shows the capture of nine of the ten men at the U.S. weather station on Kiska, the island's only inhabitants. William Charles House managed to elude the Japanese until he surrendered 51 days later.

weather station consisting of three wooden huts overlooking Kiska Harbor. The Coast Guardsmen had heard of the attacks on Dutch Harbor in the days before and were expecting an assault by Japanese forces. They had burned all of their code books and dismantled the weather monitoring gear lest it fall into enemy hands. Most of the men were asleep when the duty watch woke them to report enemy troops converging on the weather station. Bursts of machine-gun fire rattled them awake as shards of glass and splintering wood exploded about the hut. A bullet tore into the leg of one man as the others rushed to get out of the erupting cabin. All fled, but all save one man were rounded up over the next two days.

Senior aerographer's mate William Charles House managed to escape and eventually made it to Kiska's western side, where he dug himself into a muskeg-covered cave. He planned to hide out there until American troops arrived—in a day or two, he hoped. For 51 days House held out, living on moss and grubs he found under rocks. He was once strafed by a plane while he was foraging along the shore. Later he could feel the ground shake from the impact when American bombers finally struck out at the island, but his liberators never followed. Starving and emaciated, House limped into the Japanese camp and surrendered. He remained on

Japanese aircrews on Kiska are briefed prior to a mission.

Kiska for three months, labouring for the Japanese, but his captors treated him fairly well considering they too were living under harsh conditions. They even taught him some Japanese, and on one occasion a crewman from *I-25,* which had stopped at Kiska on a return journey, told him how they had shelled the Oregon coast. The American joked with the sailor about the possibility of dropping him off in Oregon if they were to make another trip. Politely, the Japanese submariner apologized, saying he did not think that it would be possible. House was sent to a prisoner-of-war camp in Japan where he finished out the war.

At dawn on June 8, the senior officer of the Kiska landing forces, Lieutenant-Commander Hifumi Mukai, stepped ashore on the island with 1,200 Japanese soldiers and ran the Rising Sun up the flagpole. An enemy force occupied United States soil, something that had not happened since the War of 1812. In this desolate, isolated, and windswept archipelago, thousands of American, Canadian, and Japanese troops came to fight. Many would die in this barren place. The harsh weather of the Aleutians claimed more casualties than did men or machines, however, meting out punishment indiscriminately to ally and enemy alike.

Captured Territory

9

Now that Japan had captured the two Aleutian islands, some wondered if they were worth keeping. Without Midway to complete Japan's "sphere of prosperity" in the mid-Pacific, the army argued, the value of holding the Aleutians was lost. Prime Minister General Hideki Tojo, supreme commander of Japan's armed forces, was against wasting troops to hold on to these godforsaken islands of little apparent importance. He wanted to proceed with the invasion of Australia instead. Tojo believed that the terrible Alaskan weather would prevent the Americans launching a campaign from the Aleutians in the winter. Yamamoto disagreed, insisting it was imperative to hold the islands for Japan's defence against American attacks from the north. Besides, some measure of victory had to be salvaged from Midway, and for now Japan held the upper hand in the Aleutians. It would be best for Japanese troops to remain in possession of this tiny piece of the United States.

The Japanese public was unaware of the Midway loss and was left in ignorance until after the war. Families of those killed were led to believe their men were still in the South Pacific, fighting for the homeland. Tokyo news broadcasts claimed Dutch Harbor, Anchorage, and Sitka were in Japanese hands and that 3,000 civilians were killed in air raids on Fairbanks. Canadian POWs in one Japanese camp told of having to listen to a broadcast that foolishly claimed Japanese planes had destroyed the non-existent bridge between Vancouver and Victoria. Playing wildly with the facts in a desperate public relations ploy, Japan's War Ministry tersely claimed, "The diversion of Midway has assured Japan of the devastating success of the great Aleutian victory. All objectives have been met."[1]

Admiral Hosogaya set about fortifying Kiska, largely by transporting more troops and equipment to the island. Kiska, and Little Kiska Island within its harbour, were armed with 75-millimetre dual-purpose guns, 13.2-millimetre anti-aircraft batteries, and many small but versatile 22-millimetre mobile guns. Six four-engined Kawanishi flying boats, as well as eighteen Rufes (float-equipped Zeros for amphibious takeoffs and landings), were also deployed. Construction and road-building equipment was imported to begin work on a runway for land-based fighters. On the uninhabited island of Agattu, the most westerly of the Aleutians, the Japanese set up a tent encampment, but soon abandoned the island, moving the troops to Attu instead.

By June 10 the Americans realized the Japanese had indeed occupied islands in the western Aleutians. Until then, Admiral Robert Theobald's North Pacific Force cruised north of the islands in the Bering Sea, following up on reports that Admiral Kakuta's strike force was in the area, although no one knew exactly where. Strict radio silence and the incessant fog didn't help the situation, but through a break in the clouds an American pilot spotted a cluster of warships in Kiska Harbor and brought his four-engined Liberator down for a better look. A barrage of anti-aircraft fire greeted his approach, and the shaken crew hightailed it to Cold Bay and reported that Japanese ships were in Kiska Harbor.

The following day, June 11, brought a rare clear morning in the Aleutians. B-24 Liberators of the 21st Bomber Squadron and five B-17 Flying Fortresses of the 36th Bombardment Squadron took off from the steel-matted runway of Umnak's Cape Field, where they had stopped on the way from Cold Bay to refuel and bomb up. Four hours after departing Umnak, the Liberators spotted Kiska's brooding volcano and went in for the run on the Japanese encampment surrounding Kiska Harbor. Around the bay, the Japanese had placed 75-millimetre dual-purpose guns, which could be used for cannon fire or to throw up bursts of flak. Through a break in the clouds they spotted the bombers and quickly calculated their range. Their first barrage of flak blew one Liberator to pieces and damaged two more before a single bomb was dropped. The remaining two heavies let go their charges over the harbour, only to have them explode harmlessly in the water as the planes wheeled back to Cold Bay.

Colonel William Eareckson's five B-17s of the 36th Bombardment Squadron were up and winging their way to Kiska shortly after reports of Japanese guns came in from the first wave of bombers. Eareckson was known for his loose but confident discipline that endeared him to

The deck gun of the Nissan Maru, *sunk by Allied bombing.*

his men but made enemies of his superiors. Appointed head of the 11th Air Force Bomber Command, Eareckson refused to remain at a desk and personally led missions out to Kiska, assuming every position on the plane from left-seater to tail gunner. Always a maverick—caustic, outspoken, and contemptuous of red tape—Eareckson was regularly passed over for promotion to brigadier general, remaining a colonel until his retirement from the army in 1954. Alaska, with its uncooperative climate and hardships, was just the place for officers such as him, who bucked the status quo, to do penance. But their unconventional style and disregard for regulations served them well in this theatre, which demanded wits and instinct over pointless protocol. In typically inspired thinking, Eareckson planned to approach the harbour from the landward side, winging his way through the narrow peaks and valleys of Kiska to surprise the Japanese gunners, who would be expecting another wave of bombers from the sea.

Roaring in over the island, Eareckson's crews had little time to pick and choose their targets, and all made for the warships reported to be anchored in the harbour. In a low sweep, the five Fortresses let go their loads as machine-gun fire opened up and massive water geysers erupted in the harbour. Returning to Cold Bay, the weary crews were disheartened to learn that not one bomb had found a target. The following day Eareckson led a flight of five B24s and got the air force onto the scoreboard with a hit on a cruiser anchored in Kiska's harbour.

Because of the incessant fog, traditional high-level bombing produced poor results in Alaska. Most bombing runs had to be carried out by dead reckoning off the Kiska volcano and a timed run into the harbour. This method was less than ideal as the targets could not be seen and the results of blind bombing could not be verified. Eareckson turned to low-level attacks with heavy bombers, unprecedented but achieving some success. On their next mission his crews inflicted damage on two more cruisers and hit the *Nissan Maru* as it unloaded supplies and troops. Smoke poured from the freighter for several hours before it sank in 30 metres of water. A few days later a U.S. plane flying reconnaissance over Kiska confirmed the sinking, noting the ship's mast protruding from the water.

The U.S. Navy moved a squadron of 23 PBYs and the seaplane tender *Gillis* from their home base at Unalaska to Nazan Bay at Atka Island, 480 kilometres closer to the enemy. Primarily used for anti-submarine and reconnaissance patrols, the unwieldy, slow, and lightly armoured PBYs had been pressed into service as bombers even though they were hardly suited for the job. The flying boat crews armed their craft as best they could, and with their Pratt and Whitney twin-Wasp engines droning, tried to keep up with the army bombers out to hit Kiska.

As lightly armoured and hard to control in air combat as the planes were, the navy PBY crews kept up a steady bombardment of Kiska's harbour, sinking three of six four-engined Kawanishi Mavis float bombers, damaging the destroyer *Hibiki*, and earning grudging respect from the Japanese. The hourly poundings by the American PBYs kept Japanese ground crews from making much headway with airfield construction and became such an irritant to the Japanese that Hosogaya ordered his remaining aircrews to find and destroy the seaplane tender and her squadron.

The strikes on Kiska came at a heavy cost for the navy PBYs, though. After three days of steadily harassing the enemy, half of them had been shot down or damaged and more than half the aircrews were dead or wounded. Japanese float bombers finally levelled the Aleut village on Atka, but the *Gillis* and her planes had left Nazan Bay for Dutch Harbor the previous day, taking with them the Aleut populace of Atka.

With the seizure of the western Aleutian Islands, the Japanese took heart that they had won a toehold in North America, remote though it might be. The Allies could only speculate about what the Japanese might want with this barren, volcanic gulag at the ends of the earth. Many in Congress and the military believed the islands should be left to the Japanese—the capricious climate would make for a miserable and costly occupation that would eventually drive them out. Others ominously warned that the grab for the Aleutians was the beginning of a Japanese island-hopping campaign that could bring them within bombing range of major West Coast cities. And, they reminded those who preferred to leave the Aleutians to the wolves, had not Admiral Yamamoto himself stated in a speech to the Japanese parliament, "I will dictate the terms of peace on the steps of the White House"?[2]

While the Japanese had toyed with the idea of some day invading North America, there were no firm plans other than carrying out some initial reconnaissance and so much posturing. Initially the Japanese had planned to occupy Adak, then Dutch Harbor, and then stage raids on the West Coast with a view to landing forces in the north. These designs were quickly cast aside after the loss at Midway and after it became clear how difficult it would be to hold bases in the eastern Aleutians so close to North America. However, a chain of events re-enforced the American and Canadian belief that Japanese plans for an invasion via Alaska were much further along than was actually the case.

American patrol planes had spotted Admiral Kakuta's northern force sailing eastward far north of Kiska in the Bering Sea in the days following the occupation of the islands. Many believed it to be headed for an attack on Nome. In reality, Kakuta was standing by, hoping to surprise any American warships that might be sent out to menace the recently captured atoll. Furthering the misconception, American code-breakers deciphering messages from Kakuta's fleet wrongly concluded that an enemy attack on mainland Alaska—probably Nome—was imminent. They had no doubt that the Japanese, once they secured the area, hoped to use it as a beachhead from which to invade the continent proper.

When apprised of the situation, Admiral Chester Nimitz, commander of Pacific Naval Forces, decided to send the remainder of Admiral Raymond Spruance's carriers, fresh from Midway, far north to intercept and engage what he believed was a Japanese invasion fleet in the Aleutians.

The Japanese admiralty correctly assumed, although for the wrong reasons, that Spruance's fleet would head north to Alaska. They believed their feint in the Aleutians had achieved one of its objectives by drawing out the American fleet, and the admiralty bolstered Admiral Kakuta's fleet with two more aircraft carriers, *Zuiho* and *Zuikaku*. The expected showdown never happened, though, as Nimitz changed his mind and shrewdly decided not to risk the remainder of his Pacific fleet. With that decision went Admiral Yamamoto's second chance to destroy the American

This movie reel cartoon of the time depicts a buck-toothed Japanese standing in the Aleutians at the back door to North America.

carrier force. The presence of a Japanese invasion fleet, meanwhile, had become a self-perpetuating threat. Kakuta's fleet, which the Allies believed to be the advance force for an invasion of mainland Alaska, was really prowling for American warships headed for Kiska, hunting for an enemy looking for him and his so-called Nome invasion fleet.

Even if he had planned on leapfrogging down the Aleutian Islands chain to the Alaskan mainland, Admiral Yamamoto would discover it a costly, if not impossible, venture—especially so soon after the debacle at Midway. As it was, the plan to capture Adak and Dutch Harbor was abandoned after the first attack on Dutch Harbor was barely over. For now, holding Attu and Kiska would serve the dual purpose of securing Japan's northern perimeter and depriving the Allies of a land-based airfield within striking distance of the Japanese homeland. The two islands could also be used as airfields for long-range bombers making strikes on the Alaskan coast and perhaps even as launch points from which to grab islands closer to the mainland. In the longer term, aerial attacks and a full-scale submarine offensive against the North American West Coast could be dispatched from them.

Still, these two barren, windswept islands were of little consolation to Yamamoto after months of preparing for Midway, and the resulting loss of thousands of Japanese servicemen, half the Imperial navy's aircraft carrier strength, and two cruisers. The blow was not to be overcome. Japan had not established the massive shipbuilding programs the Allies had, so construction of replacement vessels fell further behind ever-mounting losses.

The capture of the Aleutians did serve the Axis cause to some extent. To the Americans, an invasion of the Alaskan mainland and perhaps British Columbia appeared imminent, creating a sense of alarm and drawing away resources that might otherwise be earmarked for the war in Europe and Asia. In Alaska, the Yukon, and northern B.C. it was now not a question of *if* the Japanese come but *when*, and preparations for home defence were initiated. Schoolchildren in Prince Rupert were taught to take cover under desks in case of aerial bombardment, while the general population was advised to take refuge from paratrooper attack in the surrounding forest. Territorial militias were quickly formed in coastal areas, including the Pacific Coast Militia Rangers, a volunteer unit made up of civilians and veterans of the First World War, which augmented reserve army units in British Columbia's remote Queen Charlotte Islands, the northern mainland coast, and Vancouver Island.

Similar home guard units such as the Yukon Rangers, formed at Dawson City, were trained as the front line for the army in the north. Recruits were issued Lee Enfield .303 rifles and trained weekly at one of the local gambling halls. While these sparsely armed units would be no match for highly trained Japanese marines and paratroopers, they were the eyes and ears of the army in Canada's remote northwest. Rendezvous points and storage caches were also secured so that local militias could fight a guerrilla war, which at least might stall a Japanese advance until reinforcements could be rushed north.

Following the attacks on Dutch Harbor, the Royal Canadian Air Force ordered the 111th Fighter Squadron of P40 Kittyhawks, stationed at Pat Bay near Victoria, to Anchorage to serve, among other duties, as fighter support for the 8th Squadron. Air Vice-Marshall Leigh Stevenson provided the 111th after Western Air Command (U.S.) in San Francisco flatly denied a request from General Simon Buckner for a fighter squadron to defend Anchorage. With only one map between them showing the area north of Prince Rupert, the planes, flying in groups of three, made the trip in stages via Prince George and Watson Lake before rendezvousing at Whitehorse. From there they were escorted into Anchorage. Remaining Kittyhawks joined the rest of the squadron over the next two weeks, and by June 24 the squadron was up to full strength of sixteen Kittyhawks and two Hudson cargo planes. This made the Canadians responsible for a good percentage of air protection for Anchorage.

Considering the low priority assigned the West Coast in terms of wartime readiness, British Columbia was actually well defended along the northwest coast. Canadian air patrols in the south extended well into the waters off Washington State, and in the north they predominated along southeast Alaska.

As Nome was presumably the intended target of the Japanese, General Buckner undertook a massive program to reinforce the area in the days and weeks following the capture of Attu and Kiska. Exploiting his sweeping power as commander of Alaskan defences, he commandeered almost overnight every military and civilian plane, American or foreign, that flew into Alaska. Within 24 hours, tons of supplies and equipment, twenty anti-aircraft guns, and 2,250 troops were rushed to the Seward Peninsula in a feat that became known as the Nome Airlift. By early July 1942, only a couple of weeks later, 900,000 tons of equipment had arrived and the population of Nome exploded from about 400 to 7,000 people.

Buckner prevailed upon General DeWitt for still more air support and was assigned the U.S. Air Force's 404th Bombardment Squadron of B24 Liberators. Originally destined for service in Africa, the planes were diverted from Arizona and arrived in Nome sporting pink desert-fatigue war paint. A contingent of Bolingbrokes from the RCAF's 8th Squadron operating out of Anchorage was deployed to join the 404th and was charged with covering thousands of square kilometres of the Bering Strait. The patrols would fly west and south over the Diomede Islands and the Pribilofs before turning north at the Siberian coast so as not to violate Soviet airspace (the USSR was not at war with Japan until 1945).

The patrols were an endless vista of icy coastline and berg-laden waters. On one patrol, Harry Bray and his crew decided to break the monotony by flying into Siberia for a change of scenery. The Soviets had an uneasy truce with Japan and both sides were expecting an attack from the other at any time. The Soviets spotted the Canadian bombers flying in from the coast, took the RCAF roundel on the wings and fuselage for the Japanese red sun, and radioed an alarm that assumed this was it—war with Japan. Upon landing at Nome, that same RCAF patrol was told that Japanese planes had been spotted over Siberia and the Soviets had requested air support. Amused, the bombers again went out to look for "the enemy," their superiors none the wiser that some bored Canadian pilots might have changed the course of history.[3]

Like every other air base and town in the north, Nome was unprepared for the influx of men and machines that war brings. As usual, the newcomers lived in tents and subsisted on tinned rations and powdered foods. Close on the heels of the military, brothels, saloons, and gambling popped up, just as they had for fortuneseekers during the Klondike gold rush. As the jumping-off point to Siberia during the Lend-Lease program, Nome enjoyed boom times that lasted the duration of the war and brought thousands of personnel through the bustling town. The only invasion the town experienced was an economic one, as a steady parade of Russian, American, and Canadian servicemen appeared on the scene looking for a place to spend their money in Nome's second "gold rush."

Army of the Tundra

10

Save for a few coastal squadrons, the whole barren coast in the area of Nome lay open with few resources to defend against, or even warn of, an enemy attack. Acutely suspicious of Japanese belligerence in the years prior to the attack on Pearl Harbor, Governor Ernest Gruening had pushed for the establishment of an Alaskan Territorial Guard since he was first elected to office in 1939. Even when an invasion seemed imminent in 1942, Gruening maintained the United States was unable or unwilling to mount an adequate defence of Alaska. The consensus in some military circles was that, in the event Japan launched an invasion through the Arctic, Alaska would be impossible to defend and should be abandoned to the enemy. On Kodiak Island, as well as in other coastal villages, civilians were issued First World War-vintage rifles with 20 rounds of ammunition and given the choice of surrendering to the Japanese or hiding out and fighting until help arrived.

Such talk angered Gruening, and he pressed Congress for funds to set up militia units in Alaska. His plan was to form native Alaskans, trappers, homesteaders, prospectors, and, most significantly, the Eskimos into a first line of defence of soldiers and scouts.[1] Eskimo soldiers, Gruening argued, were accustomed to surviving and working in a land that offered little in the way of sustenance and would surrender no comfort fighting a guerrilla war against an invader. They also had an intricate knowledge of their home terrain, where no navigable landmarks existed, and were master dog handlers and expert sailors. As to their deftness with a rifle, Gruening wrote, "Had the [enemy] parachutists come, or would they come tomorrow, the deadly accuracy of these Eskimo marksmen would bring them down."[2]

Eskimo soldiers of the Alaska Territorial Guard.

Congress, after much rallying by Gruening and Alaska Representative Anthony Dimond, shook off its indifference to the security of Alaska long enough on March 27, 1941, to sign Bill 122 authorizing formation of the Alaska Territorial Guard (ATG).

Initially Gruening was allotted enough funding and rifles to outfit two units totalling about 400 men. Once Hawaii was attacked, no limitation was put on the number of recruits the territorial guard could enlist. The army assigned Captain Carl Scheibner as an aide to the governor and made him responsible for recruitment in eastern Alaska, while Major Marvin Marston oversaw Alaska's more significant coastal and western region. Marston had served in the American army in the First World War and already had much bush experience working as a prospector in northern Quebec and Ontario. He re-enlisted in the army after precious metals mining was shut down when Canada went to war in 1939 and he was left without a job. Marston's ability to irritate the upper brass with schemes to store aircraft underground and other eccentric projects made him a prime candidate for posting to Alaska, which he readily accepted.

While many considered Alaska a punishment detail, Marston relished the opportunity to be back working in the wild country. Buckner had no time for his type, however, and described Marston as "no damn good," giving him the task of helping the governor recruit the Eskimo.[3] Governor Gruening took an immediate liking to the major and appreciated his empathy for the Eskimo. Marston's work had regularly brought him among the indigenous people before, and rather than impose white ways on the Natives, he gave himself over to learn their ways of the bush.

Gruening found that the army in general, on the other hand, was bigoted. This was evident in the substandard treatment of black construction battalions sent north, while throughout Alaska the aboriginals were treated as second-class citizens and were segregated from white society. The Eskimo could not sit in the white section of the movie house in Nome, and Native women were prohibited from performing with the United States Overseas (USO) tours in Alaska.

The worst manifestation of this attitude came when the U.S. military uprooted 881 Aleuts from nine villages on the Aleutians and Pribilofs and sent them to five camps in southeastern Alaska, where they were virtually abandoned. They were evacuated with only 24 hours notice, allowed to take one suitcase each, and were forced to leave behind personal items, cultural and religious icons, rifles, boats, and dogs. Some were even ordered to torch their villages. At Nazan Bay on Atka, the Aleuts had not even left the village before American soldiers began looting their homes for souvenirs. The internment camps they moved to were leaking, drafty, old canneries and mining camps with no plumbing or electricity. In one camp, 200 residents shared one open toilet located on the seashore. Few of the populace had even seen a tree before, and they now found themselves corralled in the dense rain forest of southeast Alaska. The treatment the transposed Aleuts received at the hands of their own country was no better than that received by inmates sent to Japanese camps. Over 10 percent of all Aleuts transported to southeast Alaska died during the two to three years of internment.

Despite these insults, Aleuts and other aboriginal Alaskans remained fiercely loyal to America. Marston's recruiting efforts took him to the remote villages of the Alaskan Arctic and the islands that lay off the Seward Peninsula: St. Lawrence, the Pribilofs, and the Diomedes. Using aircraft and boat when conditions permitted, he most often made the trek by dog-team with the help of an Eskimo guide. Despite the prevailing attitude towards them, Marston found the Aleuts and Eskimos eager to sign up.

Gruening used the recruiting drive to inform the Eskimo of their rights as citizens—most of them did not even know they were Americans—while Marston and Scheibner encouraged them to vote and even run for office. Throughout the campaign, no Eskimo recruits asked to be paid and none turned down the American government's request for help. Boys as young as twelve, as well as women, enlisted, and all of them were as good with a rifle as the average GI recruit—or better. (This eagerness to sign up was mirrored in Canada's north. Many Canadian aboriginal people saw it as their patriotic duty to enlist in a war worlds apart from their own. Some put their traditional skills, honed for survival in the Canadian wilderness, to good use in the army as scouts, observers, sharpshooters, and snipers. When asked how he came to be so accurate with a rifle, one Canadian Native undergoing training in the army remarked, "When your dinner is running away from you on four legs, you get to be a good shot.")

One of Marston's first challenges was to recruit the Natives on St. Lawrence Island, which lay north of the Aleutians in the Bering Sea about 320 kilometres off Alaska's Seward Peninsula and just 160 kilometres east of the Siberian mainland. Few residents had seen many Europeans and other outsiders, except for Russian traders early in the century. When Marston made his first trip to the island village of Gambell, he found about 50 Natives and one white man, Frank Dauherty, the Roman Catholic mission schoolteacher. Dauherty's compatriots had abandoned the island, fearing Alaska would be the next target after Pearl Harbor—and with good reason. In November 1941, before war was declared, a large Japanese warship had appeared off the island and remained for ten days. During that time the ship took soundings and troops came ashore, questioning the Natives about the number of reindeer on the island, the inventory of rifles, water sources, and other relevant details. Believing this to be part of a larger invasion force, Dauherty hid out with his eight-millimetre camera and filmed the goings-on. The ship then departed east towards mainland Alaska, but returned after many days to retrieve a shore party left on the island. The residents had observed their signal fires and later found the remains of the Japanese camp. News of the reconnaissance visit to St. Lawrence was further evidence to Gruening and Buckner that a Japanese invasion was to come from the north.

By 1943, Marston's Alaska Territorial Guard stood at 20,000 strong, including 3,000 Eskimos who—for the first time in their history—were united under a single leader into an organized army. This did not sit well with much of the white population of Alaska, and the army began to question Marston's motives. It charged him with inciting armed insurrection among Eskimos seeking to secede from the United States, and an investigation was launched. The Eskimo units' strong loyalty to Marston was scrutinized, and nearly every Native male in the ATG was interrogated—one so severely that he committed suicide in shame after being released.

Marston saw the investigation as an attempt to remove him from Alaska and for certain quarters to impose their control over the Natives. Governor Gruening was powerless to interfere with the army's investigation, but after one month of questioning, all charges against Marston and his men were dropped. Still, the incident left many of the Eskimo soldiers too disheartened to return to service.

While the Alaska Territorial Guard never saw action, it performed invaluable tasks by serving as the army's eyes and ears on the northern frontier and easing the strain on already stretched military resources in that area. Later in the war the ATG's Eskimo units were responsible for the rescue of an air force crew lost in the Arctic and the downing and recovery of Japanese balloon bombs.

While the idea of a Japanese invasion of North America through Alaska might draw scoffs today, throughout 1942 the threat appeared very real and drew considerable concern from the U.S. and Canadian governments. Japan's chief commanders had, to varying degrees, entertained the idea of some form of occupation or strikes against Alaska's mainland. Had the Battle of Midway gone in favour of the Japanese, no sea power would have been left to stop them from grabbing a foothold on the continent in Alaska, and with no significant naval opposition, Japan would be free to pursue its interests in Asia, Australia, and the South and North Pacific. Whether Japan won or lost at Midway, however, it seemed to those in the thick of events that an invasion was imminent. In this case, North America's front line of defence was to be the humble Eskimo in his army of the tundra.

Northern
Actions

By early summer 1942, Royal Canadian Air Force squadrons comprised over one-fifth of Alaska's air strength. Many of the RCAF pilots already had much experience over Europe. X-Wing, established at Anchorage under Wing Commander G.R. McGregor, who himself had received the Distinguished Flying Cross for actions in the Battle of Britain, oversaw the Canadian squadrons operating in Alaska and acted as liaison between the USAAF and the RCAF. The two squadrons based at Annette (115th and 118th) remained under Canadian control, while those based farther north (8th and 111th) fell under the command of the combined Alaska Defence Command and the 11th Air Force, United States Army—unofficially known as the Alaskan Air Force.

The 11th Army Air Force moved its American squadrons west to engage the Japanese in the Aleutians, leaving its Canadian counterparts to languish on the mainland, flying dull escort duty and anti-submarine patrol. Recording the monotony of the post, an entry in the daily log for 8th Squadron read: "Possibilities of unit seeing combat whilst based here seem extremely remote."[1]

It was obvious to Wing Commander McGregor that the Americans favoured using their own squadrons, although few had aerial combat experience. Those that did had either been in recent skirmishes with the Japanese over Dutch Harbor or had transferred from the RCAF once the U.S. entered the war. The Canadians, on the other hand, had been at war since 1939 and many had been bloodied in the skies over Europe. McGregor wrote Air Vice-Marshall Stevenson that his men were essentially treated as a convenient rear guard and proposed that they would be better used elsewhere. Much to his chagrin, McGregor was proved right time and again. When fresh American bombers of the 404th were brought up and then deployed to Nome, where action was expected, he lamented to Stevenson, "It is again evident that Canadian Squadrons will only find themselves in a location likely to result in active operations as a result of some completely unforeseen enemy attack...The greatest care will be taken to insure the Canadian squadrons will not see action if it is possible to place U.S. Army Air Corps Squadrons in a position to participate in such action, even if said U.S. Squadrons are much more recent arrivals in Alaska."[2]

Stevenson took up the matter with Air Marshall Breadner, the Canadian chief of air staff, and C.G. Power, minister of National Defence for Air. They in turn met with General Butler, USAAF, who commanded Alaska's air forces. Butler agreed that the Canadian squadrons should and would assume a more active role in the north. A contingent of six Canadian Bolingbroke bombers of the 8th Squadron was deployed from Anchorage to Nome to serve with the American 404th (Liberators) and the USAAF 56th Fighter Squadron of Bell P39 Aircobras, patrolling the far north for the expected Japanese assault during the period of the Nome Airlift. Four Boleys were sent to Kodiak to patrol the Gulf of Alaska and west to the Aleutians to look for a possible Japanese surface force and submarines, which continued to make their presence felt.

There may have been some justification for the Americans' reluctance to deploy Canadian squadrons closer to the action. The Canadian Bolingbroke squadrons in Alaska began to feel the pinch of shortages of British-made parts, to the point that they were cannibalizing aircraft to keep others in the air. By the end of July, only two of the 8th Squadron's Bolingbrokes out of Kodiak and only one from Elmendorf Field (Anchorage) were operational, out of a strength of twelve aircraft. Aircraft and parts, radar, and armoured equipment destined for Canadian units were routinely diverted to meet British needs, even though much of the manufacturing had been done in Canada. Periods of total grounding ensucd, and at one point crews could scrape together only enough spark plugs to keep one Bolingbroke in the air between Elmendorf and Kodiak. No one could argue that the overseas units weren't the priority, but the acquisitions board's failure to maintain even a minimum standard of supply to the north resulted in a mire of problems, not the least being shortages of parts that led to crews foregoing regular aircraft maintenance. This was undoubtedly the cause of some fatal aircraft mishaps.

Bristol Bolingbroke of the 8th Bomber Reconnaissance Squadron on the field at Anchorage, Alaska.

The lack of new and more modern equipment probably also caused accidents. New aircraft and engines earmarked for Canadian home squadrons were increasingly diverted to units overseas, as were tanks and ground vehicles for the army. For much of the war, Canadian navy ships had to make do with antiquated radar and ASDIC (sonar), even when providing escort in the U-boat–infested Atlantic—American and Royal Navy vessels seemed to take priority over the Canadian ships, even for domestically produced goods. War materials manufactured in Canada were regularly appropriated by the British War Ministry's Washington office. While the threat of the German enemy just across the English Channel was obviously pressing, the British often responded to Canadian concerns with a haughty rebuff or ignored them altogether. Rejecting a Canadian request for aircraft for defence of the West Coast, the British Acquisitions Board dryly ended one report with "at this very moment, Vancouver has its back to the wall."[3]

Whether in the halls of government in Ottawa or at the remote Alaskan bases themselves, some Canadians were sceptical that there was a serious threat in the North Pacific and begrudged the use of their forces to serve as backup to the Americans. To them, the real war was in Europe and on the East Coast, where German U-boats were taking an alarming toll on Allied shipping. And the demands of the war in Europe were stretching Canada's tight military resources.

The result was that, except for the Royal Canadian Navy, Canadian units in Alaska depended heavily on American generosity for food, fuel, some ammunition and ordnance, and even some clothing—much of it unofficially provided. At the Aleutian bases, where everything was in short supply, Canadian squadron leaders often had to go cap in hand to the American supply officer requesting anything from soap to aircraft parts. Canadian servicemen stationed with them observed the Americans obliged without hesitation. Whatever Uncle Sam sent north, the Canadians were welcome to as if it was their own. As one Canadian veteran recounted of his time in the Aleutians, "The Americans seemed glad to have us there and they were very good to us. They treated us A-1." He recalled that the Americans "had really good equipment, weapons, combat gear, even food, which they supplied to us...better than the junk we were issued with."[4]

Most disheartening for both Axis and Allies alike, though, was that the war in the north suffered from a lack of interest at home. Few Canadians or Americans could even locate the Aleutian Islands on a map, and because of tight government censorship on both sides, few people beyond those directly involved had any idea that there was a war being fought on the North Pacific frontier.

By the end of July 1942, no more large fleet movements of enemy ships were observed in the North Pacific and it became apparent that an attack on Nome and its subsequent invasion was unlikely. Still, the threat of enemy submarine action along the coast was very real. On July 14 the U.S. Army transport *Arcata* was transiting Unimak Pass, which separates Unimak and Akutan islands at the bottom of the Bering Sea, when *I-7* sank it with cannon fire. *Arcata*'s crewmen drifted south in lifeboats for eight days until they were rescued near Kodiak Island on July 22. Even in summer the waters of the North Pacific remain only a few degrees above freezing, a fact never far from the minds of air and ship crews facing the grim prospect of finding themselves suddenly immersed in the icy seas. Only 12 men of 22 survived the ordeal, and many succumbed to the effects of exposure.

I-9, commanded by Akiyoshi Fujii, had sunk the Matson steamer *Lahaina* off Hawaii in December 1941 and opened fire on survivors in lifeboats. Now, on June 10, 1942, it was loitering off Tanaga Island, 320 kilometres west of Atka, when, through a break in the clouds, a navy PBY spotted the sub slowly skirting the treacherous, uncharted shoals of Tanaga and went into a dive. A watchman in the sub's conning tower yelled into the intercom, and the control officer ordered her into a crash dive with anti-submarine bombs falling all around. An ear-shattering explosion blasted against *I-9*'s pressure hull. The force knocked the sub to a port list on its steep dive. The bomb shattered the glass face plates on gauges and sent icy water spraying in from sprung rivets as Fujii ordered the helmsmen to maintain full down on the sub's elevator planes. Overhead, the PBY circled like an angry wasp for a second pass, but the I-boat was gone. Inside the sub, water coursed through the damaged hull joints ever faster as the sub went deeper and the outside pressure increased. Any farther and the seams would rupture. Fujii ordered the sub levelled off to sit and wait several hours for the plane to leave while damage crews attempted to control flooding. Fujii had two choices: put in at Kiska and try to effect repairs, or risk running on the surface back to Japan. After a quick check by periscope, *I-9* surfaced and made for Kiska, 160 kilometres west.

In the spring of 1942, American submarine forces in Alaska numbered only five vintage S-class boats. *S-27* was lost in June after crashing onto one of the many uncharted reefs of Amchitka Island. Miraculously, there was no loss of life. When the first of eight new fleet-class submarines arrived on June 28, 1942, the force made its initial offensive in the sea war against Japan, taking up positions around Attu, Kiska, and Japan's northern Kuriles.

Patrolling north of the Kuriles, the submarine *Nautilus* sent one Japanese destroyer to the bottom in home waters. *Growler*, on its first war patrol, sneaked into Kiska Harbor and torpedoed destroyers *Shiranuhi*, *Arare*, and *Kajumi*. The new fleet-class submarine *Grunion* torpedoed and sank two more Japanese vessels, sub-chasers *S26* and *S27*, in the approaches to the harbour and damaged a third. On July 30, while hunting for a Japanese sub that had shelled a Soviet freighter, *Grunion* disappeared with all hands following a routine radio report to Dutch Harbor. No trace of the sub was ever found.

Off Attu, *Triton* torpedoed the destroyer *Nenohi* as it approached the island, sending it to the bottom of the frigid Aleutian waters with 200 men. In October, 800 kilometres west, the antiquated *S-31* sank the 2,800-ton merchant ship *Keizan Maru*, which was bound for the outpost with a load of supplies.

Admiral Robert A. Theobald's North Pacific Force had now expanded to include four light cruisers, nine destroyers, and the heavy cruiser *Indianapolis*—later fated to go down in shark-infested waters while returning from a secret mission to deliver the atomic bomb dropped on Hiroshima. In August 1942, under increasing pressure from General Buckner and Admiral Nimitz to take action against the Japanese, Theobald's cruiser force under Rear Admiral William "Poco" Smith set out in a blind fog for Kiska. Unable to even see the island from eight kilometres out, Smith hesitated to bring his fleet any closer as no accurate charts were to be had, and jagged volcanic reefs ringed the island fortress like huge stone sentries. Spotter planes were catapulted from the cruisers to give the gunners some bearings, but the two remaining Rufe fighters on the island quickly chased the cumbersome biplanes away. Relying on little more than dead reckoning, the cruisers' big guns opened up on Kiska and were met with return fire from the 6-inch (150-millimetre) guns the Japanese had mounted on the island. With no eyes to guide them, the cruisers' 8-inch (200-millimetre) shells whistled harmlessly over the enemy base surrounding the harbour to blast enormous craters in the other end of the island.

After only seven minutes, Smith's cruisers withdrew, their supply of mortars nearly exhausted. For all the fireworks, damage to the Japanese fortifications and main camp was negligible. Shortly after, Admiral Nimitz ordered the core of the North Pacific Force to provide much-needed reinforcement of Guadalcanal in the South Pacific. Theobald's Alaskan navy was reduced to *Indianapolis* and the light cruiser *Richmond*, four four-stack destroyers, and the remaining old S-boat submarines. Of small consolation, Theobald was given control of two Royal Canadian Navy corvettes, *Dawson* and *Vancouver*, and the three armed merchant cruisers, *Prince Robert*, *Prince Henry*, and *Prince David*. With only one heavy cruiser, *Indianapolis*, Theobald's force had little more firepower than a convoy escort group—small comfort in the face of the firepower the Japanese navy could still muster.

The RCAF
in the
Aleutians

12

General William Butler made good on his word to get RCAF units into combat. While the potential for action was present, however, no one knew just where and when it would occur. He sent Canadian P40 Kittyhawk fighters of the 111th to Umnak to relieve an equal number of American P40 Warhawks at Fort Glenn. En route from Anchorage, 1,440 kilometres east, the first contingent of Canadians fell victim to the notorious Alaskan weather.

On July 13 a detachment of seven Kittyhawks, led by Wing Commander McGregor, left Elmendorf Field in Anchorage. As the Canadian P40s had yet to be equipped with belly tanks to accommodate the long-distance flying required in the Alaskan front, refuelling stops had to be made down the Alaska Peninsula to Cold Bay. By the time the Canadians put down there, the weather had turned foul, and two planes were damaged while landing. The squadron was grounded for three days waiting for the weather to clear and for the two new replacement aircraft to arrive. At the southern tip of the Bering Sea, across frigid, storm-tossed waters, Umnak was still another 320 kilometres west. The Canadians took off July 16, but the weather continued to wreak havoc. With less than 64 kilometres left to go, they hit a wall of infamous Aleutian fog over Dutch Harbor. McGregor ordered his men to return to Cold Bay, but the pilots lost visual contact in the middle of a turn. Four Kittyhawks slammed into Unalaska Island while a fifth crashed into the sea. Amongst the fatalities was the squadron leader, J.W. Kerwin, a battle-seasoned pilot on rotation from Europe. Calls to the missing fighters by McGregor and the Dutch Harbor radio operator were met only by an eerie static. A shaken McGregor and the remaining P40 searched frantically in the fog for half an hour, trying to raise the five planes on radio, before returning to Cold Bay to raise a search patrol.

Within the span of a few days, the weather had claimed seven of the 111th's Kittyhawks—half its fighter strength—before any of the fliers had set foot on Umnak, let alone seen the enemy. When replacement fighters arrived by way of Vancouver and Anchorage, General Butler ordered them grounded until they were modified with belly tanks that would allow them to fly longer distances. In the meantime, the Canadians flew the American version of the Kittyhawk— the P40D Curtiss Warhawk with American markings. The P40 had a range of only around 1,000 kilometres, which spelled almost certain death in conditions of no visibility between refuelling stops. The addition of a belly tank effectively doubled its range.

The P40 was the most widely used Allied fighter and saw action in all theatres of the war, although it was far inferior overall to the Mitsubishi Zeros of the Japanese. Armaments consisted of one 20-millimetre machine gun mounted on the starboard wing. Later versions sported three 50-calibre guns in each wing. The P40 was powered by one Allison V-1710-81 engine that put out 1,360 horsepower for a maximum speed (unloaded) of 604 kilometres per hour. Loaded, the plane weighed in at 4,014 kilograms. The plane certainly had its good points. As veteran Canadian combat pilot Louis Cochand remarked, "It was a tough plane. You could practically fly it into a brick wall and come out the other side."[1]

Fort Glenn, the base on Umnak to which the Canadians were stationed, had been in operation less than two months when they arrived and had only one airstrip, Cape Field. The 11th Fighter Squadron (USAAF), the American P40 squadron already there, was commanded by Major Jack Chennault, whose father Claire Chennault, of Flying Tiger fame, had commanded an all-volunteer force of Curtiss Warhawks in China. The Aleutian Tigers bore a snarling Bengal tiger on the nose, while the Canadians, in tribute to the senior Chennault, emblazoned on their planes the fierce face of a tiger shark, synonymous with his fighters. The Canadians eventually got their own runway on Umnak, Berry Field, sixteen kilometres from Fort Glenn, which helped ease congestion on Cape Field.

Even for the P40s equipped with belly tanks, however, it was still too far to fly from Umnak to hit the Japanese on Kiska. This meant

Some 60 years later, the wreckage of four RCAF P40 Kittyhawks remains on Manning Point, where they crashed on Unalaska Island. Note the scorched crater surrounding the wreckage is still evident in the slow-healing muskeg. The radio (below) is from one of the crashed P40s.

they could provide only limited fighter escort for the heavy bombers that had an extended loaded range of over 3,000 kilometres. Weather permitting, the bombers could fly out of Cold Bay, 480 kilometres east on the Alaska Peninsula, pick up extra fuel at Umnak, and then harass Attu (1,600 kilometres from Cold Bay and 1,280 kilometres from Umnak). Other times they were diverted to Kiska, about 290 kilometres closer. The Japanese were never able to supply fighter protection for the far outpost on Attu, so the bombers could strike largely unchallenged from the air. Over Kiska, however, the bombers had to contend with the Japanese float fighters on their own.

It was obvious that the Allies needed an airfield much closer to the action, but Aleutian topography offered few choices. Adak was about the best option for a forward base. Situated near the centre of the Aleutian chain, 440 kilometres from Kiska and 640 kilometres from Attu, it offered a broad harbour deep enough to accommodate even large warships. Japan had initially set its sights on the island, but opted against taking it following the discovery of the airbase on Umnak. A patrol of Alaska Scouts was sent to see if there were any signs of Japanese scouting parties on Adak (there were indications of Japanese visitors on several of the other islands), but it found nothing.

An army of engineers and construction battalions sailed from Kodiak once the all-clear for Adak came through. With transport vessels at a premium, the convoy consisted of work barges, scows, fish packers, and pretty much anything else that would float. Serving as escort were four old American four-stack destroyers, the Canadian corvettes *Dawson* and *Vancouver*, and the armed merchant cruisers *Prince Robert*, *Prince Henry*, and *Prince David*.

The first troops of the 4th Infantry Regiment came ashore the morning of July 29, braving angry seas and a driving wind. They at once set up defensive positions and anti-aircraft batteries and were followed a few days later by the 807th Aviation Engineer Battalion, which arrived to build an airfield—no easy task in the muskeg of the island. The only near-suitable site was a lagoon at Sweeper Cove that flooded at high tide, so the engineers under Colonel Benjamin Talley built a dike and a collapsible floodgate at its seaward end. The gate was closed at low tide to seal off the lagoon, the remaining water pumped out, and the bottom filled in and levelled. The runway was to be composed of Marsden matting—perforated strips of steel that interlocked to make a runway when ground conditions made building one impossible—but the shipment of matting was lost when a barge sank en route. Until replacement decking arrived, hard sand was packed down, though it had to be continually re-groomed after planes took off or landed. Ten days after construction started, the first B17 landed on Adak. Serious bombing of the enemy could now begin. It was also possible to provide a full escort for the bombers, and the fighters could be used to strafe Japanese targets on Kiska.

The farther west the Americans moved down the Aleutian chain, the more difficult it became to supply the spartan line of bases. Alcohol and tobacco were rare or non-existent as space on cargo planes was too valuable to waste on simple pleasures, and even necessities were in short supply.

The Japanese had the same problems as the Allies maintaining their Aleutian bases. When a transport with earthmoving equipment was sunk, all road and runway building had to be done by hand. Japan also had to deal with the critical logistics of maintaining supply lines that stretched to the Aleutians and almost to Australia and southeast Asia. It was nearly impossible to obtain replacement aircraft as there was high-level opposition to expending resources in the Aleutians, especially after the Midway losses. Japanese airmen on Kiska, like their Canadian and American counterparts, had to cannibalize other Rufes to keep their float fighters in the air. The lack of replacement fighters became so acute that by September 1942, only 2 of 24 Rufes were still flying.

For both sides, the North Pacific was of secondary importance compared to other fronts. Hitler's Third Reich was at its farthest reaches in Europe and North Africa before a series of strikes in various campaigns started driving it back. The Canadians had just been badly bloodied in the ill-fated raid on Dieppe, while the Americans were deeply embroiled against the Japanese in the South Pacific. Official apathy conspired with the horrendous conditions of the North Pacific to bring the Aleutian war to a tedious crawl.

In August, Wing Commander McGregor assumed full responsibility for X-Wing, overseeing the four Canadian squadrons in Alaska. Leadership of the 111th was turned over to Squadron Leader Kenneth Boomer, an Ottawa native who had battled the Luftwaffe in the skies over Britain with two kills to his credit. All spit and polish, Boomer exemplified the ideal of a fighter pilot in the Royal Canadian Air Force, and when he arrived at the Canadian base at Umnak, he was appalled by the slovenliness of his new charges, who were generally a lot of spit and no polish. The formalities of maintaining proper uniform and drill had long been discarded, even among many officers. Several layers of clothing were needed to protect against wind and cold, and one wore whatever was available. American standards were no different, and men began to have their own variations of the uniforms issued them. In the case of the Canadians, it was typically the air force blue serge over a bright plaid shirt and longjohns with an American army-issue parka. When he threw his plaid shirt in with everybody else's laundry, Flight Lieutenant Ron Cox earned the ire of his compatriots when their blue air force shirts came out tinged in tacky pink.

On those rare occasions when a soldier cleaned his uniform, he would immerse it in a 45-gallon drum of gasoline, then hang it for a matter of minutes in the Aleutian wind to dry. Shortly after arriving on Umnak, Boomer ordered the squadron to fall in for inspection in 60 minutes in full proper uniform. The men grudgingly complied, after a fashion. Out of necessity, officers eased up on rules and regulations in the Aleutians, and some of them took Boomer aside and spelled out the reality of living and operating in such a remote and demoralizing setting. Boomer relented, but implored his men to at least wear their uniform caps on the base for the sake of appearance.

Adding to his frustration, not one serviceable plane could be found when he wanted a fly-around of the base. The new squadron leader's main priority was to keep the aircraft operable and maintain fighter patrols. In late August, Wing Commander McGregor flew from Anchorage to inform Boomer that a group of pilots from the 111th would move out to Adak to take part in direct combat missions against Japanese-held Kiska. Only one week after completion of the Adak airstrip, five Canadian Kittyhawk fighters and twelve of Jack Chennault's P40 pilots flew from Umnak to Adak to assume combat duties against Kiska.

The Japanese were by now aware of the new base at Adak. With their remaining two Rufes they launched erratic strafing runs against the airstrip over a five-day period, but there was little to damage. Once fighters took up residence on the island, the Japanese, not wanting to risk the last of their Rufes, ceased their bothersome flyovers. On September 14 the Americans carried out their first fighter missions against Kiska, employing P39 Air Cobras and P38 Lightnings. Flown by the 54th Fighter Squadron, the latter was a new double-fuselage, twin-engined fighter that was being used for the first time in combat.

On September 25 the first fighter-escorted bomber missions took place, with Jack Chennault leading the 343rd Fighter Group of Aleutian Tigers and four RCAF P40s of the 111th under Squadron Leader Boomer flying escort. The fighters took off from Adak at eight in the morning to

Squadron Leader Kenneth Arthur Boomer of the 111th Kittyhawk Squadron, a veteran of the Battle of Britain, downed a Japanese Rufe fighter over Kiska in September 1942. His was the only air kill of the Canadian Home War establishment, and he became the first Allied pilot to have both German and Japanese kills to his credit. He was later shot down over France in October 1944.

make the treacherous 400-kilometre trip to Kiska. Overhead the fighters rendezvoused with seven B24 Liberators of the 36th Bombardment Squadron flying out of Cold Bay. Nearly two hours later the Canadians regrouped east of Kiska. They would attack the harbour from the east while the Americans would come at it from the west.

The Liberators first plastered the harbour with incendiaries to soften up Japanese gun positions. Six minutes later it was the fighters' turn, giving the enemy on the ground enough time to come out of the bunkers.

The Canadians made the first run on Kiska where, because of unusually clear weather, the Japanese spotted them with time to send up their two remaining Rufes. Pom-pom bursts of flak went up from Little Kiska, the small island sentinel in the harbour, as Kittyhawk machine guns threw back tracer fire. At dock in the harbour's north head were some of the larger Japanese float planes—the big four-engined Mavis bombers and Pete twin-wing reconnaissance planes.

The Kittyhawks ripped through them as the aircrews frantically scrambled to get them into the air. Once past the harbour, the Canadians sent the construction crews that were returning to work on the roughed-in airstrip diving for cover. Immediately on the tails of the Canadians, Chennault's Tigers appeared to take their turn at tearing into the float planes in the bay and the shore gunners firing on the swarming fighters.

The Canadian planes regrouped over the uninhabited west side of the island and had come back over the harbour when Squadron Leader Boomer saw a Rufe on the tail of a Warhawk, laying into him with machine-gun fire. The battle-seasoned Boomer pulled back hard and, in his words, "climbed to a stall practically, pulled up right under him. I just poured it into him from underneath. He flamed up and went down."[2] The pilot rode it down as long as he could, then bailed out, hitting the water before his chute opened. The plane exploded on impact. Jack Chennault brought the other Rufe corkscrewing down, trailing a plume of black smoke.

Anchored in the harbour were two RO-class submarines and one of the large I-boats. The sub crews opened fire with machine guns on the swooping P40s, which tore up the deck of one submarine and killed three gun crews. After three minutes it was over for the fighters and they headed east for home, taking time on the way out to empty their magazines on Japanese gunners on Little Kiska.

It was the strongest show of force yet against the enemy, and the first combined U.S.-Canadian fighter mission of the Alaskan war. The attack on Kiska had claimed as many as eight Pete float planes in the harbour and the two Rufe fighters and had severely damaged the submarine *RO-65*, with the loss of three gun crews. These RO subs were an obsolete British Vickers design, sold abroad to foreign navies. The boats had been commissioned long before the war, in 1925, at Mitsubishi Shipyard in Kobe, Japan. Outdated by the start of war, they had been relegated to training and coastal patrol, but were pressed into active service once the naval war began to turn. This class of RO boat was 76 metres long; sported one 76-millimetre cannon, one 50-millimetre machine gun, and six 53-centimetre torpedo tubes; and had a crew of 48 officers and ratings.

A few days later one of Chennault's pilots, Captain Wilbur Miller, dropped a 250-pound (110-kilogram) bomb on the damaged sub, sending it to the bottom of Kiska Harbor with all hands except for the skipper, Lieutenant Shoichi Egi, who was not aboard at the time. Miller was then killed when he flew into a flak burst.

A National Park Service diver explores the wreck of the Japanese submarine RO-65, sunk at Kiska.

Both American and Canadian pilots involved in the attack on Kiska were awarded the American Air Service Medal for their hazardous 800-kilometre over-water flight. The RCAF pilots were Squadron Leader Ken Boomer, Pilot Officer H.O. Gooding, and Flying Officers Robert Lynch and Jim Gohl—the latter an American who had joined to get his pilot training through the Commonwealth Air Training plan and had stayed on. For his downing of the Rufe, Boomer earned the double distinction of being the only Canadian and the first Allied pilot to shoot down planes from both Germany and Japan. He had claimed two Germans in the Battle of Britain and one Japanese over Kiska, and he would later add two more Luftwaffe planes when he returned to the war in Europe, for a total of five. He himself was killed over France in 1944. Boomer's was also the only aircraft kill credited to the Home War Establishment, which commanded all units of the armed forces that were charged with the home defence of Canada.

In late August, the navy seaplane tenders *Casco* and *Gillis* and their PBY charges returned to Nazan Bay on Atka to resume harassing Japanese supply ships trying to reach their Aleutian bases.

On August 30, Commander Tatsudo Tokutomi in the submarine *RO-61* had slipped into Nazan Bay and was calculating a run on *Casco*, which was anchored in the bay, when the appearance of the destroyer USS *Reid* changed his mind. If he attempted an attack now, the destroyer and seaplanes would surely find him in the shallow bay. Firing on the destroyer was out of the question because the antiquated RO boats had no stern torpedo tubes, and turning around to fire would reveal his whereabouts to the listening enemy.

Tokutomi settled his submarine onto the floor of Nazan Bay, virtually shutting down his boat. There was to be no unnecessary talking, the noisy air circulators were shut off, and food was handed out cold and uncooked. Men relieved themselves into collection buckets as the water pumps that flushed the head were turned off. The arctic water of the Bering Sea outside quickly dropped the temperature in the submarine to a few degrees above zero Celsius, and the crew, already bundled in oilskins and blankets, suffered bouts of shivering.

The next 32 interminable hours dripped by like the rivulets of cold condensation that ran down the bulkheads and dripped off every gauge face and electrical panel. The old RO boat was well beyond its submerged endurance—after 28 hours the air inside the submarine started turning lethal. The carbon-dioxide scrubber filters were saturated, and Tokutomi had sodium sprinkled freely around the quarters to help absorb some of the increasing gas. Meanwhile, the lack of oxygen gave each of the trapped submariners an excruciating headache.

Attuned to every sound of a surface ship's engine, the crew listened intently as the drone of *Reid's* engine slowed significantly and the clutch then re-engaged. Thank the gods! The destroyer had backed away from the floating dock and was now leaving, its engines revving ever higher but falling more distant. Giving the destroyer enough time to pass out of hearing range, Tokutomi ordered the submarine's systems brought back on. After more than 30 hours on the bottom, and with two torpedoes already loaded in the tubes, he was not to be cheated of his quarry.

Back on the surface, he fired one torpedo that drove itself up on the rocky beach and failed to explode, then another that crashed through *Casco*'s engine room, killing 5 crewmen and injuring 20. The remaining crew was able to beach *Casco* to keep from sinking and sent a distress call. USS *Reid* responded and reversed course back to Atka, guided to the enemy's position by two PBYs that had also picked up the call and were now pummeling *RO-61* with anti-submarine bombs. Tokutomi dived his tortured ship, but bombs from the PBYs had ruptured the fuel tanks, leaving a blood trail of diesel for the destroyer to scent out. Drawing the noose tighter, *Reid* dropped depth charges that knocked out *RO-61*'s power and shattered the glass in the indicator gauges. Water sprayed into the sub, shorting out electrical panels and plunging it into the dim glow of emergency lighting. Tokutomi ordered the ballast tanks

Japanese prisoners of war, survivors of the sinking of the submarine RO-61 *off Atka by USS* Reid *on August 31, 1942, are brought ashore at Dutch Harbor, Alaska.*

purged and full altitude on the elevator planes to drive his dying vessel to the surface. When the sub breached the waves in a torrent of foam and air, the destroyer's gun crews were waiting and opened fire. The cluster of bubbles marking the submarine's ascent gave them time to set their range, rewarding them with direct hits. The boat hung with her bow pointing up, then slipped stern first beneath the water almost as fast as she'd surfaced. Five crewmen were blown clear of the drowning sub by a blast of escaping air and were picked from the frigid seas, becoming the first Japanese prisoners of war in the Alaskan war.

The war in the North Pacific was starting to wind down for the season. On August 21 the 404th Squadron (U.S.) had departed for the the South Pacific, leaving the 8th Squadron (RCAF) to assume solo anti-submarine patrol out of Nome. By November, the threat of a Japanese attack subsided with the onslaught of winter and the presence of heavy ice in the Bering Sea. Non-winterized as they were, the Boleys could not withstand the cold extremes of Nome and were re-deployed to Kodiak Island to patrol for submarines and escort the many ships bringing war materials to Alaska.

One Man's
Glory

The war seemed far removed from North America's West Coast, where life went on pretty much as it had during peacetime. Merchant ships made no attempt to conceal their course, lighthouses continued to serve as beacons to friendly and enemy ships alike, and coastal communities followed no blackout procedures. Marvelling at the lights of San Francisco one night, Zenji Orita, a crewman aboard *I-15*, recorded in his diary with some perplexity, "Don't they know there's a war on?" Another of the ship's officers even went so far as to suggest they tie up and go ashore for a night on the town as probably no one would take any notice.

Farther north, *I-25* off Oregon's coast conducted the most frequent patrols of any Japanese submarine off the shores of North America. In two previous tours it had ranged from the Columbia River separating Washington and Oregon to the Gulf of Alaska, Kodiak Island, and the Aleutian Islands. Now it was back, with a new mission. In its tiny deck hangar, the sub carried a Glen collapsible aircraft for reconnaissance purposes. The sub's flying officer, Warrant Officer Nobuo Fujita, had used it for reconnaissance missions over Woman's Bay on Kodiak in the month leading up to the attacks on Dutch Harbor. It was Fujita who had conceived the idea that perhaps this little plane could be used for more covert missions and even, in numbers, to attack West Coast cities of North America.

Fujita had forwarded his plan to Imperial navy headquarters and was surprised when, during a refit of the *I-25* at Yokosuka naval base, his captain Meiji Tagami handed him a telegram summoning him to the flotilla offices.

There, in a red-brick, three-storey building, he met Prince Takamatsu, the younger brother of Emperor Hirohito; Commander Iura of the 3rd Division-Submarines; and the former Japanese vice-consul, who until the outbreak of hostilities had been posted in Seattle.[1]

The Prince himself had endorsed the idea, Imperial headquarters had approved it, and Fujita was informed he was to bomb the American mainland. The pilot beamed with heady enthusiasm. To think that the Imperial navy had singled out his idea and he himself would execute the mission! Using U.S. Hydrographic Survey charts captured from the Americans on Wake Island in the South Pacific, Commander Iura indicated an area about 120 kilometres north of the California border in Oregon and approximately sixteen kilometres inland, where he was to bomb the forests.

Fujita was crestfallen. He had hoped to strike at some major city or other vital target. What was the sense in bombing a forest?

Noting Fujita's disappointment, the consul explained how the Northwest was full of trees. Once a fire got started, it was very hard to put out. Sometimes whole towns were burned. The reasoning was that the Americans would panic if they knew Japan could bomb "their country, their factories and homes." Taking heart that his was to be the first of many such missions to strike directly at the North American mainland, an elated Fujita returned to his submarine.[2]

I-25 left the yard at Yokosuka on August 14, and on September 2 it arrived off the Cape Blanco lighthouse on Oregon's southern coast. Incessant swells knocked the submarine about, making a launch of the Glen impossible. The weather continued for seven days, and Fujita passed the time playing cards with Captain Tagami and the ship's officers. The sub surfaced at night to recharge its batteries and dived at first light to rest on the sandy bottom of Oregon's shallow banks or to maintain neutral buoyancy at depth while the ocean gently rocked the crew to a half sleep.

On the morning of September 9, Commander Tagami viewed the Oregon coast from periscope depth, still jostled by the waves. After a few minutes of contemplation, he called Fujita to have a look for himself. The black coastline stood out against the first blue hues of morning in the east, and sixteen kilometres distant the light of Cape Blanco's lighthouse still beckoned despite recent submarine attacks. Tagami had the boat brought to the surface, where the aircrew scrambled topside and opened the watertight hanger to begin assembly of the little airplane. Two 76-kilogram incendiary bombs, each containing 520 magnesium-firing pellets, were loaded aboard. Upon detonation, the pellets would burn at a temperature of 1,500° Celsius and cover an area over 100 metres in diameter.

As Fujita and observer Shoji Okuda climbed into the plane, Commander Tagami wished them well and shook hands with the two men—a departure from the standard, stoic salute of Japan's rigid navy. Once strapped in, Fujita revved the single engine and the plane strained against the chocks of the launching catapult, while inside the cockpit the noise made it impossible for the two men to hear each other. Fujita gave the thumbs up, and with a loud hiss the compressed air was released and fired the little plane off the submarine deck. Behind him, the foreboding hulk of I-25 slipped once again beneath the waves.

Nobuo Fujita twice dropped bombs from his Yokosuka E14Y1 Glen aircraft into the forests of Oregon in September and October 1942. Fujita was launched from submarine I-25. This was the only enemy aircraft bombing of the continental United States during the Second World War. In 1992 Fujita was welcomed back to Oregon to plant a tree at the site of his first bombing in what is now Siskiyou National Forest.

On a southeasterly course, Fujita passed over Gold Beach north of the town of Brookings and climbed to about 2,500 metres. A dairy driver at an early morning stop spotted the unusual plane with its Japanese red sun markings over Port Orford, puttering along like an airborne Model T. After careful observation he phoned his sighting to the Coast Guard, which responded with an insult and hung up.

Below Fujita and Okuda, the topography quickly gave way to the dense coniferous rain forest of Oregon's coast. After about 30 minutes they released the first of their incendiaries over Wheeler Ridge. The bomb hurtled to earth, spinning end over end, splitting a young tree, and spilling the magnesium pellets onto the forest floor. Fujita and Okuda noted that they ignited like fireworks and burst into flame.

After a few minutes Fujita released the second bomb, smiling with great satisfaction. In a small way this was his personal retaliation for the previous February, when Colonel James Doolittle's B-25s bombed Tokyo and the Yokosuka base, punching a hole in *I-25*, which was sitting in dry dock. The second of the two bombs apparently failed to ignite, as neither of the two men could see any sign of fire below. To this day, under the deep foliage of Wheeler Ridge, the 75-kilogram incendiary bomb still lies unexploded.

To the northeast, forest rangers at the Mount Emily Firewatch Station watched an unusual, small-pontooned float plane skirting the tops of trees. They noted the plane in the daily logbook and made passing mention of it in their morning call to forestry headquarters.

A soldier coming off duty reported the unidentified plane as it headed out to sea at about 0630 in the Cape Blanco area. The Roseburg Filter Center, which disseminated all information regarding enemy activity in the area, now started to take seriously the notion that some enemy activity was unfolding. A squadron of P-38s were scrambled from McChord Field near Tacoma, but flew in the wrong direction, apparently because of the soldier's southern accent. His reference to Bandon was taken to mean the town of Bend, Oregon.

Later that day, forestry workers discovered a patch of small, sporadic fires covering an area about 30 metres across. They quickly extinguished the flames. Sifting through the site they found unlit incendiary pellets, metal fragments, and the nose cone of a bomb with Japanese markings. When it hit the tree, the bomb had failed to fully detonate, thereby containing the fires to a small area. Authorities at the Roseburg Filter Center were informed of the find.

Officials saw the bombing as a prelude to invasion and ordered small infantry units dispatched up and down the Coast Highway. Summing up this response, with its antiquated battle gear and only five to ten rounds of ammunition per man, one soldier observed, "We would have had one hell of a time if the enemy was serious about landing."[3]

One of the only truly effective measures the units could take was to remove road signs along the highway so that if the enemy did land amphibiously on Oregon's beaches, they would not have local road signs telling them how to get around.

While Fujita's efforts caused little material damage, they did create pandemonium in certain quarters. Some brass believed the Japanese had smuggled pontooned aircraft to remote lakes along the coast, where they would assemble them and from which they would bomb American cities. Special FBI agents spent weeks on horseback scouting the wilderness areas and "found beautiful lakes and mountains, good fishing, and mosquitoes ... but no Japanese."[4]

Fujita and Okuda made it safely back to the rendezvous point with *I-25*, which was occasionally concealed by a drifting morning fog between bursts of bright sunshine. With the Glen dismantled and stowed in the hangar, the crew was just about to go below decks when the lookout shouted, pointing to the sky.

Out of the sun roared a twin-engine Lockheed Hudson piloted by Captain Jean Daugherty, who was on routine patrol out of McChord Field when he spotted the enemy sub. Armed with two 300-pound (135-kilogram) bombs, he went in for the kill just as *I-25* cleared the surface. The first bomb detonated next to the sub and sent it rolling sharply to starboard, plunging the crew into darkness. With water seeping into the radio room and an electrical panel temporarily shorting out, Tagami ordered the boat into a crash dive.

Daugherty banked around for another crack at the intruder and let go the second bomb. The explosion went off over the heads of the submariners with a shock that rattled their teeth as the boat continued its sharp descent before levelling off around 30 metres. Tagami ordered the electric motors shut off, and the boat drifted along with the current while each station reported the extent of its damage. The effect of the attack was minimal, and after several hours Tagami ordered the electric drive motors engaged and to proceed dead slow. Silently, the submarine entered the harbour of Oregon's Port Orford and settled on the bottom. It remained there until nightfall, giving the crew time to rest and repair any damage.

For nearly three weeks *I-25* kept a low profile and in the darkness of early morning on September 29, Fujita and Okuda had the plane readied for a second bombing mission over Oregon. The I-boat took up position about 80 kilometres off the Cape Blanco Lighthouse and catapulted the Glen off the submarine deck. After flying inland for half an hour, Fujita dropped two incendiaries into the forest eleven kilometres east of Port Orford. Noting their flashes as they disappeared into the dense bush, he believed he had ignited a forest fire. Once again forest rangers sighted the strange little plane buzzing Oregon's forests and reported it to the Roseburg Center, but search and fire crews found no sign of fire or incendiaries.

Fujita made it back out to sea and circled the predetermined rendezvous point, but there was no sign of *I-25*, only the endless green rolling sea. As his compass had on occasion been terribly inaccurate, he returned to the coast to take a new heading off the Cape Blanco lighthouse. Spotting an oil slick on the water, he followed it and a short time later saw the black outline of *I-25* running partially submerged. The two airmen made it aboard and Fujita reported to Tagami that there were several fires burning out of control, but this was only wishful thinking. Due to an unusually wet September in 1942, any fire started by Fujita and Okuda would likely have burned itself out quickly. Although a section of burned ground was discovered some time later in the targeted area, rangers concluded a lightning strike or other source could also have caused it.

Five days later, on October 4, while patrolling Oregon's southern coastline about 80 kilometres west of Coos Bay, Tagami spotted the 6,600-ton tanker *Camden*. Loaded with 76,000 barrels of gasoline, it had developed a serious mechanical problem that caused it to shut down its engines and sit dead in the water. Tagami lined the tanker up in his attack scope and fired two torpedoes. The first passed astern of the ship, but the second slammed into its side and erupted into a wall of flame. Civilian and military vessels came to *Camden*'s rescue and brought the fire under control before towing the vessel towards Seattle.

The fire continued to burn, and on October 10 it again raged out of control and engulfed the ship. Under the weight of so much water poured on the fire, *Camden* settled lower and lower until it finally sank off Gray's Harbor, Washington, six days after being torpedoed.

Still lurking off Oregon's southern coast, Tagami came upon the tanker *Larry Doheny*, loaded with 66,000 barrels of oil. It regularly transported petroleum between Puget Sound and Santa Barbara, and in December 1941 had escaped an attack by *I-17*.

Racing on the dark surface to intercept the unsuspecting ship, Tagami ordered one torpedo away, but it petered out by the time it hit the target and failed to detonate. The *Larry Doheny* steamed on, unaware of the deadly calculations with slide rule and triangle taking place at that moment aboard the enemy submarine. With co-ordinates for a second shot relayed into orders, the crew fell silent and listened as another torpedo whirred out of the tube on its long trajectory to the tanker. Executive Officer Lieutenant Tatsuo Tsukudo leaned casually against the elevated rail of the console as he clocked the run with his stopwatch. A tremendous explosion reverberated back to *I-25* and the crewmen cheered, a few of them clapping hands.

Above, the tanker had become an inferno, its buckling steel screeching as if in agony. It sank the following day as rescue crews stood by. Forty men made it to lifeboats and were later put ashore at Port Orford, while six others died in the attack. Escaping to safety, Tagami decided, after conferring with Fujita and Executive Officer Tsukudo, to abandon further flights over the American mainland and conclude their third patrol to the West Coast. The submarine still suffered from the surprise aircraft attack a month before, leaving a telltale trail of fuel oil, and it was down to its last torpedo, while the compass on the Glen had proved unreliable.

As Tagami headed northwest about 1,200 kilometres off the rugged Washington–British Columbia coastline on October 11, his soundman alerted him to the unmistakable noises of two distant ships. Tagami followed the sounds to two submarines, which he assumed to be American, then switched to silent running on electric motors so as not to be heard. Positioning his boat so the targets would pass in close range, he fired his last Mark 95 torpedo. The result was an explosion so severe it shattered gauges, light bulbs, and the porcelain toilets aboard his own sub.

Unbeknown to Tagami, the target of his attack was *L-16* of the Soviet navy's Pacific fleet, en route to the Panama Canal with sister sub *L-15*. The stricken sub sank in twenty seconds with all hands, while *L-15* immediately opened fire on *I-25*, but to no avail.

Despite their belief that they had sunk an American enemy, there was no joy aboard *I-25*. The instantaneous destruction of the sub was shocking, and they knew it was unlikely there would be survivors. Tagami's crewmen also knew they could easily suffer the same fate as those whose lives they had just taken. After the gruelling 70-day patrol, *I-25* pulled into Yokosuka navy base in November 1942. It was not until 1973, 31 years later, that Tagami learned *L-16*'s identity and nationality.

As for Warrant Officer Fujita, he took pride in the fact that he had struck directly at the enemy in his homeland. Fifty years later, on September 9, 1992, he returned to Oregon at the age of 80 to plant a tree at the site of his first bombing in what is now Siskiyou National Forest. He died in 1998—the lone warrior who bombed America.

War— Northern Style

By December 1942, the onset of winter slowed the pace of the war in the Aleutians to almost unbearable monotony and compounded the already harsh conditions of life so far north. If existence at the remote Alaskan bases was generally dismal, it was even more so in the Aleutians. For the Japanese as well as the Americans and Canadians, the weather more often than not determined the conduct of both military operations and daily routine.

With few permanent structures built for accommodation, Allied servicemen slept five to a tent, in tents that had no floor and were pitched into the muskeg up to the roof to prevent them blowing away. An oil stove burned continuously, but in colder months it was so inefficient that the men would be standing in freezing mud up to the knees while sweltering above the waist—an 80-degree difference between floor and ceiling. Guide ropes connected the tents to the latrines so men would not get hopelessly lost and possibly freeze to death when they ventured a few metres outside. Winds routinely exceeded 200 kilometres per hour and snapped the wind meter off its pole at Adak. Despite precautions, it was not unusual to return from the mess tent to find one's quarters and everything in them had blown away. Often crews just skipped dinner, as a walk to the mess tent took too much effort.

Life was somewhat better for the Japanese on Kiska. They had constructed permanent wooden huts, and the volcanic caves that lace the island provided ready-made bomb shelters. An infirmary and storage room were constructed at the end of one of these long lava tubes, safe from enemy bombs, while the Japanese had also built saunas and participated in daily exercise routines, with rations of saki and gin brought in for the men. Ack-ack guns, manned round the clock, now surrounded the harbour to greet Allied planes with heavy groundfire. But even the most basic items such as firewood had to be brought in by freighter, an increasingly difficult task once marauding bombers began flying from Adak to close the gap of ocean between the Kuriles and the Aleutians.

Because it was too far north for the Americans to mount any regular effective action against it, Attu for the most part escaped the severity of bombardments the Allies meted out to Kiska. In September 1942, Admiral Hosogaya abandoned Attu and moved the 1,500-man garrison to Kiska, but by the end of October the Japanese high command decided to reoccupy the base over winter. The Americans were moving down the Aleutian chain, having occupied the Pribiloffs, Tanaga, and Adak in an apparent bid to mount some sort of offensive. From Attu, the Japanese reasoned, the Americans could deploy long-range bombers to hit their navy base at Paramushiro in the Kuriles. To head off that prospect, they re-occupied the island in November with 1,100 soldiers ready for a long winter.

While the Americans lost nine planes to enemy fire in the ensuing months, Alaska's weather claimed 63 during the same period. The Canadians fared no better, losing more aircraft to the weather in the North Pacific than in any other theatre of the war. Patrol planes simply failed to return to base, swallowed up by the icy seas after digging into the waves. Heavy icing also forced planes down into the water, while blinding snow produced whiteout conditions that sent others crashing in the vast forests of the West Coast, their skeletal remains to be found only decades later.

The Japanese, subjected to the same capriciousness of the weather, also had to contend with bomber attacks—sometimes several times a day. On December 30 alone, Kiska was pummelled with 20,000 kilograms of bombs that amounted to little more than an early New Year's display of fireworks save for the destruction of a derelict transport.

That same month, Admiral Theobald resigned as commander of the North Pacific Force in disgust, the result of professional differences with General Buckner and the depletion of his ships to little more than an escort force. His replacement, the gruff Admiral Thomas C. Kinkaid, took over in early January 1943 and immediately set to work. In his view, concluding the war in Alaska meant somehow bringing it to the enemy rather than maintaining long, arduous flights over open water in ridiculous flying conditions and hit-or-miss missions. The Allies would have to move farther west down the chain to be within better range for the fighters and in position for a seaborne landing to be staged. Amchitka Island, only 112 kilometres east of Kiska and some 320 kilometres closer to the action than the nearest base on Adak, was ideal for his purposes. From there it was possible to fly regular runs by heavy bombers and harassment by fighter aircraft against Attu, which heretofore had been targeted only intermittently.

On January 11, 1943, a platoon of Colonel Lawrence V. Castner's Alaska Scouts paddled silently to Amchitka as they had to Adak five months before. On shore the scouts found remains of Japanese encampments, but the enemy had long since left the island.

Standing by were Kinkald's ships, now under command of Rear Admiral Charles H. McMorris, who had replaced Rear Admiral "Poco" Smith as squadron commander. At dawn the Alaska Scouts flashed the "all clear" signal, and the landing of 2,100 engineering and construction personnel and tons of equipment began. Not all was smooth sailing. Destroyer *Worden* hung up on one of many uncharted rock pinnacles and capsized, taking fourteen men to the bottom of Constantine Harbor. Another destroyer grounded hard on Amchitka's black volcanic shoals, and a dock had to be constructed to offload it.

By this point in the war, the Japanese had flown in a few replacement aircraft to shore up air defence of Kiska. Within days the planes discovered the Americans building a short runway on Amchitka and flew the short hop from Kiska to harass them, killing three engineers and shooting up some construction equipment. Mavis bombers twice bombed the island, but there was little to hit except for the dirt airstrip that was being groomed. Sporadic as they were, and launched by a handful of pontooned aircraft, the attacks did little to prevent completion of the runway. It was built of Marsden matting, as the Adak runway had been, and was soon able to accommodate a group of the dependable P40s. When Rufe fighter planes next attacked Amchitka, they were chased off by the Warhawks. After that, enemy air strikes against the island became rare.

In January, American bombers sank two Japanese transports en route to their Aleutian bases: *Kotohiro Maru* approaching Attu and *Montreal Maru* attempting to resupply Kiska. Some weeks later an American submarine prowling off Attu reported several enemy ships anchored in Attu's Holtz Bay, and McMorris steamed for the island in his flagship, the cruiser *Richmond*.

Japanese troops on Attu making the most of the weather.

A rare break in the weather allowed McMorris's squadron to reach Attu hours ahead of the estimated time, only to find that either the submarine reports were wrong or the enemy had given them the slip. McMorris decided that even if the enemy had no ships in the area, he could at least rattle them. From eight kilometres offshore, the big guns of *Indianapolis* and *Richmond* pounded Chichagof village and Holtz Bay. While the island provided few obvious targets, the shelling killed 23 soldiers and shattered some of the wooden Aleut buildings now used by the Japanese. After a two-hour barrage, McMorris withdrew his ships to the waters between Japan's northern Kuriles and the western Aleutians. It was time to turn up the heat on the enemy.

With such a small contingent of warships—the 9,800-ton heavy cruiser *Indianapolis*, the 7,050-ton light cruiser *Richmond*, and four destroyers —Admiral Kinkaid reasoned that the only effective use of the force would be a naval blockade of the islands. The strategy was to intercept enemy vessels attempting to resupply the Aleutian bases and thereby starve the Japanese out of Alaska.

Loaded with supplies and fresh troops, the 3,100-ton transport ship *Akagane Maru* was the first to run afoul of the blockade when *Indianapolis* easily sank it as it headed to Attu. In the following days Kinkaid's fleet forced more than a dozen other supply ships to return to Japan.

By March 1943 the Japanese had lost or suffered damage to more than 40 ships supporting the Aleutian garrisons. Proportionately, fighting the war in Alaska had become a very costly endeavour. Supply ships cunning enough to slip the blockade had to contend with enemy fighters and bombers flying out of the new base on Amchitka Island. Once anchored at Kiska, the supply ships were sitting ducks for marauding planes. Four were destroyed in the harbour and its approaches. Bombing had intensified greatly since the Allies took up position on Amchitka. They subjected the Japanese to hourly poundings when weather permitted, driving them into the island's damp caves and lava tubes for shelter. When power from the diesel generators to the pumps was knocked out, the infirmary at the end of a long cave flooded, leaving the wounded knee-deep in cold water.

With the monotonous military routine broken only by intense bombing from the air, shortages of food, spare parts, and equipment whittled away the renowned stoic resolve of the Japanese. When a transport went down, letters, small gifts, and personal ties from loved ones back home went with it. The Japanese line of supply had been virtually cut off, except for submarines or the occasional ship that managed to dodge the blockade.

Such was the case on March 9, when convoy ships that had eluded the American gunboats reached Attu and Kiska. Those left on Attu watched the lone transport unload overnight, then weigh anchor and slip out of Chichagof Harbour. Other than the odd submarine, it was to be their last physical contact from home.

A Spy in
Our Midst

In October 1942, American intelligence uncovered an Axis conspiracy. Intelligence had been monitoring transmissions from Yakichiro Suma, Japan's ambassador in officially neutral but, under the fascist government of Francisco Franco, pro-Axis Spain. American intelligence revealed to its Canadian and British counterparts that Suma had requested Spain open a consulate office in Vancouver, British Columbia, to look after Japanese interests. Suma claimed to be concerned about the Japanese Canadians removed to internment camps in the B.C. interior, but his request was actually a thinly veiled attempt to bring an agent in the service of the Japanese to the West Coast. Suma approached Alcazar de Velasco, a good friend in Madrid and the number one agent in SIM— the Spanish external spy agency—who agreed to provide someone for this purpose.

Under General Franco's regime, German and Japanese agents had a free hand to recruit Spanish diplomats, whose consulates were centres of intelligence-gathering for the Axis powers. Many Spanish ship captains and crewmen also acted as Axis agents, sending coded messages to waiting Nazi U-boats after they spotted Allied convoys on North America's eastern seaboard. De Velasco boasted that he was personally responsible for helping sink 800 Allied ships because of information he had passed on to the Axis.

The German government also wished to have a spy in the Pacific Northwest as it had little information on the route being used for the all-important supply line to the eastern front via Siberia. The Japanese were interested in West Coast shipping activity—particularly the amount of material moving up the coast to supply the Aleutian war effort and the ships carrying the material—and in possible Allied plans to invade Japan via the Alaskan islands. According to Robert Wilcox in his book *Japan's Secret War*, the Japanese were also highly interested in secret atomic research being conducted at the Hanford Nuclear facility in southwest Washington State. They were doing their own research into nuclear fission and its potential for weaponry.[1]

The Axis intended that a Spanish agent would investigate the placement of naval establishments and airfields on the West Coast and in Alaska and would report heavy movements of troops and aircraft—particularly long-range bombers—to the north. Boeing Aircraft, headquartered in Seattle, was turning out the B-17 Flying Fortress, the mainstay of American bomber forces, and a plant in Vancouver was contracted to build PBY (Canso) flying boats. The Japanese were also interested in knowing the number and condition of roads between Alaska and the continental United States, and the status of communication facilities, shipping activity, and local labour attitudes.

De Velasco recruited Fernando de Kobbe de Chinchilla, a low-level career diplomat to whom he had taken an immediate dislike, for the Vancouver post. De Velasco, an ex-bullfighter with a reputation for arrogance, found Kobbe to be silly and effeminate. His estimation was hardly improved when Kobbe, who insisted that their first meeting with Ambassador Suma take place at a Madrid café to avoid suspicion, showed up with a girlfriend, both of them dressed as "spies" in long coats and dark glasses. Displaying a penchant for the theatrical, Kobbe drew the curtains around the group and enquired as to the whereabouts of "enemy agents."

"The whole meeting appeared a contradiction," De Velasco wrote. "He [Kobbe] was not inconspicuous."[2]

At the meeting, Suma provided Kobbe with a set of priorities to investigate while in Vancouver and a payment of 50,000 pesetas, with a promise of more later. The spy ring out of Vancouver would be known by the Japanese word TO, which translated means "door"—short for "door to the west." Allied intelligence simply referred to the ring as Span-Nip. The Americans were onto Kobbe before he even left Madrid.

Spain applied to the Canadian government to reinstate a consulate office in Vancouver to oversee suspended Japanese-Canadian interests. The U.S. State Department and the Federal Bureau of Investigation encouraged London and Ottawa to grant Kobbe's application for a visa as they believed it might prove useful to monitor the Spanish agent's actions. After the Canadians approved Kobbe's visa application, Kobbe and his 21-year-old, London-born daughter Beatriz departed Spain on November 28 on the SS *Marques de Comillas*—a Spanish liner well known to the Allies for its suspected work passing convoy information and carrying enemy agents for the Nazis. Kobbe and Beatriz arrived in New Orleans in December and journeyed to New York, where they spent Christmas, all the while followed by the FBI. When they crossed into Montreal, the Royal Canadian Mounted Police took up the tail.

From Montreal, the pair took a Canadian Pacific train across the continent, finally arriving at Vancouver's Burrard Street train station in mid-January 1943. In the following days, Kobbe secured an office for the Spanish consulate at 325 Howe Street in Vancouver's downtown core. For the time being, Kobbe kept a low profile, conducting regular affairs of a consul—apparently oblivious to the RCMP's round-the-clock surveillance. Kobbe befriended members of Vancouver's Spanish community, enjoying the hospitality of local Spanish businessmen. Given that most of his compatriots still seemed loyal to Spain's recently deposed monarch, Kobbe told them nothing of his work. Every week he visited the ports and took excursions into Washington State, playing into the hands of the Allies.

Duel in the North Pacific

By early 1943, the frozen northern islands of volcanic rock that many in Japan's military had seen as useless had become paramount to Japan's survival. They alone stood in the way of an all-out assault on the home islands by the Allies from the north. While the Aleutians served as potential stepping-stones to North America, their strategic location was a double-edged sword that also worked against the Japanese. Loss of Japan's bases there would leave the Allies free to establish forward bases from which to launch bomber strikes on Paramushiro in the Kuriles and, before long, on Tokyo itself as a prelude to invasion. A large enemy naval force would surely follow the bombers to the Aleutians, with implications too terrible to consider.

Although possession of the Aleutians could give either side an advantage, however, both gave them low priority. The war in Alaska had become a costly headache for the Japanese and Americans, who saw the deployment of aircraft, munitions, and troops to the Aleutians as secondary to maintaining a shaky hold on territory in the South Pacific and other theatres. For the Allies, at least, supply lines were improved by the completion of the Alaska Highway and by the fact that the Japanese seemed unable or unwilling to maintain an effective submarine offensive against West Coast shipping. Still, maintaining the war effort in Alaska meant diverting millions of war dollars, machinery, and manpower that could be better used elsewhere.

For Lieutenant General Hideichiro Higuchi, commander of all Japanese land forces in the North Pacific, McMorris's blockade was an ever-tightening noose strangling the vital supply line to his Aleutian bases. Seeing the navy as the only hope for his beleaguered Alaskan garrisons, he prevailed on it to deal directly with the blockade. On March 22, 1943, Admiral Hosogaya responded by ordering the heavy cruisers *Maya* and *Nachi*; light cruisers *Akubunka* and *Tama*; destroyers *Wakaba*, *Hatsushimo*, *Ikazuchi*, *Usagumo*, and *Inazuma*; and transports *Maru Sanko*, *Maru Sakito*, and *Maru Asaka* from Paramushiro. It was time to smash through the American fleet.

On the morning of March 26, Admiral McMorris's task group, made up of flagship *Richmond* accompanied by the Pensacola-class heavy cruiser *Salt Lake City* and destroyers *Monaghan*, *Dale*, *Bailey*, and *Coghlan*, was 160 kilometres south of Russia's Komandorski Islands— a 600-kilometre extension of the Aleutian chain. *Salt Lake City* had recently replaced the cruiser *Indianapolis*, which was now heading to the West Coast before assuming duty in the South Pacific, where its last act would be to deliver the atomic bomb that finally brought Japan to heel.

From high up in the crow's-nest the lookout reported five vessels— mere specks on the horizon topped by columns of smoke. McMorris believed he would only be engaging an enemy supply convoy as the repeated sounding of an alarm bell brought the ships to an about-face.

Alerted by his bridge officers to approaching ships on the southern horizon, Admiral Hosogaya ordered the launch of scout Pete aircraft to verify their origin. Receiving confirmation that it was indeed the American blockade ships moving north for an engagement, he changed course to broadside the enemy fleet. His ships outweighed and outgunned the American boats by two to one, and from a point eleven kilometres off they opened fire with their 10-inch (250-millimetre) guns to bracket the cruiser *Richmond* with towering water geysers.

Salt Lake City replied with its forward gun turret, landing shells just below the bridge of the *Nachi* and knocking out power to the forward turret. *Nachi*'s electricians soon had the turret back in action, but almost as quickly, *Salt Lake City* scored three more hits on *Nachi* in the same vicinity. This time power to the main guns as well as the bridge was cut, the main mast was wrenched askew, and three officers on the bridge were killed, with Hosogaya himself narrowly escaping death.

Return fire from the Japanese cruisers landed shells squarely on *Salt Lake City*'s main deck, crashing below into the engine room and buckling a watertight bulkhead. A defect within the cruiser's steam-powered steering system, resulting from firing the ship's big guns, had already reduced the *Salt Lake City*'s manoeuvrability, and now sea water seeping in through the damaged hull plating threatened to short out the main generators. Noting the cruiser's speed drop to a few knots, the Japanese force formed an ever-tightening arc with their guns fixed on their quarry.

Salt Lake City took a heavy shot below the waterline, and the icy North Pacific began welling up in the port side engine room, adjoining voids, and compartments and shorting out fuses. The switchboard room, aft 5-inch (127-millimetre) handling room and ammunition room, and shaft alleys three and four were flooded. Diesel fuel, hydraulic fluid, and oil from a ruptured lube oil tank swirled around ladders and fittings. At 1147 hours its engines stopped. Other ships of the Alaskan fleet pulled in closer to put up a defensive smoke screen around *Salt Lake City*, which had run up three signal flags indicating "MY SPEED ZERO" after salt water in its fuel injectors choked off the propulsion machinery and quenched the steam boilers. The cruiser was also listing five degrees to port, and the gun crews had expended all of the large bore ammunition. Two men were dead and several wounded. In the engine room, engineers and oilers worked to purge the contaminated fuel from the supply lines and switch over to the starboard fuel tanks, which were still not breached. McMorris considered ordering *Salt Lake City*'s crew to abandon ship, but that would leave *Richmond* open to the four Japanese cruisers.

The battle had raged for nearly four hours, and the Japanese had also made direct hits on the *Bailey* with their 8-inch (200-millimetre) guns as the American destroyer attempted to divert action from the stricken cruiser. It was now only a matter of delivering the coup de grâce to *Salt Lake City*, but the Japanese, believing American bombers from Adak were surely on their way, and having no air cover of their own, broke off the attack and retreated west.

It was a lost opportunity for Hosogaya. Despite the American navy's request for air support and the eagerness of Eareckson's crews to join the fight, the army bombers remained idle on the airfield at Adak as all their bombs were frozen to the ground.

Upon returning to Japan, Admiral Hosogaya was relieved of command for his poor assessment of the naval engagement and subsequent withdrawal from the battle. For the remainder of his career he was relegated to naval reserve. Admirals Kinkaid and McMorris claimed a victory for the Americans, and the Battle of the Komandorskis went down in history as the longest naval artillery duel in modern naval warfare and the last "big ship" duel of the Second World War.

17

The Battle
for Attu

At the Casablanca Conference in January 1943, British prime minister Winston Churchill and U.S. president Franklin D. Roosevelt approved plans to recapture the occupied Alaskan islands. As the main enemy base in the Aleutians, Kiska was originally the first target, which was probably the prospect anticipated by the Japanese. The Allies ultimately favoured retaking the smaller island of Attu first, however, for it would leave Kiska in the centre of a pincer movement and vulnerable to a greater concentration of forces. The earliest opportunity for an invasion was late spring, owing to treacherous seas in the long winter and incessant heavy fog in the short summer. The San Diego Conference in March set the date for the attack—code-named Operation Landcrab—as May 7.

General John DeWitt requested for the assault the 35th Infantry Division under Major General Charles H. Corlett and General Eugene Landrum, both of whom already had intimate experience in the Aleutians. He received instead the 7th Motorized Division, which had just completed desert warfare training in California and was destined for the war in North Africa. The unit was commanded by Major General Albert E. Brown, a career soldier who had gained combat experience in the trenches of France in the First World War. Buckner and DeWitt protested that a mechanized unit would prove useless in the Aleutians, where the muskeg and hilly terrain caused wheeled and tracked vehicles to bog down. Every piece of equipment and supplies moving to the front line would have to be packed in on the backs of men, they argued, and for that an infantry unit was the only viable option. The two generals were overruled, but found support from Admiral Kinkaid, who held

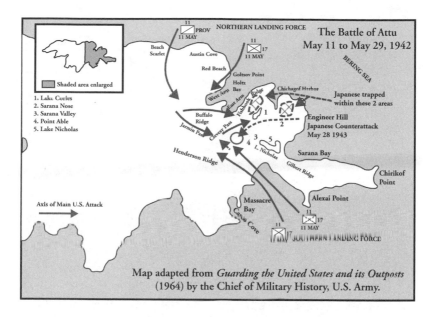

Map adapted from *Guarding the United States and its Outposts*
(1964) by the Chief of Military History, U.S. Army.

that if a desert unit was to be used, it should at least be commanded by someone with knowledge of the Aleutians. Their protests again came to nothing, and General Brown's command was affirmed. Though he did not bother to make so much as a cursory air tour of the battlefield, Brown was experienced enough to note that even unopposed, his soldiers needed at least a week to make it across the hilly terrain of Attu, when plans called for them to take the island in three days.

DeWitt's superiors did make a minor concession by assigning the 4th Infantry Regiment as reinforcement for the 7th Division. The 4th had been languishing at outposts throughout Alaska since the Americans entered the war, and Buckner felt obliged to use it in the re-occupation of the islands. To his chagrin, however, the 4th had no amphibious training, suffered poor morale due to its quarantine in Alaska, and was scattered far and wide around the territory, so had no time to train as a cohesive combat unit.

To safeguard the secrecy of the upcoming invasion, the soldiers of the 7th Division were led to believe they were headed for a battlefield in the tropics. After training in amphibious landing on the beaches of California, in conditions totally opposite to those of the Aleutians, they shipped out 10,000 strong from San Diego to what they thought was the Solomon Islands in the South Pacific. Loaded aboard were crates of gear marked "Australia." Two weeks later, following a cramped

General Simon Bolivar Buckner (second from left), commander of all Allied forces in Alaska.

trip in five transports up the stormy coast of the Pacific Northwest, they arrived at Cold Bay, Alaska.

On April 18, Japan suffered another in what was becoming a succession of devastating losses. Admiral Isoroku Yamamoto, the great naval strategist who planned Pearl Harbor and almost solely directed Japanese destiny in the Pacific, was assassinated while touring his South Pacific bases on a morale-building exercise. After American code-breakers determined his itinerary, P38s ambushed his plane and sent it down in flames into the jungle of Rabul. Speculation about the reason for the assassination ranges from a desire to avenge Pearl Harbor to a wish to strike a blow at Japanese morale given their fanatic worship of military heroes. In any case, all of the American fighter pilots involved in the ambush were quickly removed from the South Pacific theatre and reassigned to separate squadrons in Europe.[1]

News of the admiral's death was a particularly serious blow to the morale of Japanese troops on Attu. All contact with the homeland, apart from radio, was gone, while food, medical goods, and even such basics as kindling were in very short supply. The Americans also stepped up their harassment of the island as the day of invasion approached. In one week alone, 90,000 kilograms of bombs fell on the tiny outpost, although most failed to do any damage other than rattle the enemy, and the weather often forced the planes to dump their load onto the now secondary target of Kiska. This increased activity helped confirm the Japanese belief that Kiska was the primary Allied objective.

In March, American code-breakers intercepted the first communications from TO and agent Kobbe out of Vancouver to Argentina, where they were relayed to submarines off South America and eventually to Japan. The intercepted messages told of a convoy of American transports loaded with troops heading for Alaska, which was consistent with the route of the U.S. 7th Division up the Pacific Northwest coast at the time.

The western press was also taking note of the Aleutians war when only days before the average person would have been hard pressed to find the Alaskan islands on a map. In early May, American radio broadcaster Walter Winchell closed one of his nightly broadcasts with "Keep your eyes on the Aleutians!"[2] By now there was no doubt the Japanese were well aware of U.S. plans for an invasion in the Aleutians, and the Americans, sensing the threat to the operation, requested even tighter surveillance on Kobbe. A Mountie managed to infiltrate Kobbe's residence by striking up a relationship with his daughter Beatriz. For now a tight check could be kept on the enemy agent, and the RCMP could also gather evidence to expose the Spanish foreign ministry, which the Allies knew to be a hotbed of Axis spy activity but were unable to prove.

The focus of all this frenzied activity, Attu was little more than a barren heap of moss-covered rock, standing alone at the western extremity of Alaska's Aleutian chain. Only 30 kilometres at its widest point and 64 kilometres long, it reaches 914 metres above sea level at its highest volcanic peaks. Colonel Yasuyo Yamasaki, who had arrived on Attu in April by submarine, faced the impossible task of holding this lonely outpost at all costs with fewer than 2,000 troops and no hope of reinforcements until late May. His best defence lay in commanding the steep ridges above Holtz and Massacre valleys, 2,700 to 3,600 metres inland at the head of the bays. By moving his men, mobile guns, mortars, and machine guns from the two main defence sectors at Holtz Bay and Chichagof to the high ground, he planned to force the invaders to make their way up the valleys to reach the Japanese encampments.

While Japanese troops in the jungles of Asia and the South Pacific had dense foliage and tropical growth to use as camouflage, the Alaskan tundra afforded no such protection. Instead, Yamasaki had his men dot the terrain with foxholes and dig two-man mortar and machine-gun posts into the muskeg, from which the Japanese weapons, although not highly accurate, would give off no flash to betray their position. A few well-hidden men in posts displaced throughout the terrain could pin down superior numbers of men—a tactic successfully employed by Vietcong guerrillas two decades later in Vietnam. Possibly Yamasaki hoped his soldiers could fight a delaying action long enough for promised reinforcements to arrive from Japan or Kiska.

At Cold Bay, the men of the 7th Division were sequestered in the convoy ships that had brought them to Alaska since there was simply no room to house them on land. The desert army had no opportunity to train on Aleutian beaches for amphibious landings, and it lacked proper cold-weather gear as all available stocks were consigned to Europe. Many of the men were of Hispanic or aboriginal origin from America's Southwest and had not even seen snow before. Now, with neither proper training or equipment, they were to go into battle against a Japanese army well accustomed to the deprivations of the Aleutians.

By late April 1943, the American invasion force had moved west into the islands and dispersed at bases along the Aleutian chain, spread out over hundreds of kilometres as there was no one place large enough to accommodate the influx of troops. The force comprised members of the Alaska Scouts, three infantry divisions—the 7th, 17th, and 32nd, with the 4th Infantry Regiment held in reserve—four artillery battalions, an engineering battalion, and supporting units of medical and service personnel. The ground troops totalled almost 20,000—surely adequate to dislodge 1,600 starving Japanese.

Naval support consisted of the battleships *Nevada* and *Pennsylvania*, salvaged from the carnage of Pearl Harbor, battleship *Idaho*, and an escort force of six cruisers, nineteen destroyers, and an aircraft carrier. Together with McMorris's blockade fleet of three cruisers and six destroyers, as well as a phalanx of army and navy aircraft, they steamed west on May 4 to Attu.

At 0100 on the 11th, in heavy fog and with the temperature standing at -12° Celsius, 244 scouts of two combat units disembarked from the submarines *Narwhal* and *Nautilus* and paddled for Austin Cove on Attu's northeast shore. There the two units split into two platoons each and filed out towards the mountains that separated them from Holtz and Massacre bays, where the main assault forces would land. In their packs were only enough rations for 36 hours.

The rest of the day the scouts followed a creek up the sharp slope of the first range that peaked over Holtz Valley. By nightfall, two groups had made it to the mountaintop, where they bivouacked in the fog, though subzero temperatures and a heavy covering of snow made for a shivering, sleepless night. At 0400 the two groups began their descent into the valley, out of sight of each other and maintaining communication using runners only so as not to alert the enemy to their presence. As they slid down the snow-covered slopes, laughing at the absurdity of it all like schoolboys given a day off because of a heavy snowfall, Japanese snipers opened with sporadic machine-gun and artillery fire. Shooting back as they went, the four platoons continued their advance into the canyon, but were pinned solidly down by late afternoon. Whenever a scout showed his head he drew a burst of machine-gun fire, while the Japanese moved freely about to support the batteries or edged closer to the Americans.

At 1800 on May 12, the scouts of the 7th brought up their 81-millimetre mortar and sent the advancing Japanese scurrying like ants into the protective wall of the valley. From positions on the hill and to the right, however, the enemy gunners kept the scouts hunkered down throughout the night and into the next day. A supply plane droned overhead in the fog, then turned away, unable to spot the scout groups, which had by now nearly depleted their rations. In the late afternoon, scouts of the 7th Cavalry Reconnaissance had made their way into the canyon to join the advance party, and by nightfall, using their combined strength, they managed to drive the enemy back temporarily. The Japanese quickly regrouped, now bolstered by reinforcements who had moved up the valley from the west arm of Holtz Bay, and again tied the Americans down with machine-gun fire.

The scouts burrowed into the snow to shelter their wounded and made tiny fires of ration wrappers in an attempt to warm frozen fingers. Even the unconscious shivered in the damp cold of the fog that swirled around them like ghosts. Through the darkness, between bursts of machine-gun fire that bounced off the canyon walls above, they could hear insults hurled in broken English: "Damn American dogs, we kill you…we massacre you."

Well into the afternoon of May 12, the main Attu invasion force still bobbed around off the island's east shore. William Jones, an army private heading for the landing beach, recognized the first sign of trouble when the landing craft were unable to find the shore because of the dense fog. Finally, a radar-equipped craft picking its way towards the island announced that the beach was 450 metres ahead. The other

American troops head for Attu's shore on May 10, 1942. It was expected the island would fall in just three days, but the Japanese held out for nineteen days in one of the bloodiest battles of the Pacific war and the only land battle fought on North American soil.

craft followed to undertake the American army's first ever amphibious invasion. With one assault force landing at Red Beach, just north of Holtz Bay, and another at Massacre Bay thirteen kilometres south, separated by mountainous terrain, the plan was to trap the main Japanese force in a pincer movement on the peninsula at Chichagof. In a tactic that became typical of the Japanese throughout the Pacific campaigns, the landings were unopposed to draw the invaders inland, where they would face a well-entrenched Japanese force.

Leading the main landing force at Massacre Bay, Company F under Lieutenant Charles Paulson had one section of light machine guns and 60-millimetre mortar. Once on the beach the company headed north into the mountains at the head of the bay, across the peculiar terrain of the Aleutians for which they had not been trained. Between the rocky shore and the incline of the mountains lay a few thousand metres of spongy tundra covered in deep snow. The men sank to their hips with their first steps. Had the Japanese set up machine-gun nests to take advantage of this obstacle, many GIs would have been stopped cold as they struggled through the muskeg.

The volcanic slopes rising from Massacre Bay's shores were so steep in places that the invaders had to use ropes to haul their weapons up. The first platoon had not landed until about four in the afternoon and spent the night travelling north over the first range of hills. When morning came the men could see the Japanese scattered around a small lake on the other side of the valley. The Japanese also saw them and opened fire with sporadic bursts of their machine guns, but were too far away to inflict any casualties. The platoon worked its way along a mountain ridge and into the valley heading towards Clevesy Pass before hunkering down for the night. Two patrols of Alaska Scouts returned to report enemy soldiers ahead in Clevesy Pass and at Sarana Nose—a promontory at the head of Lake Cories across the valley.

By daybreak the Japanese had formed a big horseshoe in front of the Americans and had circled behind them, closing off the route by which they had entered the valley. In an exchange of fire, Sergeant Alonzo Atkinson was badly wounded while trying to help cover his platoon's advance. A couple of men dragged him away and left him with the medic in a small rock enclave until a party could evacuate them.

As the Americans worked their way up Clevesy Pass, several Japanese set up a light machine gun at the bottom of the hill and opened fire. Dropping next to a large rock, Sergeant Leland Larson managed to pick off three of them as they tried to re-man the machine gun, and his own group made the top of the hill. From here they saw about 300 Japanese at Sarana Nose digging in and moving artillery pieces. Many of the American company were now sick from hunger and exhaustion. They had not slept since landing at Massacre Bay two days before, rations were nearly depleted, and neither their radio nor walkie-talkie worked, leaving them completely out of touch with the other landing parties. When the platoon separated to take up defensive positions on either side of Sarana Nose, one group became hopelessly lost in the fog and tried to retrace its route back to Massacre Bay. In the morning a shadowy figure appeared in the fog ahead of the lost group. When challenged, it crouched down while firing several shots. A grenade blasted the figure, sending it tumbling down the slope.

The first squad had by now made it up the north slope of the valley and over the ridge, where the men spent the night in a terrific wind that whipped them with snow and ice. In the morning they stumbled on an observation post dug well into the mountainside and manned by a handful of Japanese. The ensuing firefight compelled the Japanese to leave the cover of their post to get a good sight of the enemy, bringing the two sides within fourteen metres of each other. The Americans drove the Japanese back to the shelter of a ridge, where they huddled under a large outcrop of rock until a well-placed grenade killed the group.

Having made its way out of the valley, the lost squad appeared on the hillside, where it was fired upon by American beach gunners. Because they had lost radio contact, they did not know the colour code of the day and failed to display the orange cards identifying them as friendly troops. A corporal eventually made his way down to the beach, and his freezing comrades were brought down by the beach party, weak from hunger and shaken from the rattling by American gunners. A rescue party sent to find Sergeant Atkinson and the medic who had stayed with him arrived too late. Their bullet-riddled bodies had been dragged into the snow, which all around still bore the unmistakable prints of the enemy's hobnailed boots.

The northern landing point, Red Beach, was a small cove with less than 100 metres of smooth terrain, impeding progress considerably. Just around its southern corner, Holtz Bay offered a much larger beach, but the Japanese guns at Chichagof overlooked it. In the hope of securing Holtz Bay and conducting the northern landings from there, the battleship *Nevada* pounded the area with 14-inch (355-millimetre) projectiles, but to little effect. F-4F Wildcats from the carrier *Nassau* then strafed the area and scattered the Japanese gunners, but the gunners soon returned to continue their harassment. Army bombers from Amchitka settled the matter when they roared in and saturated the enemy with 100-pound (45-kilogram) bombs, allowing 4,000 American troops to land on Attu by the end of the first day on May 12. Four 105-millimetre Howitzers became bogged down less than 100 metres up the beach at Holtz Bay when the tracked cats towing them were unable to make any headway in the mushy tundra, but sheer brawn eventually got them trained on enemy mortar positions on a ridge overlooking the Holtz area.

Three days after the main landings on Attu, the Americans had still not made a dent in the enemy's defences. Upon landing at Massacre Bay, the 2nd Battalion of the 32nd Infantry was ordered to proceed inland and take an enemy strongpoint in Jarmin Pass, where the Japanese were keeping the American advance pinned down with light machine guns and mortars. Moving into the pass at 0630 on May 14, the battalion suddenly came under withering fire from behind after the Japanese let them proceed so far, then opened up. Wildcat fighters from the *Nassau* again swooped over the enemy positions, but three of them ploughed into the canyon wall. At day's end the Japanese still controlled Jarmin Pass.

The army's inability to supply GIs with proper cold-weather gear severely hampered the American effort, with casualties due to frostbite and exposure outnumbering those inflicted by the enemy ten to one. Water soaked through leather boots and froze the soldiers' feet, making walking impossible. William Jones recalled American troops were issued leather boots, which soaked up water, rather than rubber boots. "A lot of men developed frost-bite and had to have their feet or legs amputated."[3] One man remained standing up when he slipped into unconsciousness due to the cold. His compatriots were unable to rouse him and he died in the night. In an attempt to stay warm, Americans stripped winter boots, hats, and coats off the dead enemy and donned the gear, which caused confusion when the shooting started. In the unrelenting fog, supply planes found it impossible to spot landmarks on the ground and scattered supplies to no one's use around the mountain ranges.

While plans called for Attu to be taken in three days, the Japanese had not given up a centimetre of ground after day five. The three passes at Clevesy, Jarmin, and Holtz-Chichagof Valley, as well as the approaches leading to the Chichagof Peninsula, were still firmly in Japanese control, while the northern (Holtz Bay) and southern (Massacre Bay) American forces had not even linked up. The southern force made another bold frontal assault on Jarmin Pass, but was again forced to withdraw after coming under intense fire from three directions. The northern force, moving into the mountains lining Holtz Valley, found it exhausting, numbing work as the hills beyond the beach gave way to a steep incline covered in heavy snow. Japanese gunners in a camp at the top of a hill commanded a panoramic view of Holtz Bay and the valley behind. They were able to pin down the Americans filing into the hills. The American advance stopped due to the enemy resistance, and men and equipment backed up all the way to the beach because of the stalemate up in the hills.

For two and a half hours the battleships *Pennsylvania* and *Nevada* pounded the hill from more than thirteen kilometres away with all their heavy projectiles, but to no avail, while a frontal assault left 56 Americans dead after two days. A break in the impasse finally occurred when an observer crept unseen to within sight of the Japanese camp and directed the 14-inch (355-millimetre) guns from battleship *Idaho*, which tore the encampment apart. The Americans in the north were now able to advance east into the valley for the first time since the landing. The wily Japanese fell back towards Chichagof, however, to take up positions on each succeeding ridge and begin the stand-off all over again.

Private William Jones, who had been made squadron leader because so many soldiers were dying, gave his first order, directing a 38-year-old father of seven to advance while other squad members covered him. The man took a bullet and later died in Jones's arms. That same day Jones received terrible news—the soldier who was killed was to have been immediately sent home due to his age and family stature.[4]

For C Company—one of the scout battalions of the 7th Division—which had landed in the wee hours of May 11 and been pinned down for nearly five days, relief could come none too soon. Rations had run out four days before, and frustrated aircrews were unable to resupply them in the thick fog. A lack of wood ruled out building a fire, which would have drawn enemy attention in any event. Eleven scouts had been killed in the fighting, and 90 percent suffered from exposure. During the night of May 15 the enemy cleared out of the canyon, not wanting to be caught or divided by Americans now advancing down from Holtz. In their haste to withdraw towards Chichagof, the Japanese in the north left behind ammunition, guns, and their dead strewn about the command post. Limping out of the canyon, the 7th scout patrol killed three Japanese snipers and made its way to Holtz Bay.

Under pressure in Tokyo to relieve the beleaguered Japanese garrison, Admiral Shiro Kawase finally agreed to send a force of three cruisers to Attu. After leaving Paramushiro, however, the ships were recalled following reports from scout planes of the size of the American navy force standing off Attu. A couple of I-boats managed to penetrate the fleet and attack the *Pennsylvania* and a troop transport, but without success. Another submarine, *I-31*, got within range of the battleship *Nevada* and fired a spread of five torpedoes, which also missed before U.S. destroyers sank it with depth charges.

General Brown's original assumption regarding the difficulties in taking Attu were proving correct, and he requested that the 4th Infantry Regiment Buckner was holding on Adak be dispatched to Attu. Buckner and DeWitt, however, added to Brown's tactical obstacles by playing backroom politics. They continued to view him with disfavour as an "outsider" and, although they more than anyone knew the difficulties involved, insisted that the island should have been taken in three days as originally planned. They refused to accept the magnitude of Japanese resistance encountered by Brown. Even though Brown's troops were making headway—despite lack of training in the Arctic, a dearth of proper equipment, and spotty support from the air corps and navy—DeWitt's negative opinion of the general was fuelled by confusion between army and navy assessments of the situation. Ultimately, DeWitt ordered the 4th Regiment in, but not before relieving Brown of his command and replacing him with DeWitt's original choice, General Eugene Landrum.

All supplies to the front lines on Attu had to be packed in, sourdough style, on the backs of men, 25 kilograms at a time. Eventually road-building equipment brought in to plough up a creek relieved the large numbers of men from serving as pack animals for a portion of the trek to the front. The transfer of men and equipment to and from the support ships slowed to a trickle, however, as only three of the 93 original landing craft were still in operation. Most had come to grief on Attu's treacherous approaches. Some that swamped went straight to the bottom, drowning their load of troops or wounded.

As the Japanese withdrew in the north, B company of the 17th Infantry followed them across Holtz Valley and up to a ridge at Davis Hill, where the enemy had now concentrated. In gritty hand-to-hand fighting, the company took many casualties before driving the Japanese off the ridge. As the drifting fog cleared, marauding navy fighters from the *Nassau* flew over, strafing their own men—unaware the hill had just changed hands.

The northern force continued its push on May 17, attacking a ridge just east of Holtz Bay towards the Chichagof Peninsula. By now more than 12,500 American troops were on Attu, while the Japanese numbered fewer than 1,600. The ridge fell into American hands shortly before midnight, squeezing the Japanese farther into the Chichagof. Unbeknown to the Americans, the enemy had already abandoned Jarmin Pass, which had earlier proven impenetrable. On guard against ambush in the silent, fog-shrouded confines bordered by towering hills on either side, the southern force soon encountered machine-gun posts littered with dead enemy soldiers and signs of a hasty retreat. On May 18, patrols from the northern and southern forces linked up at the pass, closing an arc and turning eastward to push the Japanese onto the Chichagof Peninsula with their backs against the sea.

Still the enemy forced the Americans to fight for every centimetre of ground. In orderly withdrawals, they fell back to well-defended positions that commanded the high ground. Clevesy Pass, a high natural promontory on Point Able at the east end of Gilbert Ridge and the last route into the Chichagof, remained firmly in their hands. It housed heavy machine-gun and mortar power, while Cold Mountain, equally heavily defended on the left flank, had a crest so narrow that troops would practically have to attack in single file.

The Americans planned to launch a co-ordinated assault on both flanks of the pass in the early morning of May 19. At 0430, the 17th Infantry's I Company clawed its way up to the crest of Cold Mountain, where the barren slopes offered little to conceal the advancing soldiers. They opened the attack by lobbing grenades into the enemy camp, but these rolled harmlessly down the steep slope and only served to alert the Japanese, who counterattacked with bayonets. American machine gunners mowed down the charge, which included one officer brandishing his Boshido sword, but Japanese machine guns managed to drive the attackers downhill and inflicted many casualties. Across the valley, the distant sounds of gunfire and shrieks of men signalled that the attack on Point Able had also begun.

Rising 610 metres above sea level, the geography of Point Able was similar to the narrow crest of Cold Mountain. As one American soldier described it, "The whole damn deal was rugged, like attacking a pillbox by way of a tightrope ... in winter."[5] The first assault troops made it to within 600 metres of the stronghold under the cover of thick fog before it suddenly lifted, leaving the Americans exposed. Enemy machine guns drove them back with heavy losses. Company C of the 32nd Infantry attempted a second assault in the evening, climbing up to Gilbert Ridge from a point near the beach at Massacre Valley. Patrols moved in from three sides, with one advancing directly down the centre of the ridge. Coming up the hill, one of the flanking patrols was within 40 metres of the enemy post when the fog again lifted. The Japanese kept it pinned to the ground, oblivious of the other patrol coming up the centre, which in turn opened up on the Japanese. As heavy gunfire and screaming echoed through the pass, the fog rolled in. In the confusion, the first patrol withdrew to hold a line 230 metres from the enemy camp.

Company E, the third patrol, continued its nail-clinging advance along the west side of Clevesy Pass and could hear the fighting overhead. The men were also nearly at their target site when the fog lifted, and they too found themselves face to face with Japanese soldiers. Both sides exchanged gunfire and dropped for cover, where E Company became pinned down, spending the night shivering behind each little rock, unable to move and generate warmth for fear of drawing enemy fire. After a terrific mortar barrage followed by a machine-gun assault, Point Able finally fell to the Americans on May 20. In the infamous Japanese fighting spirit, every Imperial soldier died defending this frigid outpost. Not one enemy soldier survived Point Able.

American engineering and construction battalions made continual inroads into the island's hostile topography. Creekbeds were forged into roads, allowing soldiers to move artillery guns to strategic points and supplies to the front lines. The wounded could be more easily evacuated from a series of clearing stations, taking a further burden off the foot soldier. On Engineer Hill, artillery guns were hauled up and concentrated on the enemy at Sarana Nose, three kilometres east, where the Japanese had formed a defensive line. The lack of vegetation often made it impossible to approach the enemy, leaving the alternative of hitting them with artillery. In one case where gunnery observers did manage a close-up look, they noted five enemy soldiers walking along a ridge and radioed the gun crews. Shells soon exploded on the unsuspecting Japanese, leaving piles of smoking fabric where the men had stood seconds earlier.

Under cover of artillery, Buckner's 4th Infantry Regiment advanced up Sarana Nose, duelling with enemy snipers before the Japanese abandoned their position on the night of May 22 to fall farther back

A U.S. artillery crew fires on a Japanese position.

onto the Chichagof Peninsula. American gunners on the beach at Holtz Bay had been lobbing shells at the Chichagof unceasingly. There Colonel Yamasaki still believed his garrison would be rescued by submarines, unaware that U.S. destroyers had driven them and any chance of evacuation away.

To afford some relief to Yamasaki's beleaguered men, a squadron of sixteen twin-engine Mitsubishi Betty bombers launched an airstrike from Paramushiro against the invader's gun positions. American radar picked up the enemy planes heading towards Attu, and six P-38 Lightnings scrambled into the air from Amchitka Island. When their radios inexplicably changed to Japanese frequency, American gun crews on Attu were unaware of the signal's origin and listened to the conversation among the enemy bombers as they closed in. When the P38s thundered over their position, the men on the ground realized what was up, while the enemy apparently did not and calmly continued chattering over the radio. Suddenly the voices became excited and erratic, then stopped altogether, one after the other. Seven enemy bombers eventually made it back to Paramushiro, jettisoning their bombs harmlessly around Attu to evade the pursuers. Two P-38s were lost on the mission.

After a one-day respite, the northern and southern forces attacked enemy positions on, respectively, the west and east faces of Chichagof Valley on May 23. Simultaneously, the army's air corps demolished the Japanese camp at Chichagof Harbor, then swung back and accidentally bombed its own troops of the 2nd Battalion, which were preparing to attack Fish Hook Ridge to the north of the valley. Fish Hook Ridge fell on May 27, followed by Buffalo Ridge to the west of the valley after three days of hard fighting. By now the Americans had poured 16,000 soldiers onto Attu, while Yamasaki was down to

800 able bodies and 600 wounded, his back to the sea and facing the enemy on three sides.

His command reduced to a circle of peaks overlooking what remained of the main camp, Yamasaki received word from home that there would be no evacuation from Attu and to expect no relief until perhaps early July. His men had totally depleted their food caches several days earlier and no longer had enough firearms or ammunition to sustain them. Leaflets dropped by American bombers on May 27 called for their surrender, but for Yamasaki, a loyal soldier of the Emperor's Imperial army, this was out of the question. He would fight on to the death if necessary, depending on another option with a slim chance of success. His plan was to concentrate all of his troops and mount frontal banzai night attacks at the enemy line, capturing weapons, supplies, and food. His force would then keep moving and regroup in the mountains to the southwest, buying Admiral Kawase time to send reinforcements. He hoped the Americans, faced with Japanese determination to keep Attu, would withdraw from the island. As the sun dipped over Siberia to the west, Yamasaki sent a final message home: "Most of our positions on the front line have been captured by the enemy and today we are barely able to hold the remaining positions. The remaining force will attack the enemy and will display the true glory of the Imperial army in carrying out the final attack." Then he ordered all wireless sets and codes books destroyed, so never received the return message from home: "We received reports of your resolute determination and fine morale and are filled with deep gratitude. We wish you calm sleep as the pillar of our northern defence."[6]

Yamasaki gathered all the wounded who were too incapacitated to walk or fight into bomb craters and administered the last of the morphine while a Shinto blessing and praise to the Emperor was said over them. Hand grenades were then tossed amongst them to spare the wounded the disgrace of capture. Armed with bayonets tied to broom handles, sharpened poles, swords, and what little ammunition remained, Yamasaki's battered army then moved off in the early morning of May 28 under the cover of darkness and the ever-present swirling Aleutian fog.

Stealthily they moved up the Chichagof Valley to the southeast shore of Lake Cories, where B Company of the 32nd Infantry had set out to establish a line across the valley. Yamasaki's men caught the enemy completely off guard as they threw themselves into the American line. Fighting fanatically, the Japanese seemed everywhere at once around the small group, shooting and thrusting their bayonets against a

A row of dead Japanese soldiers following the battle for Attu. Many died in frenzied banzai charges or by their own hand after placing a grenade to the temple.

backdrop of fog turned an eerie red by bursting flares and tracer streaks. The Americans were scattered and disorganized in the confusion of flashes and noise, darkness and fog, scampering black shadows, screaming, and death.

A few led by a company captain managed to withdraw back to the command post of the 3rd Battalion, 17th Infantry, while others straggled in, wounded and in shock. The news they brought of a Japanese counterattack was almost unbelievable. As the chief of the command post gave the order to clear out and fall back, rifle shots and the shouts of men erupted. A soldier apparently roused from his sleep, coatless and barefoot, charged into the tent yelling, "The Japs are here! They've broken through!" No sooner had he said this than the enemy burst in, led by an officer slashing a sword as his men thrust bayonets and discharged carbines at the surprised group. The Americans scrambled over each other as they tried to get away, erratically firing side arms at the intruders.[7]

A small group of men that had been ambushed in the valley made it back to the command post only to find it overrun. They made for Engineer Hill, an American strongpoint a few kilometres west of the front line. At a medical evacuation station across from Engineer Hill, men were awakened by the sound of gunshots ringing through the valley. Grenades exploded outside their tents as a screaming mob of Japanese soldiers came streaming over a dirt embankment. The enemy ripped through the tents and overwhelmed the hapless men, all the time screaming, with a

A Shinto prayer card found among the Japanese dead on Attu.

few words of English thrown in to demand grenades and cigarettes. A few men found cover in a nearby hole and watched the enemy tear up their camp, unable to move for fear of enemy voices in every direction. A force of American soldiers from across the valley arrived in pursuit of the enemy, and the Japanese retreated in a hail of bullets, leaving several dead and wounded in their wake.

At the base of Engineer Hill, a large army tent had been set up as a medical clearing station where the wounded lay in cots while medics provided first aid. Stabilized casualties were to be moved to the evacuation stations, like the one that had just been overrun, and then to hospital facilities on board one of the ships off Attu. There was talk at the station of a Japanese counterattack that had breached the American line, but rumours abounded with the wounded who passed through daily. The medical crew was therefore not overly concerned by the latest reports, in spite of the sound of shots coming up the valley in the early morning. In their eyes, the battle for Attu had wound down to flushing out isolated groups of Japanese holdouts, so those medics not on watch bedded down for the night.

At a little past 0400, the relative calm of the tent was broken when the company quartermaster burst into the tent yelling, "The Japs are coming!" One man already on his feet was felled in a hail of machine-gun tracers that ripped through the fabric and tore into the portable oil stove with a clang. Outside, the Japanese descended upon stacks of rifles and ammo belts belonging to the wounded with wild cheers, and their foreign chatter filtered clearly into the tent. Encroaching dawn cast their silhouettes on the canvas walls, and occasionally one of them would knock the fabric inward as they jockeyed for a weapon. In frantic whispers, the patients begged the able-bodied not to leave them behind.

The Americans held their breath, waiting for one of the Japanese milling around outside to come through the flaps. One pulled back the canvas door but withdrew in disgust at the sight of a dead patient's shattered head. Then another came in looking for food. The Americans played dead as he stood among them, and an officer was about to shoot him when he was unwittingly saved by a voice calling him back outside. When some of the wounded started moaning in pain, a sergeant crawled around the tent floor to give them morphine, but in their drug-induced sleep they began to snore and had to be repeatedly shaken awake. Miraculously, the Japanese still did not know any of them were alive, although medical officer Captain G.S. Buehler, peering through a bullet hole in the canvas, caught one of the enemy soldiers glaring ominously at the tent with a grenade raised above his head. The soldier armed the device by tapping it twice on the side of his helmet, but fate intervened on the side of the Americans when an officer told him to put it away. Barely daring to breathe, the men trapped inside remained still throughout the whole day and into the next morning— their fate resting on the few steps it would take the Japanese to venture inside for a serious look.

Most of the Japanese left the medical station to push their way up Engineer Hill, where the Americans had positioned artillery, a mobile canteen, and a supply depot. Early in the morning the men atop the hill ambled through the cold towards the chow lines, refreshed by their first sound sleep after days of intense activity in which the constant movement of troops had afforded little rest. With the front lines a kilometre away, and believing the enemy completely cornered, those on kitchen duty rarely carried weapons, so were virtually defenceless when the Japanese came crashing through the mess tents. Some of the marauders headed straight for the food, but were killed when a grenade went off amid the confusion, felled by their own hunger.

With the enemy at their heels, some of the Americans scattered up the hill to a camp at the summit manned by two support battalions— the 50th Engineering Battalion and the 7th Medical Battalion. Soldiers in these units were startled awake as their comrades fled into the camp with the Japanese in dogged pursuit. General Archibald Arnold and Colonel James Bush immediately formed the disorganized, frantic camp into a defensive line against which the enemy charged headlong. Fierce American resistance forced the Japanese back down the hill, but throughout the day they mounted successive attacks in ever-dwindling numbers. American groups that had been scattered by the initial surprise attacks regrouped into small pockets of resistance to hit back at the enemy, while the battalions on Engineer Hill had now become used to the screaming, mad rushes of the Japanese and were no longer intimidated by them. At the kitchen site that had been previously overrun, an intense gunfight broke out in which 47 Japanese were killed.

Finally, as the realization of defeat with no hope of rescue dawned on the tattered remnants of the Attu garrison, most committed suicide by putting grenades to their temples. Yamasaki had died earlier that day, sword in hand, as he led one of the banzai charges up Engineer Hill.

The men trapped inside the tent at the medical clearing station had lain motionless for over 30 hours while the enemy held its post outside. The sounds of gunfire drew ever nearer into the afternoon, and when it was almost right on top of them, the few remaining Japanese abandoned the camp and pulled back across the valley. The surviving Americans burst into a chorus of yelling as soldiers from their own side approached, preparing to lob grenades into the tent that had been their sanctuary.

The battle for Attu officially ended after nineteen days of brutal fighting when the Americans moved into Chichagof on May 30, although small pockets of Japanese resistance remained to be mopped up well into June. Where the enemy had holed up in caves or foxholes and refused to surrender, the Americans would simply toss in a few grenades, wait, and then toss in a few more. Several large groups of men had simultaneously taken their own lives by huddling around a grenade and detonating it, while many lone Japanese died by their own hand in a modern ritual of *hari kari* by holding an armed grenade to the temple. The invading Allies were to see this form of suicide many times in the South Pacific campaigns. Of the original 2,800 Japanese on Attu, only 26 were taken prisoner.

The Japanese dead were originally buried on Attu, but were later disinterred, cremated, and the remains re-interred at the Fort Richardson cemetery in Anchorage. The Americans lost 549 in the battle, and casualties were buried at Little Falls Cemetery on Attu, the most westerly and probably the loneliest cemetery in the United States.

Little Falls Cemetery, where the 549 Americans killed on Attu are buried.

Canadian war graves from the Aleutians campaign at Fort Richardson Military Cemetery in Anchorage, Alaska.

West to the Enemy

18

The beginning of 1943 saw further Canadian involvement in a front-line role in Alaska. The 111th Squadron, operating in Alaska since the previous June, had taken part in the first fighter-escorted bombing raid on Kiska in September 1942 and now provided fighter support for the U.S. Navy from Umnak and the Chiniak Point airfield on Kodiak Island. Still, its fliers were anxious to escape this tedious routine and get into combat.

General Buckner requested Air Vice-Marshall Stevenson to replace the tired old Bolingbrokes of 8th Squadron with another fighter squadron in the Aleutians. Western Air Command quickly acquiesced, sending the 14th Fighter Squadron from B.C., but again Stevenson had to push General Buckner for a more active Canadian role. Buckner was happy to oblige, especially after his own requests for another squadron from Washington were repeatedly denied.

When Canada declared war on Germany in 1939, many Americans made their way north to join the RCAF or RAF with the intention of returning to the United States once it entered the hostilities. By agreement, American airmen trained in Canada could stay with the RCAF. If they chose to return to the U.S., their homeland would reimburse Canada about $50,000 per man for the cost of their training—no paltry sum in those years. One allowance made to the Americans exempted them from swearing allegiance to the king, which would have resulted in loss of their U.S. citizenship. At its peak, American enrolment in the RCAF accounted for about a third of the pilot trainees prior to American entry into the war.

Among them was Forest "Frosty" Young, who had left his home in Huntingdon, West Virginia, with five friends and enrolled in the British

Commonwealth Air Training Program in September 1941. Upon receiving his wings, he flew Hurricanes with the 133rd Squadron in Lethbridge, Alberta, and then moved with the unit when it was transferred to Boundary Bay in Delta, British Columbia. Frosty and two friends, fellow American George Miller and Manitoba native George Costello, volunteered for RCAF overseas service in February 1942 when the United States ordered him to report to Alabama for duty. Young, who received the same pay as Canadian officers and who, like many of his countrymen, had close ties in the RCAF, decided against going back home to enlist. Of the five friends with whom he had originally journeyed north to join the RCAF, only one left for the American air corps.

Young, Costello, and Miller all got their wish to see overseas service—after a fashion. They were transferred to another Vancouver unit, the 14th Fighter Squadron based at Sea Island in Richmond, B.C., which had been selected to go "overseas" to Alaska to replace the 8th Squadron. They began the long trek north in mid-February 1943. At Port Hardy the flight was grounded for four days, some of the planes putting down at the remote Kwakuitl village of Alert Bay, which had a rough landing strip courtesy of the air force, and for nine more days at Annette Island. Bypassing Yakutat because of fog, the squadron was forced to land at an emergency strip 130 kilometres away in Yakutaga. Four more days were lost ferrying fuel from Yakutat to Yakutaga, and bad weather continued to dog the flight from Anchorage to Cold Bay. The fifteen Kittyhawks of 14th Squadron finally assembled at Umnak on March 18, a month after leaving Vancouver. In retrospect, ferrying the planes from the West Coast to the East Coast of Canada would have been a shorter and simpler feat.

The RCAF had established its own satellite airstrip on Umnak at Berry Field, a few kilometres from Fort Glenn. There Young, Miller, Costello, and other new pilots were acquainted with the idiosyncrasies of Aleutian flying. Their P40s had a range of only about 2,000 kilometres with the addition of belly tanks and a top speed of 550 kilometres per hour at 4,500 metres, compared to the highly versatile twin-engined P38 Lightning, which made its wartime debut in the Alaskan campaign. The Lightning had a range of 4,200 kilometres, so it could easily make the round trip between Amchitka and Attu without belly tanks while carrying more firepower. The P40s were therefore relegated strictly to missions against Kiska, only a short hop from Amchitka. The Kittyhawk wasn't fancy—veteran pilot Louis Cochand of St. Marguerite, Quebec, recalls that it was like flying a chunk of lead.[1] Because of the P40's

Members of the 14th Fighter Squadron at Umnak, Aleutian Islands, Alaska, in 1943. The 14th and 111th RCAF squadrons rotated between anti-submarine duty / convoy escort from Kodiak and front-line combat duty at Amchitka.

Pilots of the Royal Canadian Air Force 14th Fighter (Kittyhawk) Squadron prepare for a sortie against Japanese-held Kiska in the Aleutians. Some RCAF pilots had flown in USAAF formations against the enemy-held island in Alaska.

A Kittyhawk of the RCAF 14th Fighter Squadron on Umnak.

attributes, or rather the lack of them, both American and Canadian models were configured to carry a 500-pound (225-kilogram) bomb strapped to the underbelly and assumed a role as dive bomber. This modification brought its own unique problems as Arthur Fanning, a Canadian P40 pilot who flew combat over Kiska, recounts. Upon sighting the target, the routine for a P40 pilot was to bring his plane into a steep bank at 4,000 metres and at 460 metres reef back on the elevator stick to release the bomb. The sudden release of the 500-pound payload and the haul back on the stick would send the plane hurtling skyward with enough G-force to render the pilot momentarily unconscious. Fanning explains, "You would come to, spinning wildly upward with no idea where you were before the plane was brought under control. That was the routine."[2]

Wing Commander Robert Morrow, who had replaced McGregor at X-Wing, devised a system to rotate twelve RCAF fliers from the two Canadian squadrons with an equal number of American fliers from one of the front-line P40 units. As the USAAF was now flying newer and updated P40s with six 50-calibre machine guns, the Canadians would initially fly the American planes with U.S. Army Air Force markings to blend into the 11th and 18th Warhawk pursuit squadrons. The Canadian 14th Squadron drew the first stint to the front, and on March 31, twelve of its pilots flew forward to Adak to join their U.S. counterparts. Typically, high winds blew the anemometer apart after hitting the maximum 110 miles per hour on the indicator, and a blizzard kept the mission grounded until April 17, when it flew on to Amchitka, only 112 kilometres from the Japanese camp on Kiska.

The 14th Squadron had its first taste of combat in Alaska the next day after escorting a formation of American Liberators that bombed Kiska, returning to attack enemy gun emplacements. Against heavy but "amazingly inaccurate" ack-ack fire, Flight Officer Louis Cochand released his 500-pounder to blow apart one gun battery and leave a gaping crater in its place. On another escort mission, the P40s bombed and strafed the marine ways near Salmon Lagoon, where three Ho Kyoteki—Japanese two-man submarines—were mounted on the rail line. The enemy had brought six of these midget submarines to Kiska, but there is no record that they were put to use, and all were destroyed on land. Japanese notes recall, "20 planes attacked and it was so severe it was strange that I survived" and "10 enemy air attacks. They made a direct hit on a gun position and killed 12 men."[3]

Soon after their arrival the Canadians were housed in their own tent camp on Amchitka, and when possible they flew together as a unit, sometimes on "all-Canadian" missions but also filling in whenever the American units were short of fliers. Eventually those American P40s designated for the Canadians were painted with the RCAF roundel, but with the blue diagonal band of the United States 11th Army Air Force across the tail of the fuselage. The nose was adorned with the gaping profile of the tiger shark that came to be synonymous with the P40. The Canadians were warned that if the Japanese captured them in an American plane, the enemy might torture them or execute them as spies.

As the last shots of battle resounded on Attu, plans were already unfolding for an Allied invasion of Kiska. In discussions at the Pacific Joint Board on Defence, the Americans had suggested to Canada's chief of the General Staff Kenneth Stuart "that it would be appropriate if Canadian forces co-operated in the removal of the existing [enemy] threat in the Aleutians."[4]

The idea had great support from Generals DeWitt and Buckner, the former pressing the issue with the General Officer Pacific Command, Major-General George Randolph Pearkes. General Stuart also pursued the matter with Pearkes and asked him for a report on the possible involvement of Canadian ground troops in the Aleutians.

Japanese Ho Kyoteki, two-man midget submarines, at Kiska. Six of the subs were brought to the island but were put out of commission early on by U.S. and Canadian dive bombers. The retreating Japanese set explosive charges in the subs before evacuating Kiska.

The capture of Attu after nineteen days of brutal fighting that had cost 549 lives and thousands of casualties had been a sobering lesson for the Americans. Kiska threatened an even bloodier toll, with at least one of every five Allied soldiers expected to be killed. Enemy strength on the island was pegged at between 8,000 and 9,000 troops, compared to the 1,800 that had held Attu. (At its peak the Kiska garrison numbered 8,500 troops but was down to about 5,200 by this time, though the Allies were unaware of this.) The island was also better supplied, had heavier guns, and did not want for ammunition judging by the amount of flak and fire thrown up at marauding Allied planes. The Japanese had also dug themselves firmly into the labyrinth of volcanic tunnels lacing Kiska, while the harbour and its approaches were easily defended.

Canadian ground troops selected for the Kiska invasion were drawn from existing regiments of Pacific Command and formed into the 13th Canadian Infantry Brigade. Among them was the Rocky Mountain Rangers of Kamloops, British Columbia, currently spread around southern Vancouver Island to guard airfields and man gun

Life was tough for both enemy and ally in the Aleutians, as illustrated by the tent quarters of members of the RCAF 14th Squadron, Armaments Section.

emplacements. The 2nd Battalion of the Winnipeg Grenadiers, recently replenished after the devastating loss of the entire 1st Battalion to the Japanese in the ill-conceived defence of Hong Kong, received its transfer orders in early 1943 and headed westward out of Winnipeg by rail to again meet the Japanese. A French-Canadian infantry unit, Le Regiment de Hull (de Quebec), completed the contingent. The entire Canadian Brigade was placed under the command of Brigadier H.W. Foster, who had been recalled from service in England and was accompanied by Major W.S. Murdoch.

The three regiments had originally been consigned to Home War Defence (HWD), which did not sit well with many of the regular soldiers. Turnover was high as overseas units continuously scoured HWD ranks to supplement their own. To bring the regiments of the HWD, and specifically those destined for the Aleutians, up to strength, conscripts, or Zombies as they were less affectionately known, were added to the cadre of regular soldiers. Thousands of conscript soldiers who had refused overseas service were languishing in Canada under HWD, viewed with disdain by the Canadian public. Tens of thousands of Canadians were overseas fighting an enemy that threatened the entire world, and to stay at home for no good reason was tantamount to treason in the public view. Under the National Resources Mobilisation

Act, war objectors could be conscripted into home war defence and mobilized for combat if the country was threatened. The Japanese had attacked North America and were now holding onto a piece of Alaskan territory on Canada's very doorstep, so sending the war objectors to Alaska would fill the defence gap without diverting first-class troops from more pressing fronts. It would also save the government from public and political criticism that it was "going too easy" on the war objectors.

When Canadian troops began training for the invasion of Kiska in early May, the more seasoned among them were sceptical that they would be put to any practical use. The Rocky Mountain Rangers had trained continuously for overseas service—even making a 650-kilometre march from Kamloops to Vancouver to take up security duties at various military installations on Vancouver Island—only to find themselves still on home turf more than a year later. They watched enviously as comrades from other regiments passed through on their way east to Halifax en route to Europe, while they maintained the monotony of guard duty, watching the skies and harbour approaches.

In April 1943, nearly 6,000 troops from across Canada converged on the Nanaimo and Courtenay region to begin training under Operation Greenlight. A third of the force was stationed in Nanaimo at what is now the Malaspina College campus, with the remainder at the barracks of today's HMCS Quadra, the sea-cadet training facility in Comox. The U.S. provided landing craft and six army observers to act as advisers, and the troops trained in amphibious landing operations on the beautiful shores around Courtenay—usually used for seaside vacations rather than as assault beaches. As the Canadians were to operate with the much larger American force, they traded their British rifles for American weapons and became familiar with American light artillery and mortar pieces. They also donned U.S. helmets, puttees, and parkas over Canadian battle dress, while the Canadian officer and NCO ranks were changed to those of their American counterparts to avoid confusion. Under General DeWitt's orders, soldiers were to accord officers from either country the same respect they would show an officer of their own country.

Each soldier was to receive a minimum of four months' combat training for the Kiska operation, and to stiffen their resolve against the Japanese, effluent from slaughterhouses was dumped into pits on the training field. The soldiers in training were required to crawl and drill through this mess, the idea being it would desensitize them to battlefield

Troops of the 13th Brigade, Pacific Command, Canadian Army, head north for the pre-invasion island of Adak in the Aleutians. Note the American helmets over Canadian battle-dress uniforms.

horrors. When the local press got hold of the story, a public outcry went up and the exercise stopped—no doubt to the delight of the reluctant recruits.

By June 14 the Canadian invasion force had been brought up to full strength with the infusion of troops from other regiments. Some of the units suffered absenteeism as high as one-third the number of conscripts. The French-Canadians, who were most vocal against the war nationally, surprisingly had only six desertions in their regiment—the lowest number of all the conscripted units. Brought in to support the Canadian contingent were the Canadian Fusiliers (Edmonton); the 24th Field Regiment; the 24th Field Company, Royal Canadian Engineers; the 46th Light Anti-Aircraft Battery; a machine-gun company of the Saint John Fusiliers; and the 25th Field Ambulance, Royal Canadian Army Medical Corps.

On July 12, 1943, the Canadian contingent of 5,300 combat troops sailed from Nanaimo and Chemainus in four U.S. troopships bound for Adak. For the first time in the country's history, a fully trained invasion army sailed from Canada and headed directly to the war front.

19

"The Gods Have Forsaken Kiska"

With Attu now fully in American hands, the air force turned all of its attention on Kiska. Bombers hit the island with every break in the clouds, raining down 82,000 kilograms of incendiaries in one twelve-hour period alone. If the Japanese on Kiska were to put up any serious defence, they needed land-based fighters and bombers. In one attempt to bring in fighter planes, disassembled in crates on the deck of a freighter, the whole shipment was lost when navy PBYs sank the ship.

At Salmon Lagoon the Japanese worked feverishly to complete a runway that would allow the island's defences to be reinforced by air from Paramushiro. In the most ambitious scenario, long-range bombers operating from Kiska and capable of striking as far as the North American mainland would once again throw the Americans onto the defensive. It was a plan that literally never got off the ground; when compact road-building equipment was crated in aboard submarines, the Allies destroyed it on the half-built runway. The Japanese then tried to complete the field with picks and shovels, but any headway they made was continually foiled by Canadian and American P40s cratering the field.

Yunosuke Osawa, a Japanese news reporter whose notes were later found on Kiska, described the air attacks on the island. "Sometimes they swoop down through cracks in the clouds dropping their bombs and hitting everything indiscriminately. I expressed my wonder at the fierceness of the enemy bombardment."[1]

While Allied planes ruled the sky over Kiska, the Japanese still had the island heavily fortified and sent up great shards of deadly flak against the incoming planes. The bombers were especially vulnerable, as they had to come in fairly low, below the fog, for a visual drop. The P40 units would attack the runway and the anti-aircraft guns surrounding the harbour and on Little Kiska Island. The fighters sometimes swooped down the valley leading to Kiska Harbor, coming out of the west and right up behind the enemy at altitudes as low as 60 metres. Eventually the Japanese strung a heavy wire cable across the valley, which several aircraft on a return trip narrowly missed. From then on the fighters kept clear of the valley and were no longer able to jump the enemy from behind.

When fog permeated Kiska, the dive bombers would conduct a timed run from Amchitka, diving through the clouds to come roaring down on the harbour in total blindness. Describing the attacks, P40 pilot Arthur Fanning of Winnipeg recalls: "The Japanese had the altitudes pretty much pegged and the anti-aircraft batteries would start chattering off when the planes peeled down out of the sky. But once the bombs started hitting and the shooting started, they would scatter."[2]

Osawa wrote: "The bullets travel through the atmosphere with the spirit of our brave soldiers in them. As I watch the action, the bullets seem to be chasing the enemy planes. So, our bullets surely find their intended target."

When the air raids knocked out the generators and sump pumps installed to clear the continually dripping water that pooled in the volcanic caves, the enemy huddled in the dark and damp cold of the shelters. Outside, the dive bombers subjected the island to terrific poundings as they sought the bunker entrances, while free to tear apart the Japanese buildings at will. Slowly and methodically they made life untenable for the Japanese and ground down their resolve to hold on to this forsaken piece of Alaskan rock. The Japanese logged: "0900 hours—11 heavy bombers attacked for 20 minutes and caused 10 casualties, 9 of whom were killed. Fourteen army personnel were buried alive in their air raid shelter."[3]

The campaign was no picnic for the Allied pilots either, however, as RCAF Wing Commander Robert Morrow discovered when he narrowly escaped with his life after bailing out of a damaged Kittyhawk over Umnak. Jumping clear of the cockpit, he was struck by the plane's tail, which knocked him unconscious and left his legs paralysed. Miraculously, the impact caused his parachute to open and he came to just before hitting the water. With the chute dragging him under the frigid water, Morrow managed to struggle free into his inflated dinghy, but the wind began pushing him away from Umnak towards open sea.

Morrow slipped over the side of the raft and, despite his injuries, swam for shore where a group of American soldiers waded out into the surf and pulled him to safety. Sent to recuperate in Vancouver, he described to reporters the little-known air war for Kiska. "Fliers spend a short period at the forward base and are then transferred to a rear base. While at the forward base they are in the air almost constantly as long as the weather permits. During a day when weather conditions are as good as can be expected in the Aleutians, a single pilot will be back and forth from Kiska and his base about six times."[4]

Over spring and into the summer of 1943, the Americans and Canadians continued their bombardment of Kiska. On a rotating basis, the 14th Squadron completed two tours of duty to rack up nearly 400 hours of direct combat operations, while the 111th Squadron logged almost 300. While this was considerably less flying time compared to other theatres of the war, it was a remarkable effort given the proximity of the enemy base (only minutes away) and the amount of time the planes were grounded by the weather. Typical excerpts from squadron logbooks for the period are: "...attacked enemy guns, submarine in harbour; radar installation attacked; destroyed auxiliary buildings; hit landing strip (again)," and as often as not "...weather very poor, no flying today." Despite the perils of enemy flak, the weather posed the main threat to the Aleutian pilots, and often they would return to their base at Amchitka to find it completely fogged in. "The flak didn't bother us too much," Fanning recalled. "The worst part was not knowing if you'd be able to find the runway when you got home."

Even as the Japanese were being overrun on Attu, Colonel Benjamin Talley's engineers had started laying airstrips on the east side of Massacre Bay and on the tiny island of Shemya. A flat rock surface situated 40 kilometres east of Attu and measuring less than four by seven kilometres, Shemya was the only level surface in the Aleutians capable of supporting the experimental new long-range B29 Super Fortress bombers. On July 11, 1943, after refuelling at the new Attu airfield, six B24 Liberators took off to bomb the Japanese on their own territory at the Imperial navy base at Paramushiro in the northern Kuriles. The mission was aborted when they were diverted to attack four enemy transports attempting to run the Kiska blockade. The B24s sank two of the ships, but the lead Liberator took a flak burst and was forced to make a crash landing on Adak.

On July 18, six B24s from Adak again refuelled at the Attu airfield before attempting the 1,050-kilometre jump to Paramushiro. This time

The Canadian camp at Adak in 1943.

they were more successful and dropped their 500-pound (225-kilogram) bombs on the enemy airfield as three of the Liberators broke off to hit the navy base. The surprised enemy sent up twenty float fighters and five Zeros but could not catch the retreating bombers heading out to sea. All of the attacking planes returned unscathed, marking the first time in the war that land-based bombers had taken off directly from United States territory to strike at Japan. It was also the first time the Japanese homeland had been bombed since Colonel James Doolittle's carrier-launched Tokyo raid of February 1942. Three weeks later, on August 11, nine Liberators flying out of Adak made a second successful attack on Paramushiro, with the loss of one bomber.

The four transports carrying the 5,300 Canadian troops of the 13th Brigade arrived at Adak on July 21 to join the American contingent. Among the American units were veterans of the Attu campaign from the 7th Division, Alaska's 4th Regiment, and the ever-reliable Alaska Scouts, as well as the 87th Mountain Combat Group, which had been preparing for service in Italy. Rounding out the invasion force were 2,500 troops of a Canadian-American commando regiment—the First Special Service Force (FSSF)—a crack unit of paratroopers embarking on their first combat mission. This elite unit would go on to win renown in Europe as the Black Devils, immortalized by Hollywood in the film *The Devil's Brigade*. The entire invasion force numbered about 35,000 strong and was known as Corlett's Long Knives after its American commander, Major General C.H. Corlett. Every soldier wore a shoulder patch depicting a long black dagger on a blue background.

Fearing the Japanese were aware of Allied invasion plans, Buckner and DeWitt decided to move the invasion ahead by two weeks, to

August 15. Whether the Spanish agent Kobbe had advised the Japanese of the movement of troops and ships north was immaterial, as it would have been nearly impossible to keep secret the tremendous buildup of resources at Adak. Following full-scale invasion exercises on Great Sitikin Island north of Amchitka, the massed force now stood poised, awaiting the order to invade Kiska. There, anticipating a fate similar to that of his comrades on Attu, Japanese soldier Kishichiro Miyazaki wrote in his diary, "All is lost … the gods have forsaken Kiska."[5]

Japanese supply runs to Kiska had already been reduced to a trickle of support by I-boats that managed to slip through Kinkaid's blockade, but these, too, suffered heavy losses. Of the thirteen submarines Admiral Kawase assigned to the northern runs in March, one was sunk off Attu and four others were listed as missing in western Aleutian waters. In June Kawase lost three more subs trying to evacuate troops from Kiska, including the 5,000-ton *I-24* as it was returning to Japan with 150 troops. On June 13, the *I-31* was sunk as it headed home between the Aleutians and the northern Kuriles with another 150 wounded soldiers. The *I-7* had to be beached at Little Kiska after being shelled by the destroyer *Monaghan*, only to be finished off in a subsequent attack by Allied planes as it limped into Kiska's Gertrude Cove. The big guns of the U.S. Navy returned on July 6 to pummel Kiska in a 22-minute barrage and followed it with another attack on the 22nd. The Japanese diarist sombrely wrote: "Everyone is exhuasted from the terrific bombing, day after day, and all are sound asleep."[6]

On July 26, radar-equipped PBYs detected a column of seven vessels off Attu, steaming towards Kiska. Believing they were headed to reinforce or evacuate the Japanese garrison, Admiral Kinkaid sent the battleships *New Mexico* and *Mississippi* and the cruisers *Portland*, *Wichita*, and *San Francisco* to intercept the mysterious column that was now reported within sixteen kilometres of Kiska. The American ships saw no craft of any kind, but with their radar still picking up the signals they opened fire on the suspected area. After a half-hour the signals dropped off the radar screens one by one as mysteriously as they had appeared, with no fire ever returned and no wreckage or debris ever found. While not discounting the possibility of enemy submarines submerging and resurfacing to trick the American surface fleet into expending its resources, the subsequent navy enquiry attributed the radar signals to a magnetic anomaly peculiar to the Arctic. Japanese records make no mention of enemy naval action at this time, and their northern force was some 300 kilometres away to the south, although five Japanese I-boats standing off Kiska reported they had been shelled by American gunboats and quietly submerged when the enemy projectiles came too close.

Short on fuel and ammunition after engaging the invisible "targets," Admiral Kinkaid's force withdrew to meet up with supply ships off Amchitka, then returned within 72 hours to set up a tight noose around Kiska. A heavy fog had rolled in and Kinkaid's ships began pounding Kiska almost daily, while the air force stepped up its bombings as a precursor to invasion. On one run the bombers showered Kiska with 60,000 leaflets cut in the shape of Kiri leaves, a symbolic reference to an ancient Japanese play about the fall of the house of Toyotomi. The leaflets suggested the Japanese Empire would fall, just as the reigning family had fallen like the Kiri leaf.

There was a conspicuous lack of activity on Kiska. Air force crews reported no ack-ack or return fire from the enemy guns and no ground movement, while aerial photos revealed that vehicles remained stationary and other mobile equipment had not changed position. It was possible the Japanese had moved underground to their labyrinth of tunnels and

The joint U.S.-Canadian invasion force assembles at Adak in August 1943.

shelters, preparing to fight a guerrilla-type war using small, well-placed squads. On August 13 a force of 35,000 men and an armada of more than 100 warships slipped away in the fog for Kiska.

In the last bombing sortie against the island prior to the invasion, pilots of the RCAF's 14th Squadron reported the island to be "eerily silent."

Thousands of these Kiri leaves were dropped on Kiska in an attempt to play on Japanese superstitions. The script on the leaf, taken from Japanese literature, describes how "the Master's house will fall like the Kiri leaf."

Kiska—An Enemy Lost

In the early hours of August 15, hours ahead of the main invasion force, the first and third units of the First Special Service Force (FSSF) paddled ashore in the dark and fog in separate landings on the southwest sector and a rocky peninsula on Kiska's north. The plan was to approach Kiska Harbor from the west and capture and hold the high ground overlooking the Japanese base until the main invasion force landed. The second unit of the FSSF waited back on Amchitka's metal runway to be called into action and parachuted onto the island if fierce enemy resistance was encountered.

After landing on the northern spit, the unit found it was not covered in gravel, as had been reported by reconnaissance flights, but by house-sized boulders. Still, the men managed to drag their rubber boats past this obstacle to traverse Lake Kiska and continue inland. Several Japanese artillery pieces and machine-gun posts protected Kiska Harbor, and as the unit approached the slopes overlooking the Japanese camp, the men broke into small groups to disable these emplacements.

All was still as Canadian Staff Sergeant Lawrence Storey slipped into the observation bunker for a 6-inch (150-millimetre) artillery piece farther up the slope. His commando training had taught him to move like a ghost into these bunkers—and to kill the enemy occupants just as silently. Moving stealthily in the dark, he discovered a grenade under the stairs leading into the bunker. It had been cleverly set to detonate when triggered by the weight of a man's foot. Posting a warning note for the troops behind, he then noticed a braided tassel hanging from

Canadians landing at Broad Beach, Kiska, in the Aleutians, August 1943.

the ceiling. It had been rigged by a system of pulleys to the trigger cord of the 6-inch (155-millimetre) artillery cannon. Counting on the natural inclination of an inquisitive mind to pull on the tassel, the Japanese had pointed the gun squarely at the dugout.

On Kiska's east side, landing craft fitted with the plywood silhouettes of troops made for Gertrude Cove to divert enemy attention from the main assault on the island's west side—but drew no fire. French-Canadian troops of Le Regiment de Hull were leading the main attack at Green Point. As the only unmarried NCO in his unit, Sergeant George Mulholland was selected to lead the first wave of Kamloops' Rocky Mountain Rangers onto Broad Beach at Witchcraft Point. Moving inland, the soldiers could hear through the fog the distant chatter of a machine-gun fight and the shouts of men, which seemed to indicate the presence of the enemy.

By the end of the first day the Rangers made it to the observation post marked out earlier by commando Storey, where they dug in for the night. Venturing into the abandoned post, Lieutenant Sidney Vessey became the first Canadian casualty on Kiska when he stepped on the rigged stairway and was killed. The enemy, it turned out, had mined the most innocuous objects, such as a tape measure that blew up and killed one soldier as he pulled out the tape.

Signs of the Japanese were everywhere, but so far not one enemy soldier had been encountered. Only a few stray dogs, happy to have human companionship again, greeted the arrival of the Allies to the camp where the enemy had left such slogans as "We will get you" on the bunker walls. Somehow the entire Japanese garrison had skillfully and silently abandoned Kiska. The machine-gun fire heard after the landings turned out to be two American squads that had tragically engaged each other in the disorienting fog. After the war the Allies learned that during the 72 hours in which Admiral Kinkaid's North Pacific Force had withdrawn from Kiska to refuel on July 26, eight transports of a fifteen-ship Japanese convoy had slipped into Kiska Harbor and evacuated almost the entire 5,183-man army. Fifty men left behind to destroy documents were later evacuated by submarine. Just as they had sneaked into the Aleutians fifteen months before under cover of a blanketing fog, the Japanese had also departed.

Twenty-five Americans died from mined traps and friendly fire in the reclamation of Kiska, as did three more Canadians. Gaston Boisclair and Gerard Desjardins of the Quebec regiment died when they set off traps in a Japanese bunker. Private Peter Poshtar of the Winnipeg Grenadiers was also killed on heavily mined Kiska. Another Canadian soldier died in hospital in Vancouver one month later from mine-inflicted wounds. Another 121 Americans and 25 Canadians were wounded in retaking the island.

An actual battle on the island, heavily fortified as it was, would have been a costly and bloody fight. The Japanese were well entrenched in the series of tunnels in which they could hide or move from point to point. Sacks of rice used as sandbags around machine-gun emplacements served the double purpose of giving excellent camouflage when their

The funeral for Lieutenant Sid Vessey, killed in a mined Japanese gun post.

Canadian troops of the 24th Field Regiment inspect a Japanese dual-purpose gun.

contents sprouted, as well as providing food for the defenders. In the baffling fog, there is no doubt the enemy could have held out with dogged resistance to the last man, at the cost of thousands of Canadian and American lives until, like Attu, the island inevitably fell.

By forcing the Allies to divert thousands of troops, more than a billion dollars, and numerous aircraft, ships, and other equipment from more urgent theatres of the war, the Japanese were in one minor sense successful in their Aleutian campaign. Now, however, these same resources were poised to strike at Japan's northern gate, putting Imperial leaders in an uncomfortable position. It appeared an invasion by this route was imminent, and it was now Japan that had to redirect badly

Rocky Mountain Rangers of Kamloops on a Japanese tank.

needed troops, ships of a decimated navy, and scarce resources to protect the Kuriles and the northern frontier.

After the conclusion of the Aleutian campaign, the RCAF squadrons in Alaska quickly returned to Boundary Bay Field outside Vancouver, B.C. The 14th and 111th Squadrons soon became the 442nd and 440th Squadrons, and the members of the 118th distinguished themselves over Europe, becoming one of the first Allied fighter units to land in occupied France after the D-Day invasion. The Canadian army's 13th Brigade remained on Kiska for four long and tedious months, departing in late December 1943 after an invasion of Japan via Alaska was overruled owing to the ungodly weather and the drastic downturn of Japanese fortunes in the South Pacific.

French-Canadian troops with an admiral's pennant of the Japanese Imperial navy.

Still, the war continued to stumble along in the north. The new American Super Fortress B29 conducted its first mission against Japan, flying from the base at Shemya east of Attu to strike Paramushiro. Alaska's 11th Air Force also made repeated attacks from the bases at Attu and Shemya, while the small contingent of ships retained by the North Pacific Force rattled the northern Kuriles with broadside salvoes. Japanese planes attempted bombing runs against the airfield at Attu, but accomplished little for their efforts.

The North American public was virtually unaware of the war fought on its northern doorstep as government censorship had tightly controlled the media going in or out of the Alaskan theatre. Reports of enemy submarine actions along the West Coast were also suppressed, and "cause of explosion unknown" was given as the reason some of the ships sank along the coast. As the Alaskan campaign wound down, it was quickly eclipsed by more prominent theatres of the war, and what little was heard of Alaska, the Aleutians, and the North Pacific theatre soon faded from media attention. In the end, most Canadians and Americans never knew how close to home the war in the Pacific had raged.

When the United States asked Canadian permission to present the Pacific Star medal to Canadians involved in the Alaskan war, the government politely refused. Negative feelings still ran high against the Home War Defence troops, even though General Corlett, who led

Graves of four Canadians killed in the reoccupation of heavily mined Kiska, Alaska.

the international force at Kiska, had commended the Canadian Aleutian soldiers on their high degree of professionalism. The majority of Canadian soldiers and airmen involved in driving the enemy from North American soil went on to fight in Europe, but the harsh climate, the miserable conditions, the suicidal tedium, and the deprivation of the North Pacific were among their worst experiences of the whole war. Even by today's standards, Canada's commitment to the Alaskan campaign dwarfs our involvement in most high-profile peacekeeping operations. Yet formal acknowledgement of those Canadians' involvement in this small and obscure war on what remains Canada's forgotten front is not forthcoming.

Desperate Measures

In January 1944, the RCMP in Vancouver intercepted a letter to the Spanish spy, Fernando de Kobbe, from his superior in SIM, Alcazar de Velasco. The letter contained a $1,000 cash payment, the latest code-name changes for ship and troop movements, and a formula for brewing invisible inks. The Allies now had proof of the Spanish foreign ministry's direct involvement in spying for the Axis, and Kobbe and his daughter Beatriz were arrested.

According to de Velasco, Kobbe "confessed everything under interrogation, even telling more than what was asked of him."[1] He revealed the names of several agents operating in North America, which included Spanish diplomats and journalists, most of whom fled to Argentina following Kobbe's arrest. The arrest was instrumental in bringing about the downfall of the Abwehr, the German intelligence-gathering organization in North America, as well as the Japanese information service. It also embarrassed Spain's foreign ministry and deterred further spying activities on behalf of the Axis. Kobbe and Beatriz were expelled in February and escorted to the international border by RCMP officers, where they were handed over to American FBI agents. They left New Orleans for Spain on February 6 aboard the Spanish liner *Magallenes*. A short time later de Velasco himself was apparently accosted in Madrid by three Allied agents—a British, a Canadian, and an American. According to de Velasco, the Canadian was particularly agitated and threatened to kill him if he continued to spy for the Axis. De Velasco disappeared, surfacing again only after war's end.

While the loss of the Aleutian Islands and the closing of their intelligence-gathering service TO effectively ended Japan's activities in

North America, the Japanese continued to make sporadic forays against the West Coast. At midnight on April 16, 1944, the U.S. Army transport *John Straub* was blown in half by two terrific explosions some 400 kilometres west of Kodiak Island. Explanations for the sinking have been inconclusive due to the speed of the violent end of the ship, but torpedoes from *I-180* probably sent it to the bottom as the enemy submarine was in the vicinity at the time. The transport went down in minutes, taking 55 of the 70-man crew to an icy grave. Days later the *I-180* was picked up on radar and caught on the surface by the American destroyer USS *Gilmore* in waters southwest of Kodiak Island. The I-boat had been on a mission to reconnoitre the navy anchorage at Woman's Bay when *Gilmore* challenged the vessel by Aldis lamp. It attempted to escape by diving, but the *Gilmore* boxed in the intruder, laying down grids of anti-submarine projectiles for 2.5 hours before a terrific underwater explosion 90 metres below sent an expansive slick of diesel fuel boiling to the surface. Launched in January 1943, *I-180* had been in service less than fifteen months. It was 100 metres long, carried six 21-inch (533-millimetre) torpedo tubes, and had a crew of 80. All perished in the sinking.

The last known I-boat incursion along the West Coast met with a similar fate on October 28, 1944. Under Commander Kaneo Kubo, the *I-12* was one of Japan's newest submarines, launched only six months previously. Designed for long-range escort and supply, it measured 118 metres long, carried a crew of 100, and with smaller engines and extra fuel tanks had a cruising range of 35,000 kilometres. It carried a Glen reconnaissance plane and boasted the latest in German radar technology. Midway between San Francisco and Honolulu, in roughly the same area where *I-26* sank the *Cynthia Olsen* 23 months before, Kubo sent two torpedoes into the American Liberty ship *John A. Johnson*, which he then finished off with gunfire. The sub returned to harass the survivors with machine-gun fire and smashed through liferafts clustered together. Survivor H.L. Clarke recalled about 15 Japanese crewmen were on the deck of the submarine, yelling at the men in the water and shouting "Bonzai." One even fired at them with his sidearm.[2] A Pan American Airways passenger plane spotted the burning ship, alerting the navy at San Francisco, and the following day survivors were picked up by USS *Argus*. All 70 crewmen had abandoned the ship safely, but by the time they were rescued, 10 were missing and presumed dead. Five survivors suffered gunshot wounds.

Two weeks later, while escorting six ships in the same stretch of water, USS *Rockford* detected an underwater contact shadowing the convoy. Stealthily the *Rockford* turned to attack with forward-firing anti-submarine projectiles and a pattern of depth charges. A tremendous explosion followed a minute later, sending a huge oil slick and a stream of bubbles coursing through the water. With air whistling from her ruptured pressure hull plates, the sub rose bow first almost straight into the air, then quickly slid below the surface thousands of metres to the ocean floor with all hands.

The death of *I-12* ended operations by enemy submarines off North America's West Coast, while increasing military setbacks forced Japan to use her undersea navy to ferry troops among her dwindling and beleaguered possessions in the Pacific. The newer and vastly superior American fleet subs had thrown a tight picket line around the home islands, and Imperial navy boats could hardly hoist anchor without the Americans knowing. In desperation, the Japanese resorted to radical and questionable weapons and techniques, such as the infamous kamikaze fighter pilots, who would crash their planes into enemy ships. Along the same lines were manned torpedoes called Kaiten; Fukuryu, frogmen who volunteered to use themselves as human mines; and Shinyo, motorboats packed with explosives.

One new weapon employed directly against North America, and which could have had more sinister applications had the project not been thwarted, was Fugo—terror balloons. On Sunday, May 5, 1945, in Bly, Oregon, Pastor Archie Mitchell drove with his wife Elsye, who was five months pregnant, and five children from his congregation to Gearhart Mountain in the Fremont National Forest for a day of picnicking and hiking. Reaching their destination, Mitchell let his wife and their charges out while he parked the car. Shortly after, Mrs. Mitchell called to her husband from about 95 metres away that they had found something when a terrific explosion suddenly engulfed the group, killing her and all the children. Their tragic discovery had been a "fusen bakudan," a Japanese army balloon-bomb. Sadly, both the Canadian and American governments knew that such weapons had reached their countries' shores, but had remained silent about them so that Japanese intelligence would not know of their effectiveness.

In November 1944 the Imperial army and navy conducted a series of tests that sent balloons carrying recording and transmitting instruments to North America. Having established the existence of a perpetual jet stream high in the stratosphere that moved from west to east, the Japanese embarked on a program to send armed balloons as unguided missiles against the North American continent. With a moderate payload of less than 170 kilograms, Japanese scientists determined, a balloon could ride eight kilometres up, which put it beyond the reach of radar and most aircraft patrols. Travelling at speeds of up to 480 kilometres per hour, it could cross the Pacific from Japan to North America in about three days.

The balloons were made of laminated paper panels shellacked together with a type of potato paste produced by nimble-fingered school girls in the service of the Empire. Food was now so scarce in Japan that supervisors at the balloon factory had to be constantly vigilant, on guard for workers who would steal the paste to eat. Initial production of the balloons took place in scattered, small-scale locations, such as school halls, judo dojos, and auditoriums, before more permanent quarters were established at the Kokura Army Arsenal on Kyushu.

Measuring ten metres in diameter, the fully inflated balloons held 6,100 cubic metres of hydrogen for lifting. They were equipped with a pressure-relief valve that released air as the balloon drifted between higher and lower pressures at different altitudes, and they could reach a height

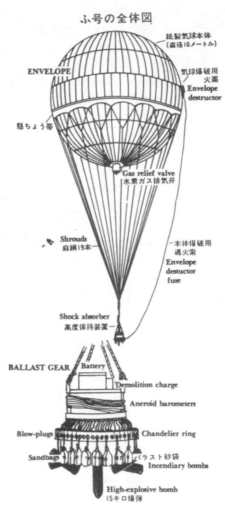

ふ号の全体図

紙製気球本体
(直径10メートル)

ENVELOPE

気球爆破用
火薬
Envelope
destructor

懸ちょう器

Gas relief valve
水素ガス排気弁

Shrouds
麻縄19本

一本体爆破用
導火薬
Envelope
destuctor
fuse

Shock absorber
高度保持装置

BALLAST GEAR   Battery

Demolition charge

Aneroid barometers

Blow-plugs

Chandelier ring

Sandbags   バラスト砂袋
Incendiary bombs

High-explosive bomb
15キロ爆弾

The Type A Paper Balloon

One of the 9,300 balloon-bombs launched from Japan against North America. British Columbia recorded the highest number of balloon-bomb sightings at 57. The only known fatalities were five children and a pregnant woman in southern Oregon.

of 10,000 metres. Sixteen-metre shroud lines suspended the weapon, which consisted of two aluminium rings with a series of 75 blow plugs. Batteries, aneroid barometers, and altimeters controlled gunpowder charges that intermittently released sixteen pairs of sandbags serving as ballast. By the time the balloons were over North America they would ideally have released all of their sandbags. The devices were usually armed with four five-kilogram magnesium incendiaries for starting random fires in the forests of the West Coast, and a 15-kilogram anti-personnel bomb. A one-kilogram picric acid block would destroy the remaining device, while magnesium flash powder ignited the remaining hydrogen in the balloon. The entire apparatus stood 21.3 metres from top to bottom.

The Allies, who at the time were totally unaware of the existence of the jet stream, initially had no idea where the strange devices originated. It was inconceivable that they could come from Japan, more than 8,000 kilometres away, and theories abounded as to their source. Among them were enemy submarines off the West Coast and even landing parties on the very beaches of North America. Some suggested that the balloon-bombs were secretly deployed from camps in which Nikkei had been interned, while others more accurately surmised that they came from nearby South Pacific atolls.

When a balloon or its remnants was found, the military would analyze them. It had already established that the weapons were of Japanese origin from markings on the metal components and by studying paper balloon fragments, and it slowly realized that the weapons were indeed launched from Japan. The Military Geology Unit of the United States Geological Survey was brought in to pinpoint exactly where in Japan the balloons originated and embarked on a piece of sleuthing work worthy of the best forensic criminologists. Employing geologists, paleontologists, micro-paleontologists, mineralogists, and petrologists, the survey team painstakingly analyzed the sand contents of recovered ballast bags that narrowed the search to beaches with rivers flowing from sources having the same ratios of mineral concentration. The team also discovered the sand to be totally devoid of coral, indicating that the river source was in colder waters above the 35th parallel. Telltale signs of granite further revealed inland streams that meandered through bedrock, while grains of quartz, augite, and glass were evidence of a volcanic region. Minute crustaceans and fossils native to a very confined area of Japan's east coast were also pulled from the sand samples. Slowly and steadily, scientific deduction narrowed down the whereabouts of

This intact Japanese balloon-bomb is at the Canadian War Museum storehouse in Ottawa.

the balloon-bomb factory to three sites on the east coast of Honshu, northeast of Tokyo. Each had rail lines and an arsenal for storage of the weapons, as well as hydrogen generators and storage tanks for the ascending medium.

While the military had maintained strict silence on the existence of the balloon weapons invading Canadian and American airspace, the six deaths in Oregon prompted it to issue public warnings about the devices. Approximately 9,300 fusen bakudan were launched against North America, landing as far north as the high Yukon Territory, as far east as Michigan, and well south into Mexico. British Columbia recorded the highest number of balloon-bombs shot down or recovered—57. Two were sighted over Port Hardy on March 13, one of which was brought down by gunfire while the other escaped. Two intact five-kilogram bombs were recovered with their ballast gear on Denman Island near Campbell River, and in 1972 loggers found the remains of another exploded balloon bomb in the coastal forest. Bombs also landed in Williams Lake, Boundary Bay, the Gulf Islands, the Strait of Georgia, the Queen Charlotte Islands, and Prince Rupert. Cowboys reported one in the Thompson River valley near Ashcroft, and another crashed into Vancouver's Coal Harbour near the entrance to Stanley Park. The last balloon-bomb was shot down on April 20, 1945, near the Huntingdon-Sumas border crossing, after two children

spotted it through a break in the clouds. A Kittyhawk piloted by P.V. Brodeur scrambled out of the RCAF base at Abbotsford and brought it down over Vedder Mountain for a joint Canadian-American investigating team to recover intact.

Almost 50 more balloons or their remains were found in Alberta, Saskatchewan, Manitoba, the Yukon, and the Northwest Territories, while the U.S. coastal states of California, Oregon, Washington, and Alaska recorded 135 incidents together. On March 10, 1945, a balloon-bomb caused a power outage for three days at the Hanford nuclear production facility when it came into contact with hydro lines from the Bonneville dam in Washington. Ironically, the plant was processing plutonium isotope for use in the atomic bomb that would be dropped on Nagasaki.

In May 1945 American B29s took out two of the three balloon-bomb production facilities at Ichinomiya, Nakoso, and Otsu.

The fifteen-kilogram anti-personnel bomb payload was recovered intact with an entire balloon-bomb assembly.

Between the bombing and the lack of feedback from the American media as to the effectiveness of the balloon-bombs, Japanese decision-makers cancelled the program, unaware that more than 300 balloon bombs or parts had been reported or recovered in Canada and the United States. Thousands more likely crashed into the remote forests, and their remains were still being discovered as recently as 1992. While the Allies speculated that the Japanese would eventually use the balloon-bombs to transport chemical or biological weapons, no enemy data uncovered after the war supports that assertion.

War's Legacy

With the end of the Second World War, alliances realigned along ideological lines. Security clamped down in the Aleutians because of their close proximity to the Soviet Union, and the western islands became virtually inaccessible to anyone without official business in the area. The United States expanded the Adak base to nearly 5,000 personnel, Shemya became a super-secret listening post, and Attu a Coast Guard Loran station. The displaced Aleuts were relocated to islands in the eastern end of the chain: Atka, Unimak, Umnak, and Unalaska.

Amchitka Island, from which Canadian and American bombers relentlessly pounded the Japanese on Kiska, became the site of a series of American nuclear tests in the 1970s. Operations Long Shot and Milrow were followed by Cannikin on November 6, 1971. It was the largest underground nuclear explosion in U.S. history. The construction of an air force base on Amchitka was shelved when the Cold War ended in the late 1980s. Today the United States Department of Fisheries and Wildlife administers Kiska and most of the other islands. Kiska and Attu, as well as their ruins, have been declared national war memorials and can only be accessed by permission.

In 1989, the U.S. National Park Service's Submerged Cultural Resources Unit (SCRU) and the United States Navy set up a program to locate and catalogue the relics above and below the water on Attu and Kiska. SCRU identified and filmed the wrecks of the *Nissan Maru* and the submarine *RO-65* in Kiska Harbor. Captain Wilbur Miller's P40, which sank *RO-65* before being shot down, is believed to be close by. A pile of rifles rises up from the harbour floor, thrown overboard by the Japanese abandoning the island as Canadian and American troops massed for the invasion.

On land, Japanese 6-inch (150-millimetre) guns still overlook the harbour, while other artillery pieces point skyward in readiness for the return of enemy planes. A rusting two-man submarine lies broken, sinking into the soft muskeg. A wooden barracks, walls covered with bits of Japanese pin-ups, still houses a wood stove at its centre—a must for survival in the frigid islands.

Along remote West Coast beaches in British Columbia and Alaska, gun turrets that were built to fend off the expected mighty Japanese navy, but which now lie empty and deserted, are a canvas for today's graffiti artists. These deteriorating relics and the few surviving veterans who served in these remote outposts are all that remain of a war that brought the enemy to our very shores, yet remains virtually forgotten.

This was the war on our doorstep.

The Union Jack of the Canadians at Kiska flies proudly over the vanquished Rising Sun.

Recovered from Kiska, these Japanese weapons—a Japanese Hotchkiss heavy machine gun type 92 (top) and a Nambu light machine gun (bottom)—are part of the collection at the Minto Armoury Regimental Museum of the Royal Winnipeg Rifles. Allied troops found several of the guns in well-placed positions, stocked with plenty of ammunition. Had the Japanese stayed to fight, they would have inflicted withering casualties on the Allied army.

Bow section of the Nozama Maru *on Kiska Island, Alaska.*

A Japanese barracks with wood-burning stove on Kiska, 60 years after the invasion.

A midget submarine is surveyed by members of the National Park Service's Submerged Cultural Resources Unit.

A Japanese midget submarine on Kiska today.

Notes

Chapter 1

1. Minoru Yakota was known as Hosegawa, but changed his name to Yakota following the war. For clarity he is referred to as Yakota.
2. At this time the world was not on a standardized time format. Many countries had their own formats that did not conform to other time zones.
3. The only explanation presented to this day is that Yakota must have confused his time and attacked an hour before the attack at Pearl Harbor—although he insisted his time was correct.
4. A derogatory term commonly used by Western media to describe the Japanese during the Second World War.
5. Quoted in *The Silent Siege III* by Bert Webber.

Chapter 2

1. Quoted in *The Thousand Mile War* by Brian Garfield.
2. Alaska did not become a state until 1959.
3. The S-boats were called pigboats because of their blunt bow. However, the crews came to refer to them as such due to the deplorable living conditions on board.
4. *Yorktown* was damaged in the Battle of the Coral Sea and repaired just in time for the Battle of Midway.
5. Quoted in *The Thousand Mile War* by Brian Garfield.

Chapter 3

1. The description of the 8th Bomber Reconnaissance Squadron's war experiences is drawn, with permission, from H. Layton Bray's article "Northern Exposure," *Legion Magazine*, May 1994.
2. The Curtiss P40 was the most widely used fighter plane of all Allied air forces. It was referred to as the Kittyhawk in the RCAF, Warhawk in the USAAF, and Tomahawk in the other Commonwealth air forces.
3. John Wallace in an interview with a newspaper in Halifax, his hometown (no date given).

4. Royal Canadian Air Force Inquiry February 26, 1943. File 1022-C-2378 and File ROX1022-C-2453.
5. Quoted from an RCAF document "Attacks on Submarines: Official Report of Attack RCAF WAC Bolingbroke No. 9118—115 Sqn. July 7th, 1942."
6. From an interview with Jim Johnston, RCAF, September 1995.
7. A common saying at the time, quoted in *The Thousand Mile War* by Brian Garfield.

Chapter 4

1. In the Bataan Death March, 76,000 American and Filipino prisoners of war captured by the Japanese in the Philippines were forced to march 88 kilometres through jungle from the south end of the Bataan Peninsula. An estimated 10,000 POWs died from exhaustion, beatings, dehydration, and executions. It is considered one of the worst atrocities of the war.

Chapter 5

1. Cited in *The Alaska Highway: Papers on the 40th Anniversary Symposium*, edited by Kenneth Coates.
2. Ibid.

Chapter 6

1. Some critics suggest it was our own or American ships doing the shooting rather than the *I-26*. However, American author Bert Webber interviewed several ex-crewmen of *I-25* and *I-26* in the mid-1970s, and all related the same story, even though many had not spoken with each other since the war. An unexploded shell recovered at Estevan in 1972 was confirmed as belonging to a 5.5-inch Japanese gun. The incidents are recorded by Commander Mochitsura Hashimoto in his book *Sunk!* Long after war's end, Japanese sources revealed that the presence of the radio-direction installation was known, and it was this post rather than the lighthouse that was the primary target. Japanese submarines relied on Allied navigational aids along the treacherous West Coast as much as any other vessels, so destroying them would have been a questionable strategy.
2. The incident is described in *The Silent Siege III* by Bert Webber.
3. Following the First World War, the *Gorgas* (formerly the steamer *Prinz Sigismind*)had been seized as a prize of war from the Germans and purchased by Libby, McNeill of Seattle for its Alaska cannery operations. The U.S. government in turn appropriated it at the start of hostilities with Japan.

Chapter 7

1. Description of the incident is drawn with permission from H. Layton Bray's "Northern Exposure" in *Legion Magazine*, May 1994.

Chapter 8

1. From *Alaska At War*, a documentary produced by the Alaska State Historical Commission.

Chapter 9

1. From *Alaska at War*.
2. Technically Yamamoto did make this seemingly inflammatory statement. However, it was within the larger context of a speech in which he stated, "If hostilities break out between Japan and the United States, it would not be enough that we take Guam and the Philippines, nor even Hawaii and San Francisco. To make victory certain, we would have to march into Washington and dictate the terms of peace in the White House." American propagandists got hold of this phrase and twisted it to mean that Yamamoto claimed he *would* dictate the terms of peace in the White House.
3. From an interview with H. Layton Bray of RCAF 8th Squadron.

Chapter 10

1. The four aboriginal groups in Alaska are the Inupiat, Central Yupik, Alvtiiq, and Siberian Yupik. The general term Eskimo is still used to refer to them.
2. Quoted in *Men of the Tundra* by Major Marvin Marston.
3. Letter from Lieutenant General Buckner to Governor Ernest Gruening quoted in *Men of the Tundra* by Major Marvin Marston.

Chapter 11

1. Quoted in *The Creation of a National Air Force* by W.A.B. Douglas.
2. Ibid.
3. Ibid.
4. From the author's interview with George Mulholland.

Chapter 12

1. From the author's interview with Louis Cochand.
2. Quoted in *First Steps to Tokyo: The RCAF in the Aleutians* by Flight Officer D.F. Griffin.

Chapter 13

1. The description of Fujita's plan and his meeting at the flotilla office is drawn from Bert Webber's *The Silent Siege III*.
2. Japan later built the massive I-400 series of submarines that were 400 feet in length and able to carry three Aichi M6A1 float fighters. They intended to use fleets of the subs to bomb the Panama Canal and launch attacks on Washington and New York.
3. Quoted in *The Silent Siege III* by Bert Webber.
4. Ibid.

Chapter 15

1. In his book *Japan's Secret War: Japan's race against time to build the atomic bomb*, Robert Wilcox maintains the Japanese were developing nuclear bombs—"Genzai Bukudan"—on a small island in the Sea of Japan in the days following the atomic bombing of Hiroshima. The desperate Japanese believed they might postpone the impending outcome of the war by delivering "Genzai Bukudan" to Allied invasion fleets in midget submarines or from balloons. Oddly, the Japanese army and navy worked on similar weapons projects, but rather than co-ordinating efforts, they were generally at odds and in competition for research monies. The rift was so acute that scientists on similar projects did not share information—one of a long list of causes leading to Japan's defeat.
2. Quoted in *Japan's Secret War* by Robert Wilcox.

Chapter 17

1. To the great dismay of the Americans, after the assassination western newspapers got wind of Magic's success in deciphering Japan's secret naval code, and an Australian paper broke the story. Fortunately, Japanese arrogance refused to believe the report and dismissed it as propaganda.
2. Described in *The Thousand Mile War* by Brian Garfield. Information also from author's interview with George Mulholland.
3. From the author's written interview with Major W. Jones.
4. Ibid.
5. Comment by Lieutenant Donald E. Dwincll of Company C, 32nd Infantry, quoted in *The Capture of Attu: As told by the men who fought there* by Lieutenant Robert J. Mitchell, Sewell T. Tyng, and Captain Nelson L. Drummond Jr.
6. Quoted in the Alaska State Historical Commission's *Alaska at War*.
7. As told by Captain Albert L. Pence Jr. of Company B, 32nd Infantry, to Lieutenant Robert J. Mitchell for *The Capture of Attu*.

Chapter 18

1. From author's interview with Louis Cochand.
2. From author's interview with Arthur Fanning.
3. U.S. Army Intelligence Corps, "The Enemy on Kiska" (November 1943). This previously classified document describes articles left behind by the Japanese, from weapons to handwritten notes.
4. Quoted in *The Creation of a National Air Force* by W.A.B. Douglas.

Chapter 19

1. "The Enemy on Kiska."
2. From author's interview with Arthur Fanning.
3. "The Enemy on Kiska."
4. From an interview with RCAF Wing Commander Robert Morrow, published in the *Vancouver Sun*, 1943.
5. Quoted in the Alaska State Historical Commission's *Alaska at War*.
6. "The Enemy on Kiska."

Chapter 21

1. Quoted in *Japan's Secret War* by Robert Wilcox.
2. From an interview with crewman Harold L. Yates, carried out by the captain of USS *Argus* following the sinking.

Bibliography

Books

Brebner, Phyllis Lee. *The Alaska Highway*. Erin, ON: The Boston Mills Press, 1985.

Burlingame, Burl. *Advance Force*. Kailua, HI: Pacific Monograph, 1992.

Carpenter, Dorr, and Norman Polmar. *Submarines of the Imperial Japanese Navy 1904-1945*. Annapolis, MD: Naval Institute Press, 1986.

Coates, Kenneth, ed. *The Alaska Highway: Papers on the 40th Anniversary Symposium*. Vancouver: University of British Columbia Press, 1985.

Cohen, Stan. *The Forgotten War*. Four vols. Missoula, MT: Pictorial Histories Publishing Company, 1981–1983.

Douglas, W.A.B. *The Creation of a National Air Force*. Vol. II of *The Official History of the Royal Canadian Air Force*. Toronto/Ottawa: University of Toronto Press in co-operation with Department of National Defence and the Canadian Government Publishing Centre, Supply and Services Canada, 1986.

Ferguson, Ted. *Desperate Siege: The Battle of Hong Kong*. Scarborough, ON: Doubleday Canada, 1980.

Fuchida, Mitsuo, and Masatake Okumiya. *Midway: The Battle that Doomed Japan: The Japanese Navy's Story*. Annapolis, MD: The Naval Institute Press, 1955.

Garfield, Brian. *The Thousand Mile War*. New York: Ballantine Books, 1969.

Graham, Donald. *Keepers of the Light: A History of British Columbia's Lighthouses & their Keepers*. Madeira Park, BC: Harbour Publishing, 1985.

Griffin, D.F. *First Steps to Tokyo: The RCAF in the Aleutians*. Toronto/Vancouver: J.M. Dent & Sons (Can), 1944.

Handleman, Howard. *A Bridge to Tokyo: The Re-conquest of the Aleutians*. New York: Random House Wartime Book, 1943.

Hashimoto, Mochitsura. *SUNK! The Story of the Japanese Submarine Fleet 1941-1945*. New York: Avon Publications, Henry Holt & Co., 1954.

Hoyt, Edwin P. *The Aleutians*. Vol. V of *War in the Pacific*. New York: Avon Books, 1992.

———. *Yamamoto*. New York: Warner Books, 1991.

Morgan, Lael, ed. *The Aleutians*. Vol. 7, no. 3 quarterly hardcover for members of the Alaska Geographic Society. Anchorage: Alaska Geographic Society, 1980.

Macpherson, Ken, and John Burgess. *The Ships of Canada's Naval Forces 1910-1981*. Don Mills, ON: Collins Publishers, 1981.

Marston, Major Marvin "Muktuk." *Men of the Tundra: Eskimos at War*. New York: October House, 1969.

Milberry, Larry. *The RCAF at War 1939-1945*. Toronto: CANAV Books, 1990.

Mitchell, Lt. Robert J., Sewell T. Tyng, and Capt. Nelson L. Drummond Jr. *The Capture of Attu: As told by the men who fought there*. Originally published in "The Infantry Journal" 1944. Reprinted: Lincoln, NE: Bison Books, University of Nebraska Press, 2000.

Morison, Samuel Eliot. *History of United States Naval Operations in WWII*. Edison, NJ: Castle Books, 1948, reprinted 2001.

Orita, Zenji, with Joseph D. Harrington. *I-Boat Captain*. Canoga Park, CA: Major Books, 1976.

Popp, Carol. *The Gumboot Navy*. Lantzville, BC: Oolichan Books, 1988.

Power, C.G. *The RCAF Overseas: The first four years*. Toronto: Oxford University Press, 1944.

Rigge, Simon. *War in the Outposts*. Chicago: Time Life Books Inc., 1981.

Roscoe, Theodore. *U.S. Submarine Operations in WWII*. Annapolis, MD: U.S. Naval Institute Proceedings, 1949. Reprinted as *Pig Boats*. New York: Bantam Books, 1982.

Smith, Peter C. *The Battle of Midway*. London, UK: New English Library, 1976.

Stacey, Colonel C.P. *The Army in Canada, Britain and the Pacific*. Vol. I of *Six Years of War: The Official History of the Canadian Army in the Second World War*. Ottawa: Department of National Defence, 1956.

Stephenson, William S. *The BSC Papers: The Secret History of British Intelligence in the Americas 1940-45*. New York: International Publications, 1999.

Webber, Bert. *The Silent Siege III*. Medford, OR: Webb Research Group, 1992.

Wheeler, Keith. *War Under the Pacific*. Chicago: Time Life Books Inc., 1980.

Wilcox, Robert K. *Japan's Secret War: Japan's race against time to build the atomic bomb*. New York: William Morrow, 1985.

Zich, Arthur. *The Rising Sun*. Alexandria, VA: Time Life Books, 1978.

Periodicals

Bailey, Lloyd. "The Estevan Point Mystery." *Pacific Yachting* 36, no. 11 (November 1994).

Bray, H. Layton. "Northern Exposure." *Legion Magazine*, May 1994.

Fallon, Joseph E. "The Censored History of Internment." *Chronicals: A Magazine of American Culture* (The Rockford Institute), February 1998.

Frisbee, John L. "Eareckson of the Aleutians." *Air Force Magazine* (journal of the Air Force Association, United States) 74, no. 6 (June 1991).

Hatch, F.J. "The Aleutian Campaign: Parts I & II." *The Roundel: Magazine of the RCAF*, May and June 1963.

Kelly, William. "The Guns of Yorke Island." *Pacific Yachting* 37, no. 11 (November 1995).

Lenihan, Daniel J. "Aleutian Affair." *Natural History Magazine*, June 1992.

Maclean, H. "Kiska Canucks: With the Canadian Invasion Force Aleutian Islands." *Maclean's Magazine*, October 1943.

McPhee, John. "Balloons of War." *The New Yorker*, January 29, 1996.

Morgan, Lael. "The Aleutians: Alaska's Far-out Islands." *National Geographic Magazine*, September 1983.

Paterson, T.W. "Torpedo! Torpedo!" *Victoria Colonist*, July 12, 1964.

Rearden, Jim. "Akutan Zero Part I & II." *Alaska Magazine* 53, no. 9 and 10 (September and October 1987).

Rearden, Jim. "Kiska: One Island's Moment in History Part I & II." *Alaska Magazine* 52, no. 9 and 10 (September and October 1986).

"U.S. Retakes Aleutians." *Life Magazine*, October 1943.

Weir, Christopher. "Crude Awakening." *Nature Magazine*, November 1997.

Newspapers

Montreal Gazette (May 29, 1943)

Rocky Mountain Rangers Association Newsletters (September 1992 and August 1993)

Vancouver Province

Vancouver Sun

Victoria Colonist

Films

Goldin, Laurence. *Alaska at War*. Aurora Films & The Alaska State Historical Commission, 1986.

Huston, John. *Report From the Aleutians*. Produced by Daryl F. Zanuck. 50 min. Released by the U.S. War Department, August 1943. Rereleased 1986 by United American Video, P.O. Box 7563, Charlotte, NC 28217.

Tourtellot, Arthur B. *Crusade in the Pacific: The Aleutians*. US Army Film, 1951. Rereleased 1986 by Embassy Home Entertainment, 1901 Avenue of the Stars, Los Angeles CA 90067.

Interviews / Personal Communications

Abel, John (14th Sqn, RCAF)

Association of the United States Army, Arlington VA

Betterton, Russell (Aleutian Veteran, US Army Transport (Marine))

Bray, H. Layton (8th Sqn, RCAF)

Burt, William (RCAF)

Cameron, Terry (RCMP Archives, Records Information Directorate, Ottawa)

Canadian Merchant Navy Veterans Association

Canadian veterans of the Alaska / Aleutians Campaign—RCAF, RCN, RCA (not an official organization)

Cochand, Louis (14th Sqn, RCAF)

Finlay, Roy (Canadian Merchant Navy)

First Special Service Force Association, 262 Pine Knob Circle, Moneta, VA

Fort Garry Horse Regimental Museum, Winnipeg, MB

Johnston, J.H. (Annette Island, RCAF photo tech, 1942–44)

Jones, Major William S. (Attu veteran, USA New Jersey National Guard, Retired)

Jordan, Norm (Annette Island, RCAF)

Koughan, W.H. (HMCS *Prince David*, RCN)

MacDonald, Hammish (Rocky Mountain Rangers)

Maley, Barney A. (Winnipeg Grenadiers)

Maude, George (Marine Division, RCAF)

McCann, Bill (14th Sqn, RCAF)

Members of the Rocky Mountain Rangers Association

Morris, Robert (14th Sqn, RCAF)

Mulholland, George (Rocky Mountain Rangers, RCA)

Murphy, Larry (Submerged Cultural Resources Unit, National Park Service, Santa Fe, NM)

Olsen, Ross (Attu veteran, USS *Nevada*, USN)

Pease, Robert C. (RCAF)

Richards, John (14th Sqn, RCAF)

Rodgers, Arnold (17th Infantry Division, U.S. Army)

Royal Winnipeg Rifles Regimental Museum, Minto Armory, Winnipeg, MB

7th Infantry Div. Assoc. U.S. Army, Wailuka, HA

Stevens, Harry (HMCS *Prince David*, RCN)

Stewart, Don (115th Sqn, RCAF)

Storey, Larry (FSSF veteran)

United States 17th "Hourglass" Division Association

US Fish & Wildlife Service, Homer, AK

Vandersteen, Bert (49th Field Battery, RCA)

Veterans of the Attu Campaign—United States Army / United States Navy

Welch, Arthur S. (Association of the United States Army, Arlington VA)

Whitlock, George (111th Sqn, RCAF)

Wikert, Verne (*Coast Trader*)

Documents

Hall, Henry W. *The Battle of the Aleutians*. Intelligence Section – Field Force HQ Adak Alaska, 1943. Arlington, VA: Association of the United States Army.

Lindstrom, David. *World War II: The Japanese Submarine I-25 and the Oregon Coast. Part 1 The Fort Stevens Encounter*. Hammond, OR: Fort Stevens State Park.

Murphy, Larry E. and Daniel J. Lenihan. *National Park Service Report on Archeological Investigations of WWII: Kiska Harbor*. Santa Fe, NM: National Park Service, Submerged Cultural Resources Unit (with permission from Alaska Humanities Forum), 1995. (Available online at http://www.nps.gov/scru/kis-1.htm or http://www.nps.gov/scru/AlaskaP.html)

RCAF Archives. Various weekly reports, memoranda, correspondence, log books. Available from the Directorate of History, Department of National Defence, 101 Colonel By Drive, Ottawa, ON K1A 0K2, or from Command History Officer, Air Command Headquarters, Department of National Defence, Westwin, MB R3J 0T0. Filed according to squadron numbers.

Stevenson, Leigh. "The RCAF and the Anti-Submarine Campaign in the Pacific," documents concerning 115th Squadron and 118th Squadron, and 1972 letter re: RCAF operations in Alaska in WWII. Directorate of History, Department of National Defence, 101 Colonel By Drive, Ottawa, ON K1A 0K2

U.S. Army Intelligence Corps. "The Enemy on Kiska." November 1943.

Western Air Command. Official reports on submarine attacks. Available from Command History Officer, Air Command Headquarters, Department of National Defence, Westwin, MB R3J 0T0

Websites

"Aleutian World War II National Historic Area, Aleut Internment." http://www.nps.gov/aleu/AleutInternmentAndRestitution.htm or http://www.ounalashka.com/Aleutian%20WWII%20National%20Historic%20Area.htm

"Inquiry into the Sinking of the *John A. Johnson*. Commandant 12th Naval District. Summary of Statements of Survivors. Nov 9 1944." http://www.archives.gov/research_room/nail/index.html

"Japanese Canadian Internment." http://www.lib.washington.edu/subject/Canada/internment/intro.html

Bibliography

"Montbello. Report of Casualty: U.S. Board of Inquiry. 12/23/41." http://www.archives.gov/research_room/nail/index.html

"Recollection of Verne Wikert—Crewman aboard—Re: sinking of SS *Coast Trader*." http://www.archives.gov/research_room/nail/index.html

"Report Compiled on the Shooting Deaths of Japanese Americans at Internment Camps." http://www.oz.net/~cyu/internment/shootings.html

"Statement Regarding the Montbello Sinking by Capt. Olaf W. Eckstrom. 12/23/41." http://www.archives.gov/research_room/nail/index.html

"USS *Salt Lake City* Cruise Book. The Komandorskies." http://sandysq.gcinet.net/uss_salt_lake_city_ca25/pg-14-20.htm#top

"Value of Evidence—The Redress Movement: A Case Study." http://www.rose.mygarden.com/Weblinks/485CaseStudy.html

Cohn, Werner. "Persecution of Japanese Canadians and the Political Left in British Columbia, December 1941–March 1942." http://www.werncrcohn.com/Japanese.html

Munson, Curtis B. *The Munson Report.* (October / November 1941). http://www.geocities.com/Athens/8420/generations.html or http://www.curriculumunits.com/crucible/whunts/munson_report.htm or http://www.curriculumunits.com/crucible/whunts/framesmunsonreport.htm

O'Hara, Vincent P. "Battle of the Komandorski Islands: March 26, 1943." http://www.microworks.net/pacific/battles/kommandorski_islands.htm

War Relocation Authority. "Relocation of Japanese Americans. May 1943." http://www.lib.washington.edu/exhibits/harmony/Documents/wrapam.html http://www.sfmuseum.org/hist10/relocbook.html

Worden, William (American Press reporter). "US Naval Force Repels Larger Japanese Fleet in Torrid Four-hour Duel." At sea with an American Naval Force, March 26, 1943. http://sandysq.gcinet.net/uss_salt_lake_city_ca25/paulson2.htm

Index

Photo credits

Melanie Arnis: p. 238
Canadian Department of National Defence: p. 63
Stan Cohen (*The Forgotten War*, volume 2) Admiral James Russell Collection: p. 97, p. 120
Brendan Coyle: p. 18 (b), p. 37, p. 43, p. 44, p. 89, p. 90, p. 93, p. 94 (t), p. 181, p. 214, p. 215
Jeff Dickrell: p. 137
Michael Eng (Submerged Cultural Resources Unit): p. 219, p. 220 (t)
Fort Richardson Chaplain's Office: p. 184 (b)
Fort Steven's Museum: p. 94
Brian Garfield, (*The Thousand Mile War*): p. 208
Donald Graham (*Keepers of the Light*): p. 24
Bob Harvey, p. 78
Jill Holmgren: p. 201
Japanese Navy File: p. 105
Jim Johnston: p. 52, p. 55, p. 60, p. 61, p. 62, p. 65, p. 66
Ken Macpherson and John Burgess (*The Ships of Canada's Naval Forces 1910-1981*): p. 41
Barney A. Maley: p. 217
Major Marvin Marston (*Men of the Tundra*): p. 125
George Maude: p. 56
Bill McCann: p. 187 (t), p. 188, p. 191
Wally Mulholland: p. 193, p. 198, p. 203, p. 204, p. 206, p. 207
National Archives of Canada: p. 50 (Stan Cohen), p. 92, p. 131, p. 141, p. 187 (b)
Royal Winnipeg Rifles Regimental Museum: p. 218
Stewart/Ashman collection: p. 57, p. 59, p. 64
Rich Thistle, www.richthistle.com: front cover
United States: p. 156, p. 170, p. 104 (t), p. 190
U.S. Army: p. 38, p. 74, p. 178, p. 180
U.S. Army Archives: p. 100, p. 103, p. 106, p. 107, p. 108, p. 109, p. 110, p. 111, p. 114, p. 166
U.S. Fisheries and Wildlife Service: p. 220 (b)
U.S. Marine Corps Archives: p. 113 (#315172)
U.S. National Parks Service, Submerged Cultural Resources Unit: p. 13, p. 117, p. 143
U.S. Naval Institute: p. 200
U.S. Navy: p. 18 (t)
U.S. Navy Archives: p. 145, p. 148
Vancouver Maritime Museum: p. 87, p. 88
Bert Vandersteen: p. 205
Bert Webber (*Silent Siege III*): p. 16, p. 20, p. 90 (t), p. 212

Maps provided by Brendan Coyle, reproduced by Heritage House.

Author Biography

Brendan Coyle was born and raised in New Westminster, British Columbia, the youngest of ten siblings. He always had a keen interest in ships and all things nautical, and he was determined to work in B.C.'s historic maritime industry. He earned his basic SCUBA certification at fourteen and worked his way through the "ranks" from stints as a deckhand and commercial diver to journeyman fabricator / welder in the fishing and boat building industry. He is now employed as a maintenance planner in ship repair.

Brendan's freelance articles appear often in the *Victoria Times Colonist*. He has also written for the the *Vancouver Sun, Vancouver Province, Diver Magazine,* and the *Canadian Diving Journal*. His interest in Canadian and American military history, vintage aircraft, and Canada's north led him to write about the unknown war on North America's West Coast.

Brendan Coyle lives in Steveston, B.C., with his wife, Melanie Arnis, and two daughters, Meghan and Rhianna.

Back cover photos (clockwise from left): A Second World War searchlight camouflaged beside Fisgard Lighthouse in a "fisherman's shanty," the Director's Tower and gun placement at Belmont Battery, and a balloon-bomb remnant on display in the Officers' Quarters. All photos taken at Fort Rodd Hill National Historic Site of Canada (Heritage House collection).